The Theology Frontier

Also by Ashish Dalela:

Semantic Atomism
Semantic Reasoning
The Journey of Perfection
Material and Spiritual Natures
Conceiving the Inconceivable
The Science of God
Time and Consciousness
Conceiving the Inconceivable
The Balanced Organization
The Yellow Pill
Cosmic Theogony
Emotion
Mystic Universe
Moral Materialism
Signs of Life
Uncommon Wisdom
Gödel's Mistake
Quantum Meaning
Sāńkhya and Science
Is the Apple Really Red?
Six Causes

The Theology Frontier

SHABDAVERSE
VOLUME 2

Ashish Dalela

The Theology Frontier —SHABDAVERSE Volume 2
by Ashish Dalela

Published by Shabda Press
press.shabda.co
ISBN 978-93-85384-48-6
v1.2 12/2025

SHABDA
PRESS

Contents

SERIES PREFACE

SHABDAVERSE is a series of article collections, organized by topics. The articles in these collections were originally published online on the SHABDA website over many years. A series of articles written from 2014 to 2019 were earlier published in chronological order under the series title *Western Questions Eastern Answers*. The SHABDAVERSE series organizes articles from 2019 to 2025 by categories, rather than dates. This is for multiple reasons—(a) there are enough articles in each category to produce collections organized by categories, (b) readers wanting to read topic-focused collections might find this approach more convenient and cohesive than the chronological one, and (c) the topic-focused approach allows us to make unique covers for each book, after all, in the ultimate analysis, a book is judged by its cover!

All these articles follow an interdisciplinary approach to every topic—everyday experience, empirical evidence, problems with different ideas advanced in the past and present, how ideas may have evolved historically, how certain issues were seen and understood differently across cultures, and with a solution to any and all related open and unsolved problems, which can be validated through ordinary experience, empirical evidence, and rational arguments. I often cite statements and ideas from Vedic texts, not to substantiate my claims, but to establish that my ideas are not new, and that I as the author of these articles don't claim authorship of the ideas. I only aim to present ancient ideas in a modern language, so that present audiences may understand and appreciate them based on what they already trust.

Pursuant to the science-religion divide created during European Enlightenment, we see two opposite approaches to the study of ancient texts—(a) the religious approach takes an ancient text as a divine revelation to be trusted on faith at best, and (b) the scientific approach, which rejects these texts as the personal opinion of dogmatic scribes, unprovable through or contradictory to the available evidence, and focuses on collecting evidence, followed by speculation to find an explanation that fits that evidence.

The Vedic tradition differs from both of these. Ancient texts have been preserved in a written form for thousands of years, but in every successive era, those texts were explained through commentaries. The texts and the commentaries were never merged. That trend continues today, and those who like to read ancient texts with explanations can do so. However, these explanations do not contrast their ideas with those in present-day sciences and religions, because the Vedic tradition was historically inward-looking, not outward-looking. By continuing the same trend, commentaries on Vedic texts appear to most people as different ideas, not better or true ideas, when contrasted to the ideas found in other worldviews. In fact, those ingrained in other worldviews consider Vedic texts primitive because the Vedic ideas don't match the ideas they have received through their culture and education. Therefore, the inward-looking historical trend of the Vedic texts is not adequate for the present time. For the present time, the Vedic tradition must become outward-looking, and contrast itself to the ideas of the other worldviews.

Therefore, in these articles, we—(a) sometimes we begin with unsolved problems created by prevalent ideas and theories and try to solve them using reasoning and evidence, and then connect the solution to the ideas in ancient texts, and (b) sometimes we begin with ideas and theories in ancient texts and show how they are relevant to the present time by showing how they solve unsolved or open problems.

I have seen with consternation a tendency among many authors to take ancient ideas, reformulate them in convenient ways, disconnect them from the sources from where these ideas were taken, and present these ideas as an author's original work. I think that this approach constitutes a theft, disrespectful to the teachers and texts from where ideas were taken. But more importantly, it filters the tradition of texts and teachers through the opinionated lens of the author who takes ideas without attribution, and closes the door for readers to go back to the tradition for more exploration in the future. Authors with such attitudes present themselves as prophets of original ideas, while masking the actual prophets.

I aim to show people of the present time a path to the Vedic tradition, not pretend to be a prophet of original ideas. Personally, I'm convinced that everything I have written about is a miniscule fraction of all that can be written, understood, or derived from the Vedic texts, and hopefully, future generations will do more of what I have tried to do. My primary goal is to dispel the myth that the Vedic texts are like the texts of other religions which have to be accepted on faith, rather than reason and observation. I call the dispelling of this myth, the *scientific study of Vedic texts*, pursuant to the common definition of science as truth based on reasoning and evidence, in contrast to a religion based on blind faith or belief.

Ashish Dalela

Why Theism Needs Alternative Causation

The Religious Problem of Causation

Imagine that a moving billiard ball collides with a static one, and transfers its energy, which causes the static billiard ball to start moving. The cause of the change is energy, and due to conservation, once energy is transferred to the new ball, the cause ceases to exist, and the effect becomes the new cause.

Now extend this idea to causation by God. God created the universe, and therefore He was all the energy in the beginning. But since energy gets transferred, therefore, God must cease to exist. Or even if He exists, He is like that static ball that has lost its energy because it was converted into the world.

This article discusses how this idea about causation is modified in theistic versions of Vedic philosophy.

The Abrahamic Religious Doctrine

To say that God exists fully even after the creation of the world, the Abrahamic religions adopt the *ex nihilo* idea of creation—God created the world from nothing. In short, He created the energy from which the world was produced. But how did God create energy from nothing? Isn't that a case of something coming out of nothing? Well, God is supernatural, so we don't apply naturalistic principles, and conservation of energy is a naturalistic principle. In short, God's creation is not subject to the conservation of energy, because if this principle were applied, it would entail that the energy was in God, and since it became the world, therefore

God was diminished after creation.

The pantheistic religions sometimes go a step further. They say that the conservation of energy is true, and God was the sum of this energy before creation. When the world is created, then God simply becomes the world. Therefore, He ceases to have a separate existence, and the world again becomes God when everything is destroyed. In other words, there is either God or the world, and these are merely two different states of energy—concentrated in God or distributed in the world. Supernatural ideas are not needed, because conservation of energy is upheld. And yet, right now, because the world is manifest, therefore, God doesn't exist. Your worship of God is therefore false right now.

You can see why energy conservation plays havoc with religion—if this principle is upheld, then God either ceases to exist or is diminished upon creation. If we reject this idea, then we must appeal to supernaturalism, and at the point of creation of the world, the doctrine becomes unscientific.

The Sāñkhya Philosophy Doctrine

In philosophy, examples are very important. Fire was very important to Vedic culture, so the cardinal example of causation wasn't the collision of billiard balls. It was wood being ignited into fire. You can create fire by rubbing two pieces of wood. Then, when the fire is produced by rubbing, you ask: did the fire exist inside the wood before we saw it? Or was fire being transferred from somewhere else? We can see that the fire existed in the wood as latent energy. But if it was latent, then why did we not see it earlier? Well, there are different *states* of energy—fire is *manifest*, and latent fire was *unmanifest*.

But the key problem is still there—the wood is burnt and ceases to exist when it is ignited. So, we must say that wood transformed into fire; wood doesn't exist when fire does. If this idea is extended to God, then we come to the same conclusion—when the world is manifest, then God ceases to exist. Or, at the least, much like wood is reduced to ashes, similarly, God must be reduced to ashes upon creation.

To solve this problem, a distinction between *puruṣa* and *prakriti* is drawn. The piece of wood is *prakriti*. It can have many states—unmanifest and manifest fire—and the change is caused by the *puruṣa*. Since *prakriti* is eternal, therefore, energy is eternally conserved. Since *puruṣa* is different from *prakriti*, therefore, the *puruṣa* is not diminished when the world is created: the world is only transforming the state of energy. This change in the state of *prakriti* is caused due to the free will in *puruṣa*.

However, this claim leads to a new problem—if the *puruṣa* is will, and the *prakriti* is matter, then how can will control matter? Doesn't this control violate the laws of nature? Or, should we say that there are no laws, and there is only will? But if that will is always lawful, then is it really free?

We now have two undesirable outcomes—either will doesn't control matter, and therefore, *puruṣa* has no control over *prakriti*. Or, will always controls matter, but because the control is lawful, therefore it is not free. If we reject the idea that the *puruṣa* has no control over matter, then there is no way to know the existence of *puruṣa* (after all, if something exists, then it must also have an effect). So, the only possible conclusion is that the *puruṣa* is not free will, but only the laws of nature. By this conclusion, the laws of nature are shifted from *prakriti* to *puruṣa*, but the result is the rejection of free will.

The solution to this problem divides causality into three parts—the lawfulness of matter, of soul, and of time. If you push a button, the fan will start rotating. This is the law of *prakriti*. But there is an *if*—i.e. someone must make a choice. The soul makes this choice, and every choice brings a consequence, which is called the law of *karma*. But how do we decide *karma*? If I do something wrong today, and it produces a chain of bad effects till eternity, then I'm responsible for all the bad actions till eternity. The consequences of my bad action right now will continue to punish me forever. The solution to that problem is time—time is cosmic destiny and decides what will happen, but not who will do it. So, someone is going to push the button anyway, and therefore if I push the button, then, I'm only responsible for this one action, not the subsequent ones, because they were already destined. This solution expands the Sāñkhya ontology from *puruṣa* and *prakriti* and adds *karma* and time to it.

A new problem now arises. Who is *puruṣa*? Is it God? If so, how can He be bound by the laws of nature, the consequences of actions, and the suffering resulting from these actions? The answer to this problem is the *puruṣa* is the soul, not God. This leads to two problems: (1) where is God—does He not exist? and (2) the soul is caught in the cycle of birth-and-death—does he come out of this cycle?

The solution to these two problems is then tied together. God is the person who facilitates the soul's liberation from the cycle of birth and death. God's role is not controlling matter—that is the job of destiny defined by time. God's role is not to make individual choices—that's the soul's own problem. God doesn't define the laws of matter—that is the problem of understanding *prakriti*. God has only one role—to help the soul get liberated from the clutches of the cycle of birth and death. With this solution, the Sāñkhya ontology is expanded to five things—*puruṣa, prakriti,* time, *karma,* and God.

The Vedānta Philosophy Doctrine

This is where Sāñkhya ends, but it hardly ends the problem. The new question is—what is liberation? How does God help the soul to become liberated? And why should the soul be caught in the cycle of birth and death? The Vedānta doctrine gets into the relation between the soul and God. It is stated that the soul is part of God, and as a part, the soul must serve God. The soul is caught in the cycle of birth and death when the soul stops serving God and starts serving himself. But there is a problem. If the soul is the part of God, then how can the part know the whole? The whole is infinite, and the part is finite. How can the knowledge of the infinite fit inside the finite? If God cannot be known, then how can the soul serve God? And if he cannot serve God, then how can there be liberation for the soul?

Apart from the fitting the infinite into the finite, there are other problems. Since the soul and God are different, and every type of illusion follows from the difference between the knower and the known—only self-knowledge is completely certain—then how can we be sure that we are not hallucinating about God? How can we be sure that what we call the experience of God is not merely our construction?

Now, the Vedānta doctrine is updated—the God we see is within us. The soul exists, but it is not a physical object. It is rather like a symbol—which has both existence and meaning. God is the meaning of that symbol. This meaning is within the soul, and therefore, the preliminary stage of self-realization is the existence of the soul. But a deeper level realization is that this existence also has a meaning.

But this leads to a new problem—everyone can say that they have found the meaning of their existence within themselves. Since the meaning is within us, how can we say that everyone doesn't have a different meaning? Due to this problem, the doctrine is enhanced again—the meaning within is also referential. It points to something outside us. Just like when you say the "sky is blue", there is a sentence, it has a meaning, and the meaning is about the sky. How do we know it is about the sky? We can know only if within this meaning there is another deeper reality that constitutes the reference. For example, when you see an apple, there is an external apple, and an image of that apple within you. Now, you can see the image and say that it is my hallucination. Unless, of course, there is a deeper level reality within that image which says—this image came from an external apple. That's when we know that my image is about the real external world. But we never see that real world itself. We only see the image, and something deeper within that image, which then points us toward the external world.

This understanding of Vedānta is presented as the three levels of understanding reality—Brahman, Paramātma, and Bhagavan. The soul is Brahman; the meaning of its existence is Paramātma, which exists inside the soul. But this meaning is referential, and it therefore points toward Bhagavan, outside the soul. So, you don't reach an external reality by going outward. You reach it by going deeper inward. Since you can be certain of your existence, by going deeper within, you only extend that certainty. In short, the certainty of God's existence is obtained by seeing what lies within us, not by seeing what is outside. This doesn't mean that God is inside us; it means that we are referencing God within us.

This solves the problem of liberation—we don't know our true nature, and how it is connected to God. The true nature is known when we see God within. But the God within exists as a meaning, not the object referenced by that meaning. The meaning is succinct, even if the object referenced outside is infinite. Furthermore, since the meaning is within us, and points externally, therefore, we don't need to look outside to know God, and hence the problems of epistemology don't arise. This knowledge is as certain as the certainty of the self-existence. This completes both Sāñkhya and Vedānta because the problem of liberation in Sāñkhya is explained by the soul-God relation in the Vedānta doctrine.

The Problem of Understanding Vedānta

But this raises a whole slew of new problems. The soul is described as a symbol which can represent an external reality within itself. So, even though the symbol may be knowledge (rather than illusion), it may not be *complete*. After all, saying that 'the sky is blue' is not a complete description of the sky.

This is where Vedānta is further advanced to say that the picture within is always a partial picture, and yet, this picture is part of God. Just like a person is simultaneously a father, an employee, and a citizen, but only the children see him as a father, only the boss sees him as an employee, and only the government sees him as a citizen, similarly, you see the same reality from different perspectives, and get partial views. God (as the person outside) is all those things, but we cannot see that whole truth. We only see what is uniquely defined by a relation and perspective; the soul thus has a relation to God. The doctrine of this relation is then developed into a full-fledged understanding of devotion to God. Once this relation is developed, the purpose of one's existence is revealed, and the soul is liberated. However, because God is known through a relationship, He may not be known completely. The object of knowledge is same for everyone—i.e. God—and yet, everyone has a different (partial) view of God.

Even if we see God differently, we don't say that there are many Gods. We are factually talking about a single God—or we succumb to polytheism—because the *reference* of knowledge is one. This is like saying that "John is a father", "John is an employee", "John is a citizen", etc. The attributes of 'father', 'employee' and 'citizen' are different descriptions of John. And yet, they are all about John. If John is the Absolute Truth, then everyone knows the Absolute Truth. But everyone knows this truth differently. That is not the same as someone knowing John, another one knowing Peter, Mark, etc. We don't say that there are many 'Gods', and we don't say that 'God' is always perceived in the same way. Thus, two contradictory ideas—diverse perceptions and a universal reality—are resolved simultaneously.

But this leads to a new problem. If there are so many perspectives, then how does God perceive Himself? Obviously, if He perceived Himself like the other souls, then, He would just be that soul. To be a different person, He must also have a unique perspective, not shared by anyone else. And this perspective must be the complete picture of Who He is. This leads to the conclusion that God's self-image is the original image, and from that image, many partial images are created. But this leads to the idea that the soul and its perspective must be a 'creation' of God's self-image. Just like how others view us is always a partial picture of how we see ourselves, similarly, the soul is a part of God.

Therefore, we must distinguish between the *person*, the *image*, and the *knower.* The knower knows the person, but through an image. The knower has a unique relation to the person. Unless we make these distinctions, it seems that the soul is part of God, and God is part of soul, which leads to inconceivability. But if we make this distinction, then the image of God inside the soul is not the person outside. Although the image and the person are semantically identically, they are separate individuals. The fuller solution to the problem of perception leads to tripartite nature of reality—the person is called *ananda,* their image of the person is called *chit,* and the relation to the knower is called *sat.* The interaction between the soul and God casts a picture of God inside the soul, but the picture and object are distinct.

The situation is like two mirrors reflecting each other—there is a picture of each mirror inside the other. The further complication is that the second mirror is a part of the first mirror. You can never draw a physical picture of this reflection—the whole being mirrored within its own part. And this impossibility of physically visualizing this idea leads one to conclude that the Vedānta doctrine is *inconceivable.* One aspect of this inconceivability is that we don't distinguish between the object, the picture, and the seer. Specifically, the picture pertains to the seer, and but it also pertains to the object. Even if the seer and the seen are distinct, the picture is tied to both; and this violates conventional logic.

The Problem of Understanding Sāñkhya

The problem of Sāñkhya worsens due to this conclusion in Vedānta. Recall that the soul was previously recognized as one of the five realities in Sāñkhya. But now Vedānta has concluded that the soul is part of God. If that was the fate of the soul, then what about the other three? Isn't it more consistent to extend this idea and say that the other three realities must also be part of God? Doesn't it follow that the inclusion of the soul as part of God entails that time, *prakriti,* and *karma* are also part of God?

The solution is not as easy as it might sound. If we say that these three realities are part of God, then just like God is both within and outside the soul, likewise, we must say that God is also within and outside these three realities. Thus, for instance, we would say that there is an image of the soul, God, *karma,* and time, within *prakriti,* and this image is then the cause of the *prakriti's* actions. That would be radical, because now *prakriti* is reflecting other things, so *prakriti* is also a conscious person! Now, you cannot say that matter is 'dead' or 'inert'. You must say that it is also an individual person. Likewise, time must also be a person. In fact, the soul, matter, and God are both within time, and outside time. So, we can no longer treat matter and time as physical entities; we must treat them as personalities.

So, what began as the idea of *prakriti* and time in Sāñkhya, which solved the problem of causality associated with free will, now turns out to be personalities, just like the soul and God. In fact, because *prakriti* and time are also souls, they are also spiritual. Thus, we can identify four kinds of spiritual entities—God, soul, *prakriti,* and time. The last three being the parts of the first.

Then, what is matter? Matter is that which is not part of

God, because it is not eternal. *Karma* is the only material reality. *Karma* can enter the soul, matter, and time, but matter, time, and the soul don't enter *karma*. In short, *karma* is not a person or observer; although *karma* can be observed. Every observer is eternal, and the non-observer (*karma*) is material and temporary. Since *karma* can be created and destroyed, as matter, it is certainly not 'conserved'. And yet, *karma* is also not created by God.

So, the creation of the universe is not *ex nihilo*—because the cause is *prakriti*. The creation of the universe is not by God—it is due to *karma* (a related problem is that of theodicy or evil: if God created the universe, and the universe has evil, then God must be evil; the answer is: God is not evil, and He did not create the universe; the universe was created due to *karma*, which was created by the soul). And God is not decimated by this creation, because God, soul, *prakriti* and time are eternal. Only *karma* is temporary, and it is created, and it is not a part of God. Something that is not part of God cannot decimate God. Thus, we reject all the aforementioned doctrines—(1) energy is conserved, (2) God is the creator, and (3) God is reduced by this creation because a part of Him becomes the universe.

The Problem of the Soul's Fall into Matter

A new problem now arises. The soul must fall into the world to create *karma*, but material existence is only due to *karma*. So, the soul cannot fall unless there is *karma*, and *karma* cannot exist unless there is a fall. The solution to this chicken-and-egg problem is that the soul falls due to its desire. There is hence original causation of desire, after which the subsequent causation is primarily due to *karma*.

When the material universe is destroyed, all *karma* is destroyed. The soul enters back into God's body, and God being eternal everything part of God is also eternal. Hence, *karma* doesn't exist in God's body. However, the desire in the soul remains, because it is not *karma*. Due to this desire, the soul falls into matter again and again. Unless, of course, the desire is corrected. This reinforces the idea that *karma* is material and temporary, and it only exists as long as the phenomenal universe exists. It is not reality, because it doesn't exist as part of God, and it is not a person, because it is not eternal. Simply because *karma* is not eternal, we can say that this material world is an illusion. Even though *prakriti, puruṣa,* God and time are real, the unreality of the fifth component—*karma*—makes the universe unreal.

The essence of material desire is envy—it results in competition. The essence of spiritual desire is love—it results in cooperation. The essence of *prakriti* is that it facilitates competition, and the essence of the spiritual world is that it facilitates cooperation. In between these extremes is the soul—which can exist by itself, without cooperation or competition. The soul is said to be superior to material energy, and the spiritual energy is superior to the soul. Notably, the spiritual energy, the material energy, and the soul, are all, in fact, spiritual—they are all souls. However, the competitive tendency is inferior to the self-satisfied tendency, and the self-satisfied tendency is inferior to the cooperative tendency. Accordingly, matter is called inferior to the soul, and spirit is called superior to the soul. This terminology can be confusing because we tend to forget that they are all souls—but with different tendencies.

The Novel Doctrine of Causality

Having solved all these problems, we now come to the final issue. If God has everything as His part, then why separate everything? Why divide the whole into parts, reflect the part in the whole, and the whole in the part? Why can't everything just exist as Oneness where all this complexity doesn't exist? The answer to this question is *pleasure*. God expands into His parts to enjoy with the parts. The enjoyment of the whole is that the parts are reflected in the whole. And the enjoyment of the parts is that the whole is reflected in the parts. All this complexity exists simply for enjoyment or pleasure.

The whole is the cause and the parts are the effects. The effect exists inside the cause. So, when the effect is manifest, nothing new is created, because it previously existed in the cause. Likewise, because the effect came from the cause, it is not produced *ex nihilo*. Furthermore, an effect could have been created by a different cause; if we don't know the cause, all causality would be indeterministic.

To know the cause, we look inside the effect, and we see the cause reflected within the effect. When we get effect from the cause, we overcome all forms of unrealism (e.g. that something comes out of nothing). When we get cause from the effect, we overcome all forms of indeterminism (e.g. that the same effect can be produced by another cause, so knowing the effect doesn't tell us the real cause).

Let's apply this idea to the explanation of a billiard-ball collision. We already say that the effect was inside the cause—the energy or motion of the ball was in the previous ball, and just got transferred. But the same motion could have been created in two ways—by a moving ball or by a moving cue. Just by observing the motion of the ball, we cannot know whether the ball was pushed by another ball, or by the cue. We need to see the entire sequence from cause to effect, because knowing the effect doesn't tell us the cause. Now imagine that we had to talk about the origin of the universe. We can see things moving, but the original movement that started the motion is gone. We cannot get it back, and without it, we cannot know what caused the origin. This is the problem of origin in scientific causality.

The same problem doesn't exist if we say that the cause is within the effect. We don't have to rewind the universe back to its origin to know how it started, because the cause is within the effect—right here and now. We only need to completely know the effect, to know what caused its origination. If God is the origin of the universe, then as the cause of everything, He is present in all the subsequent effects. Therefore, God is real—here and now—in all the tables and chairs and houses and phones. We don't have to look to a transcendental world, be liberated, or postulate a hypothetical entity. We only need to revise our notion of causality in which the effect is in the cause, and the cause is in the effect.

This doesn't mean we can 'see' God, just like we cannot see electrons or protons. But we postulate their existence, and we measure the effects. The effects are then used to *infer* the presence of the cause. This is knowledge by inference, rather than direct perception. God can be known by inference in the same way, but God cannot be perceived this way. This method is called *anumāna* rather than *pratyakśa*.

The Problem of Theoretical Knowledge

A simple way to understand knowledge by inference is that you send a question to someone and you get a reply. If the response matches the question, then you say that the responder exists, although we only see the received message, not the responder. Furthermore, if the response can be verified, then you also say that the responder *knows* the truth. In the same way, knowledge by inference about God is possible if we can communicate with God—send Him questions and get answers. If we get an answer, there is a person. If the answer is always correct, then the person knows the truth. This, by the way, is also how we confirm God's existence within us: we ask questions and get answers, and if the answers received by inspiration are proven true, then we say that there is true source of knowledge.

Since the scientific method is confirmation by *anumāna* and not *pratyakśa*, therefore, it is incomplete. People often mistake this incompleteness—they say that theoretical knowledge is not real knowledge. That, however, entails that there should be no books about God, because all such theoretical stuff cannot capture the nature of reality. This is a false idea. If you write a travelogue on your travels, then reading the travelogue is in one sense same as traveling, and yet not identical to traveling.

The distinction between the travelogue and the travel is that the travelogue is generally incomplete compared to the travel—you are never able to capture the full information about the travel. There are many layers of description. There is something we see, something we understand, something we learn, something surprises us, something hurts us, something we become habituated to, etc. All these constitutes parallel stories and descriptions, but you cannot capture all the stories in a linear textual description. Therefore, you use many descriptions to tell parallel stories. When people read these parallel stories, they think that these must pertain to different travels. The uniqueness about direct perception is only that it resolves this problem—all the descriptions are of the same travel.

The conclusion is that: (1) God can be known by reason, even without direct perception but many complementary descriptions may be needed to make the picture identical to the direct perception, and (2) those obtaining this multifaceted understanding may be motivated toward direct perception. Even those who believe in God, can learn the multi-faceted nature, before they perceive this reality.

Theoretical Knowledge and Current Rationality

A well-accepted fact about these descriptions is that they seem inconceivable or illogical because they necessarily involve modalities—e.g. the object, picture, and seer—which can be semantically identical and yet are different individuals. The same object can cast many pictures. The same picture can exist in many seers. And the same seer can perceive many objects and their pictures. So, in one sense, they are all distinct. But in a perception, the object, picture, and seer are identical. This basic problem of perception needs a non-dualistic system of logic, that we will leave to another occasion.

The problem is not unique to material experience. It also exists in the spiritual world. For example, the devotee sometimes misses the Lord, and in this situation, he knows that he is different from the Lord—this is *Dvaita.* Then, he sometimes sees the Lord, and understands he is related or connected to the Lord—this is *Viśiṣṭādvaita*. And finally, sometimes the devotee is so overwhelmed by the devotion to the Lord that he loses his self-identity and starts acting just like the Lord—this is *Advaita*. Similarly, the Lord sometimes misses His devotee, and then He knows that the devotee is different from Him—this is *Dvaita*. Then, when He sees the devotee, He knows that He is related to the devotee—this is *Viśiṣṭādvaita*. And finally, sometimes when He is overwhelmed with love, He acts just like the devotee—this is *Advaita*.

All three positions can be alternatively true, and yet, the are also eternally true (as a possibility). And because they are eternally and yet alternatively true, the term *Bhedābheda* is used—the devotee and the Lord are identical, related, and different. But since it is impossible to understand how the same thing can be identical, related, and different, the term *Achintya* is added to *Bhedābheda.* This inconceivability arises because the modalities of being identical, different, and related are not separately understood.

One of the modes dominates at any one moment; therefore, the Lord and the devotee are sometimes identical, sometimes different, and sometimes related. This modal existence goes beyond conventional logic. But, if logic was modified to incorporate semantic modalities, then the same thing is conceivable.

I Am the Creator, From Me Comes Everything

In practically every religion of the world God is said to be the creator of the universe. And this leads atheistic people to say: "No, the universe came from the Big Bang; no God was involved". But Kṛṣṇa says in the Bhagavad-Gita (10.8), that He is not just the creator; rather, He creates from *Himself*. If "God is the creator" is religion, then "God creates from Himself" is the science.

In Bhagavad-Gita 10.8, Kṛṣṇa says:

ahaṁ sarvasya prabhavo
mattaḥ sarvaṁ pravartate
iti matvā bhajante māṁ
budhā bhāva-samanvitāḥ

I am the creator of all spiritual and material worlds. Everything emanates from Me. Knowing this, the intelligent worship Me, embued with devotion.

Most of us tend to read this quickly, and conclude that "God created the world", but that is just the first statement–*ahaṁ sarvasya prabhavo*–or that "I am the creator". But *how* is God the creator? Some religions say that God created the world out of nothing or *ex nihilo.* This contradicts science, because energy should not be created or destroyed. If God created the energy once, then He can create it again, and that means that the energy is not merely changing *form* but it is also being created and annihilated. Thus, the statement, "I am the creator" produces an immediately unscientific proposition, or at least one that is contradictory to science.

But this is not the claim in Bhagavad-Gita, where right after saying that "I am the creator", Kṛṣṇa makes the second statement–*mattaḥ sarvaṁ pravartate*—"Everything comes from Me". In other words, the world did not come from a vacuum or nothingness. It came *out of God* like a mother gives birth to a child.

In *Damodarastakam*, Kṛṣṇa is glorified as follows:

namas te 'stu dāmne sphurad-dīpti-dhāmne
tvadīyodarāyātha viśvasya dhāmne

I worship that rope (which has bound your stomach). That rope is the residence of automatically springing light (sphurad-dīpti-dhāmne), just like (yātha) your stomach (tvadīyodarā) is the residence of the universe (viśvasya dhāmne).

On a side note, *sphura* is the fundamental difference between matter and spirit. Matter is called *jada* which means it is "inert", in the sense that there has to be some external force that acts on matter to make it move (just like a master must command a servant to do something). But spirit is *sphura* or automatically acting. This idea is explained here by saying that the rope that binds Kṛṣṇa's stomach is also spiritual, in the sense that it is source of automatically emanating light. We can contrast this idea with how we see a material rope.

We say that some light is emanated by the sun, it 'hits' the rope, and is then absorbed-emitted or "reflected" by the rope, it reaches our eyes, and then we see the rope. The rope that binds Kṛṣṇa is not like that. It is not *reflecting* light, but it is *emanating* light. In short, no sun or moon or tubelight is required to see anything, because everything is emanating its own light. The rope is self-visible, seen of its own accord. When the rope reflects light, then we can forcibly see the rope by shining light on it. But if the rope is emanating light, then we cannot see the rope unless the rope "reveals itself". This is the difference between matter and spirit — spirit acts of its own accord; even the rope is free.

Returning to the main point, this automatic emanation of light from the rope is compared to Kṛṣṇa emanating the world from His stomach. The term *yatha* means "just as". So, "just as the universe is emanated from Your stomach, like that the rope is emanating the light".

So, even when the main point is that *Damodara* is being glorified, the rope that binds Him is also glorified. And that rope is glorified as having the same nature as *Damodara*. It is not that God is spiritual, and the rope is material. The rope is also spiritual.

In this way, we must understand that the vision of the devotees is not divided between 'religion' and 'science'. These are artificial boxes that the modern world has created based on artificial religion and artificial science. The real science and religion don't have these artificial boxes. Even while praying to God, all the paraphernalia — e.g. the rope — is glorified, in the same way that God is glorified. And everything is described clearly, and even contrasted, just like Kṛṣṇa doesn't just say that "I created the world" and that's the end of the story. No. He explains how He created the world. Likewise, even if the rope is created by God, it has the same nature as God, but is not God.

Again, Kṛṣṇa explains that the intelligent worship Me in this way "embued by emotion" — *iti matvā bhajante māṁ, budhā bhāva-samanvitāḥ*. The fools don't worship God, and the mere intellectuals don't worship God. The really intelligent worship God. So, there is no contradiction between rationality and emotionality. Again, many modern so-called religious people have created some artificial boxes and they say that *jnana* is superior to *bhakti*. Or that *bhakti* is for the less intelligent. That is not a fact. Only the intelligent can worship God embued with emotion. The fools don't know God, so they cannot worship. And the dry intellectual also doesn't know, although he thinks he knows based on some book reading. Sometimes one who thinks he knows although he doesn't is more dangerous than one who knows that he doesn't know. In short, the symptom of true knowing is that emotional love "automatically springs out" just like water from a fountain. It is not that love is externally applied. That kind of forced love is artificial. Real love is automatic. This is the meaning of *sphura*.

Krishna Is Jealous and Nonchalant

Many people say that the God of Abrahamic religions is a "jealous" God. However, they don't ask: If we can be jealous, then why can God also not be jealous? Similarly, if we can be non-jealous, therefore, God must also be non-jealous. This contradiction makes it very hard to understand God's nature.

Fortunately, this conundrum is resolved in the Bhagavad-Gita, where Lord Kṛṣṇa makes two seemingly contradictory statements—one that is non-jealous followed by one that is totally jealous.

The jealous statement is BG 18.66, where Kṛṣṇa says:

sarva-dharmān parityajya
mām ekaṁ śaraṇaṁ vraja
ahaṁ tvāṁ sarva-pāpebhyo
mokṣayiṣyāmi mā śucaḥ

Abandon all varieties of religion and just surrender unto Me. I shall deliver you from all sinful reactions. Do not fear.

The "jealousy" here is the use of the term *mām ekaṁ* or "only Me". This is further affirmed by the abandoning of all other varieties of religion—*sarva-dharmān parityajya*. Clearly, Kṛṣṇa doesn't like people practicing all varieties of dharma (duties and religions) other than Him. He is therefore jealous.

However, contrary to this statement, is the statement in BG 18.63:

iti te jñānam ākhyātaṁ
guhyād guhya-taraṁ mayā
vimṛśyaitad aśeṣeṇa
yathecchasi tathā kuru

Thus I have explained to you the knowledge still more confidential. Deliberate on this fully, and then do what you wish to do.

Anybody can analyze the scriptures all over the world, and I can assure you that you will never find a single scripture that says: "I have explained to you this knowledge, now do as you please". Scriptures either describe without prescribing or definitively prescribe something. Often, they might prescribe contradictory things. But there is nothing that says: "do as you please (after deliberating)". Since Kṛṣṇa makes this nonchalant statement before the jealous statement, therefore, Kṛṣṇa is also non-jealous.

In fact, Kṛṣṇa clarifies this contradiction further in BG 18.67 and BG 18.65:

idaṁ te nātapaskāya
nābhaktāya kadācana
na cāśuśrūṣave vācyaṁ
na ca māṁ yo 'bhyasūyati

This confidential knowledge may never be explained to those who are not austere, or devoted, or engaged in devotional service, nor to one who is envious of Me.

man-manā bhava mad-bhakto
mad-yājī māṁ namaskuru
mām evaiṣyasi satyaṁ te
pratijāne priyo 'si me

Always think of Me, become My devotee, worship Me and offer your homage unto Me. Thus, you will come to Me without fail. I promise you this because you are My very dear friend.

In short, I'm making the jealous statement to you (i.e., surrender only to Me) because you are my dear friend. And don't teach this knowledge of exclusive surrender to those who might be jealous.

Therefore, God is also jealous, however, He reveals His jealous nature only to the intimate devotees. For everyone else, you can do whatever you please. This "jealousy" is the intimacy between the Lord and His devotees. Just like a wife may tell her husband—"If you look at other women, I feel jealous, so only look at me"—but she would not say that to acquaintances, because there is no intimacy. So, an increase in intimacy demands exclusivity, and a decrease in intimacy leads to nonchalance. God shows His desire for exclusivity only to those who are intimate. With those who are not intimate, He remains nonchalant.

This jealous nature of God is present in Kṛṣṇa, but the other forms of God are nonchalant. And this jealousy in Kṛṣṇa is the feminine nature present in the masculine form. Those who love Kṛṣṇa must be prepared for this jealous nature—He doesn't like His devotees loving anyone other than Himself. But those who want a nonchalant God can worship other forms of God. If you want to love a nonchalant form of God, then you cannot become intimate with Him. After all, He is nonchalant. But if you want to become intimate, then you must be prepared for exclusivity in the love. In this way, God has a jealous aspect and a nonchalant aspect. But depending on the intimacy, He reveals different aspects.

Since Kṛṣṇa demonstrates both jealous and nonchalant forms, therefore, His jealousy is not to force anyone to love Him. Rather, it is reserved for those who love Him, to ask them to love Him *exclusively*!

In this way, deep aspects about God's nature and intimate *rasa* are indicated even in Bhagavad-Gita. The basic principle of intimacy is jealousy—you cannot have any other preoccupation or interest. Therefore, as long as there is even a single alternative interest, there cannot be intimacy. In fact, even at the point of liberation, the intimate *rasa* cannot be understood. Liberation is the epitome of nonchalance. A liberated soul, who has no understanding of spiritual intimacy, will only wonder: Why is God being jealous? Why can't I have a relationship with others, along with a relationship to Kṛṣṇa? Since this jealous exclusivity cannot be appreciated or accepted until deep intimacy is established, therefore, one must not try to perform any *rasa* mental gymnastics prematurely. It is reserved for extremely advanced souls who can be spiritually in an exclusive relationship.

Voidism and Oneness in the Philosophy of Sri Chaitanya

In Indian philosophy, the voidism of Buddhist philosophy is seen as the opposition to the materialism of demigod worship and rituals. Then, classical impersonalism or Advaita is seen as the opposition to voidism in Buddhist philosophy. Finally, classical personalism or Vaishnavism is seen as the opposition to the impersonalism of Advaita. However, Sri Chaitanya's philosophy reconciles the reality of the material world (even as it rejects materialism), the emptiness of this world despite the reality of the material world (leading to the meaninglessness of this world, without factual voidism), and the interchangeability of perspectives between soul and God leading to their oneness without a factual identity.

The reality of the material world is that the world exists as meaning (not stuff) but it is *false* meaning; it exists, but it is not true. When this falsity of worldly meaning is recognized, then the world is considered empty, and only the Lord is considered meaningful. Finally, the soul has the capacity to look at this meaningless world from the Lord's perspective, and the world regains meaning in a new sense—namely, that the world is a reflection of meaning in the Lord. By the ability in the soul to see the world in the same way as the Lord, there is also the oneness of perspectives, without the oneness of the identity.

If we study the history of philosophical progression in Indian philosophy, then we see four main positions—materialism, voidism, impersonalism, and personalism—which seem contrary to each other. However, in the personalism of Sri Chaitanya, the core tenets of materialism, voidism, and impersonalism are accepted and reconciled with personalism. There is a certain sense in which

His philosophy is not materialism, voidism, or impersonalism, and in another sense, it is all these.

Our understanding of Sri Chaitanya's philosophy should begin with an alternative materialism, in which matter has three properties—it exists, it has meaning, and that meaning can be true or false. The Vedic scriptures exist, they are meaningful, and their meaning is true. Conversely, modern scientific theories exist, they are meaningful (at least to some people), and that meaning is false. Since both false and true meanings can exist, therefore, the existence of the world is not in question. Since different people can accept or reject these meanings, therefore, the meaningfulness of the world is also not in question, although that meaning is relative to the person. Finally, because this meaning can be objectively true or false, therefore, the universality of the truth of the meaning is not contrary to the relativity of meaning.

The core tenet of materialism is that the world is *real*. The core tenet of voidism and impersonalism is that the world is unreal in some sense. The world is called unreal because it is *temporary*. Things change, and whatever disappears cannot be called real in the ultimate sense of the word. However, materialism, voidism, and impersonalism conceive the worldly existence physically, which immediately creates a contradiction between realism and unrealism. How can we say that the world is unreal if the suffering is real? If the suffering itself was unreal, then why would we speak of getting out of the world?

All these contradictions are resolved when the world is described as meaning because now the world can exist, it can seem meaningful to some people, and yet it can be false. However, that doesn't mean that *everything* in the world is false. Certainly, perfect knowledge of the eternal truth can exist, so the books that embody that knowledge are possible. Even as those books may exist temporarily, the meaning in them can be eternal. As a result, the temporariness of existence is not contrary to the eternal truth of the meaning.

Thus, the contradictions between materialism, voidism, and impersonalism are immediately resolved when the world is treated as meaning. Most of the world is indeed false, but *everything* (even in the material world) is not false. Similarly, just because everything exists, doesn't mean that everything is *true*. There is no other way to reconcile the reality of the world with its unreality, other than to recognize that it exists as meaning.

However, the claim that the world exists as true or false meaning begs the question: Where did this meaning come from? If the source of this meaning is true, then how can it lead to false meanings? Materialism by itself doesn't have to deal with this problem because matter simply exists, and has no meaning. Voidism by itself doesn't have to deal with this problem because the world doesn't exist in an ultimate sense, so the whole thing is already non-existent and hence meaningless. Finally, impersonalism too doesn't have to deal with this issue because the world is false meaning, and it is caused by a malevolent agency called māyā that creates an illusory impression of meaning in us. This problem has to be dealt with in a philosophy that reconciles materialism, voidism, and impersonalism to say that the world is real, but it may not be true such that the truth is one and the falsities are many.

Personalism appears as the answer to the problem of this inconsistency between materialism, voidism, and impersonalism. In this answer, the source of all meaning is the Supreme Lord, but He is also *non-dual* in the sense that opposite meanings are present simultaneously in Him. Anything that embodies these opposite meanings at once is also non-dual, and hence, it can be called *true*. Conversely, anything that separates these opposites into separate contradictory aspects is false. Hence, falsity appears from the truth by the separation of the different aspects of the complete truth.

Since the source of everything is the Supreme Person, the ideas of impersonalism, voidism, and materialism are naturally rejected. And this rejection is classical Vaishnavism. However, this rejection is very problematic, because one can ask: If materialism, voidism, and impersonalism did not exist in the Supreme Person, then how could they appear in this world? Rejecting some ideology is very easy, but that rejection begs the question: How did the falsity appear from the truth? Surely, by the previous position of falsity being a separated aspect of the Supreme Person, materialism, voidism, and impersonalism must also be aspects of the Supreme Person, for otherwise, they could not appear in this world. Hence, they cannot be rejected *completely*, because they are aspects of the Supreme Person.

We are now led to the difficult problem outlined at the outset, namely, we have to go *past* classical Vaishnavism, which rejected materialism, voidism, and impersonalism, to advance personalism. Classical personalism got away by saying that some false ideologies exist in this world, without explaining how these ideologies appeared from a common source, so they must exist in the source as well. The difficult problem is that now personalism must be reconciled with materialism, voidism, and impersonalism.

The reality of the material world is already recognized in classical Vaishnavism, so that isn't a serious issue. The issue has been that this reality has to be understood as meaning, rather than "stuff", because only by taking the semantic position can we explain how a false world appears from the truth. If this preliminary condition about the understanding of matter is accepted, then personalism becomes consistent with materialism, but still remains inconsistent with voidism and impersonalism.

Sri Chaitanya's philosophy addresses these conundrums through three statements in His Sikśāstaka.

na dhanam na janam na sundarīm
kavitam vā jagad-īsha kamaye
mama janmani janmanīshvare
bhavatād bhaktir ahaituki tvayi

O my Lord, I have no desire to accumulate wealth, nor do I want a high birth, nor do I desire beautiful women, nor do I want liberation. I only want Your causeless devotional service, birth after birth.

ayi nanda-tanuja kinkaraṃ
patitam mām viśame bhavāmbudhau
kripayā tava pāda-pankaja-
sthita-dhuli-sadrisham vichintaya

O son of Maharaja Nanda (Kṛṣṇa), I am Your eternal servitor, yet somehow or other I have fallen into the difficult ocean of this world. Please consider me as one of the particles of dust placed on your Lotus feet.

yugāyitam nimeśena
chakśhushā pravriśhāyitam
śunyāyitam jagat sarvam
govinda-virahena me

O Govinda! Feeling Your separation, I am considering a moment to be like a *yuga*. Tears are flowing from my eyes like torrents of rain, and the whole world seems empty in Your separation.

The first statement rejects material wealth, high birth, and women, which is a rejection of materialism. However, it also rejects liberation from the material world, and requests only devotion, *birth after birth*. Repeated birth means the absence of liberation. By accepting it, the reality of the material world is accepted. Then, the second statement says that even though I exist in this world birth after birth, the world is considered a fallen place. However, the ask is not to liberate me from the material world; the ask is simply that the Lord *considers* me as one of the particles of dust on His Lotus feet. In the first statement, devotion to the Lord is requested, and in the second statement, the Lord is requested to consider the devotee as a dust particle on His feet. Then the third statement says that even though You consider me as a dust particle, still, the whole world seems empty in Your separation, and a moment passes by like a *yuga*. A *yuga* can be Satya, Treta, Dvāpara, or Kali; the shortest *yuga* is Kali, which is 432,000 years; a moment seems that long.

Classical Vaishnavism is already complicated from a theological perspective due to the doctrine of whole and part, which are "non-separable" (i.e., neither totally identical nor completely separate), but in Sri Chaitanya's philosophy, several additional paradoxes are presented. First, liberation is rejected. Second, the devotee asks for consideration from the Lord to accept him like a dust particle on the feet of Kṛṣṇa. Third, even then, the whole world seems empty. One might ask: Why not simply accept liberation, such that there would be a direct association, and one doesn't have to feel the emptiness and unhappiness of the world? The answer lies in the meaning of emptiness.

What is emptiness? It is not the factual absence of the world, but the word śunyāyitam is used to indicate how it *seems* empty. This emptiness is created by the feeling of separation from the Lord and constitutes the meaninglessness of the world. But since this feeling of separation is advocated, therefore, the pain of separation leading to the feeling of a void in this world is considered a greater position of devotion than the face-to-face meeting. The meaninglessness of this world now transforms into a *virtue* rather than a *vice*: We ask for this meaningless existence to constantly feel separated from the perfect source of all meaning. Thus, the philosophy of emptiness, void, and meaninglessness of the world, is resurrected as a perfectional state of devotion. We can no longer say that nihilism is a bad idea because it is accepted as the highest perfection. This nihilism, however, is not Buddhism; and yet, it has the classic traits of a nihilist ideology.

Then, oneness with the Lord also exists in the sense that the devotee is considered a particle of dust on the Lord's Lotus feet. Classical oneness philosophy claims that the soul merges into God's body, and the oneness in Sri Chaitanya's philosophy is like a dust particle *on* God's body. In this regard, we can distinguish between three types of oneness: within the body, on the body, and separate from the body. Even the world manifest from Kṛṣṇa is His part, but those parts are not Kṛṣṇa (as they are only parts). Conversely, every part of Kṛṣṇa's body (e.g., His eyes and tongue) are Kṛṣṇa completely (hence, food seen by Him is food eaten by Him). Then the ornaments on Kṛṣṇa's body are not *in* the body so they are not identical to Kṛṣṇa, and they are not *separate* from His body so they are more Kṛṣṇa than other expansions.

The sweat on His forehead, the clay markings on His body, and the dust on His feet are not identical to Kṛṣṇa, but they are more identical to Him than the other manifestations. In very specific terms, the ornaments, clay markings, dust, and sweat on God's body go wherever God goes; therefore, they can "see" whatever God can see, and yet, they are not privy to His feelings or emotions. These adornments of the Lord are one with the Lord in the sense that they can be as omniscient as the Lord, and yet, not identical to Him because they don't feel the happiness that the Lord feels. Since the adornments are as omniscient as the Lord, therefore, they are "one" with Him.

Philosophically, this type of oneness is being able to see the world from the vantage point of the Lord. By being situated on the Lord's body, the devotee has the same perspective as the Lord, and yet, the devotee is not identical to the Lord. Therefore, the devotee can also look at the material world in precisely the same way the Lord perceives the material world. Their perspectives are identical, so they can be called "one". And yet, despite the identity of their perspectives, they have not become the same person.

These ornaments have a unique property that they look more beautiful when worn by the Lord. Therefore, the Lord increases the beauty of the ornament, and the ornament increases the beauty of the Lord. Their interest in becoming more beautiful is fulfilled in the process of fulfilling the other's interest to be more beautiful. Both are decorating each other, so in one sense, they are united in purpose, hence "one". This sense of oneness by the unity of purpose exists in all parts of God devoted to God, so it is not unique to the ornaments. The difference is that by wearing them, the Lord makes the unity of purpose of making Himself more attractive by decorating Himself more perpetual.

Finally, the material world is also an ornament of the Lord, but one that the Lord has temporarily removed. When the same ornament is worn by the Lord, then it becomes His adornment. Therefore, using material things in the Lord's glorification is just like having Him wear ornaments manifest from Him. The "separation" between the Lord and the ornament is illusory because when the ornament is worn by others, it doesn't give the wearer the same beauty as the Lord. And even the limited beauty they get by wearing those ornaments is temporary. The temporality of the material world is the outcome of the Lord's ornaments being worn by others, and the material world is called false because those ornaments were not meant to be worn by others. However, by one person wearing another person's ornaments, the ornaments don't become false. This wearing only makes the person wearing the ornament deluded and the activity of trying to make oneself beautiful by such adornment an act of self-delusion. Thus, the realism of matter is not contrary to saying that worldly activities are illusory and temporary.

In this way, Sri Chaitanya's philosophical tenets advance personalism in three ways—(a) the world is the Lord's ornament, (b) the ornament is meaningless without the Lord, and (c) the ornament worn by the Lord is one with Him. With these advancements, materialism, voidism, and impersonalism become aspects of personalism. This kind of personalism is superior to that advocated in the other schools of Vaishnavism since these schools sometimes rejected oneness, voidism, and materialism, which Sri Chaitanya's philosophy incorporates.

The lesson to be learned from the progression by incorporating more aspects excluded from philosophy previously is this: In the initial stages of philosophy, materialism, voidism, and impersonalism are progressively rejected, but as we transcend impersonalism, then each of these is successively accepted. In simple terms, materialism, voidism, and impersonalism are rejected if they are presented either as standalone philosophies or as philosophies contrary to personalism. But if personalism is accepted as the foundation, then the progressive understanding of personalism leads to the acceptance of materialism, voidism, and impersonalism too. In the final analysis, we cannot say that the material world is false, or that it is meaningful by itself, or that it is separate from the Lord, or that the soul is not one with the Lord. That doesn't mean the acceptance of *standalone* materialism, voidism, or impersonalism, but their acceptance as *aspects of personalism*.

THE PERSONIFICATION OF KNOWLEDGE

Dualistic vs. Non-Dualistic Logic

Modern logic is defined by three principles—identity (A is A), non-contradiction (it cannot be *both* and A and not-A), and mutual exclusion (it cannot be *neither* A and not-A). In Vedic philosophy, we will call this a *dualistic* logic in the sense that the categories *neither* and *both* are logically forbidden forever. This dualistic logic is applied to knowledge by saying that knowledge must follow the rules of logic. That is, for something to be knowledge, it cannot involve or use the logical categories of neither and both.

In this article, we will explore how dualistic logic mimics *objects*, and why it cannot capture *persons*. If a person is involved in knowing, then dualistic logic fails to account for all aspects of knowing. Thus, even to correctly describe a single perception, we have to reject dualistic logic and embrace a non-dualistic logic under which the categories of both A and not-A and neither A and not-A are entertained.

The Problem of Dualistic Logic

Dualistic logic applies to *objects* but not to *persons*. For example, if you have a ball and a box, then either the ball is inside the box or outside of it. It cannot be both inside and outside, and it cannot be neither inside nor outside. However, if you have an apple and an observer, during observation, the apple is both inside the observer and outside it, and yet, it is neither inside the observer nor outside it.

- An apple is outside the observer because the apple exists even if the observer is unaware of it. Reality is said to exist if and only if it has effects even when we are unaware of them. Of course, those effects could be on other observers, but they are distinct observers.
- The same apple is inside the observer when the observer is aware of it because the apple's properties are in the observer's consciousness. Thereby, we can say that the apple has entered the observer's consciousness, and has become that specific observer's knowledge.
- Correct observation requires the observer to accept all of the apple's properties as they are, and no other properties. Hence, consciousness must be exclusively focused on the apple, and away from other things. This exclusion necessitates consciousness to be inside the apple.
- However, since the observer can know the apple partially, and mix it with other ideas, therefore, his attention may not be exclusively on the apple and thereby the observer is outside the apple. Outside the apple simply means divided attention that mixes many things.

All these problems of the observer being outside and inside but neither outside nor inside arise in the determination of various aspects of perception. If the observer isn't inside the apple, then the perception is not that of an apple. If the apple isn't inside the observer, then it is not the observer's perception. If the apple isn't outside the observer, the perception is a hallucination, not about reality. And if the observer isn't outside the apple, then the observer has no choice in knowing reality.

The observer is outside the apple if he *rejects* the apple. The observer is inside the apple if he *accepts* the apple. The apple is inside the observer if he *accepts* it. And the apple is outside the observer if he *rejects* it. Thus, two things are separated in a dualistic sense only when they are not interacting through observation. During observation, that separation is complemented by non-separation.

The Problem of Knowledge

What is knowledge? Under dualistic logic, we treat it like an *object.* We can think of it as a book, which must be impersonalized to accord to the dualistic logic, like objects. However, the problem doesn't disappear by converting knowledge into a book, because that book is also like an apple. Similarly, because the book was authored by someone, who was, in turn, perceiving reality, and the book represents that experience, therefore, it too has the non-dualistic properties of the observer.

Modern science is largely based on the idea that neither we nor the book has any property of personhood, which allows us to convert everything to dualistic logic. If, however, we are persons, then to be fully consistent (and avoid the problems of mind-body dualism, which will become a conflict between dualistic and non-dualistic logic, entailing two kinds of logic) we must also personalize the book non-dualistically.

Dualism Depends on Non-Dualism

It is often assumed that dualistic logic defines choice—something is either inside or outside—and you choose one of them. For example, you could choose to put the ball in the box or outside the box.

However, the fact is that every observation involves both inside and outside and neither inside nor outside, precisely because there is a choice of observation. In simple words, the choice of moving the ball inside or outside the box depends on observation, which in turn depends on something that is at once inside and outside, and yet, neither inside nor outside. Therefore, dualism depends on non-dualism.

This dependence is incredibly important for science in the sense that science depends on observations, which require non-dualism. However, disregarding that observation's true nature, and pragmatically using it in science to advance a dualistic study of reality, can also work. Of course, it would not produce a consistent science, nor would science ever be able to capture the nature of the observer. But the observer's choices to accept or reject a theory, or even move a ball from inside to outside a box, requires a system of non-dualism in the observer.

Failures of Dualistic Logic

If we disregard this problem and assume dualism all the way, then the distinction between *true* and *false* is lost because every hallucination, misperception, or misinterpretation is logically determined. For instance, if you are interacting with an apple, and it seems to be an orange, you cannot call your idea false because every step in this determination is logically determined. You cannot choose to observe it differently, or even choose to observe it, because those claims break dualistic logic.

Thereby, two observers interacting with the same reality can observe it differently—one of them may see an apple while the other sees an orange. However, since both outcomes are logically fixed, therefore, both are *true* although they are logically *contradictory*. You cannot say that reality is either an orange or an apple because both alternatives are logically proven in the same way. And you cannot blame the observers for not observing things correctly because that requires a choice.

Thereby, knowledge—when it is delimited by dualistic logic—must reject the idea of the *truth* and replace it with *existence*. The observers exist and their perceptions exist. Those perceptions can be different because the interaction between reality and those two observers creates different effects. Neither of these effects gives us the truth about the world. Those effects simply exist as facts.

Scientific Examples of Dualistic Failures

This distinction between *fact* and *truth* appears as relativistic effects in physics where two observers can measure the same reality differently, and you cannot say that one of them is *true.* Rather, they are both *facts,* neither of which are *true* (i.e., they don't tell us about reality). This general problem of relativism of observed facts, the absence of choice in the observation, and equivalence of all observers (due to the absence of choice) reduces all knowledge to *facts* rather than *truths*. In simple words, if you see an apple and

I see the same thing as an orange, they are both *our* facts, and neither of them is true.

In mathematics, this problem reappears as *undecidability*. Given a set of axioms, you can prove contradictory things by following different *proof paths*, which are like different observers interacting with the same reality to obtain mutually contradictory observations. Simple examples of this problem are the Liar's Paradox ("I am a liar"—if I'm a liar, then I'm truthful; if not, then I'm a liar) and Barber's Paradox ("A barber shaves those who don't shave themselves"—if the barber shaves himself, then he does not; if he doesn't shave himself, then he does). These arise because words like "I" and "Barber" have multiple meanings, and by following those meanings, you can follow different proof paths, which lead you to contradictory answers. You cannot decide if either of these answers is true. Undecidability means that you cannot decide whether X and not-X are *true* because both are equally provable.

There is hence a distinction between *provability* and *truth* in mathematics, like the distinction between *fact* and *truth* in physics. Facts are not truths, and in the same way, provability doesn't entail truth.

The Complete Collapse of Truth

Truths, under the dualistic conception of logic, simply do not exist. Facts exist and proofs exist. These facts can be empirically contradictory and proofs can be rationally contradictory. You can get around that problem by saying: *There is no truth* or that truth is undecidable or everyone can decide it for themselves. Nobody can say that your conclusion is *false* because it is logically provable.

In crude terms, your brain does a logical computation to arrive at one conclusion which is quite different from mine. Both logical computations are mathematical proofs, and they produce two different facts. So what if they are contradictory? They are both *provable*!

Despite these serious problems of dualistic logic, which have appeared in 20th-century mathematics and physics, people just can't help themselves from indulging in so-called logical arguments. It is standard practice, for example, to say that two conclusions—X and not-X—constitute a logical contradiction, and hence one of them must be false. They don't know that there is no truth with dualistic logic. 20th-century developments in mathematics, physics, and logic have completely destroyed the idea of truth.

Your brain and my brain exist. They prove some conclusions by a logical process using dualistic logic. And their conclusions are just facts, neither of which is truth. If your brain is different than mine, then its conclusions will naturally be different than mine. But who is to say that one brain is truthful? Just to do that, you have to say that one brain is the *ideal brain*, and all other brains are *non-ideal* brains. But you cannot prove which brain is ideal because ideality is beyond the scope of any fact or proof.

Objectivity vs. Personhood

The problem is that ideality lies in the realm of *choice*. Choices are ideal or non-ideal. You can also say that choices are better or worse. Facts, observations, things, and proofs are not better or worse. Rather, due to certain preferences that we chose, some facts, observations, things, and proofs are called better or worse. For example, a shorter proof can be called better. Why? Because we chose optimality over superfluity. Likewise, richness can be called better. Why? Because we chose pleasure over pain.

You cannot logically prove that optimality and pleasure are better. You must instead add them to your system of reasoning as axioms. Those who add them to the system of reasoning are making a choice. Now, you have two realms—of body and mind—the former governed by dualistic logic and the latter by non-dualistic logic. And you cannot have interactions between two logically different systems.

This is the point at which we have to realize that the only way forward is to throw away dualistic logic, and accept that everything must be described non-dualistically. This means we must entertain logical categories like both and neither. They can no longer be called *inconceivable*. We have to make them conceivable. That, of course, is not very hard. We just have to stop thinking of everything in terms of *objects* and start treating everything as a *person*. An apple, a book, and people are all persons.

Objectifying vs. Personifying

My Vedānta Sūtra commentary makes this argument, tracing the connection between the collapse of truth along with dualistic logic, the roots of dualistic logic in object thinking, its alternative in personal thinking, and the implied use of non-dualistic logics that overturn dualistic logical imperatives.

There are four parts to this connection. First, we must understand the serious fallouts of 20th-century mathematics, physics, and logic and how they have destroyed the idea of truth completely. Second, we must understand how dualistic logic originated in object thinking where one object can either be inside another or outside it; it cannot be neither inside nor outside, and it cannot be both inside and outside. Third, we have to grasp how ordinary observations necessitate the use of non-dualistic categories due to the conflicting requirements imposed by choice or will. And fourth, we have to accept that personhood, if accepted as a fundamental category as opposed to objects, can solve all the above problems.

The first three are easily demonstrable, as we have seen above. The fourth is a difficult philosophical leap in today's time because people are objectifying persons rather than personifying objects.

My thesis is factually not new because matter has always been personified as God's Śakti in Vedic philosophy, and called by names such as Durga, Sati, and Kāli. The problem is that Śaṅkarācārya depersonalized Śakti by calling Her *jada* or inert. Thereafter, Rāmanujachārya and Madhvāchārya continued the same idea by calling matter *achit* or non-conscious. Effectively, by such doctrines, the equivalent of Western mind-body dualism was created in the Vedānta tradition. As we have seen, these respectively involve non-dualistic and dualistic logics, which are mutually incongruent. When we mix two opposing logical systems into the same theory, infinite contradictions are created. The inability to resolve those contradictions then leads to the conclusion that Vedānta must be inconceivable.

Quite separately, if we personalize matter, we are required to admit non-dualistic logical categories like both and neither, which also seem inconceivable under the present hegemony of dualistic thinking.

Of course, the latter problem is equivalent to the fact that we cannot describe persons using dualistic logic. Does it mean persons are inconceivable or illogical and thereby must not exist? Or can we trace the so-called logical inconceivability of persons to the problem of observation which entails both inside and outside and neither inside nor outside in different complementary *modes*? The answer is obvious.

Conceiving the Inconceivable

Object thinking has failed along with dualistic logic. Person thinking along with non-dualistic logic is actually not contradictory because the contradiction is not in the *same* mode. For example, the observer is outside the apple in the sense that he has chosen to observe the apple. The observer is inside the apple in the sense that he has accepted the apple's reality just as it is. The apple is inside the observer because it is currently a specific observer's experience. And it is outside the observer in the sense that multiple observers can see it simultaneously.

Numerous logical contradictions are created *if* we ignore the modalities in which something is inside or outside. All those contradictions disappear if we incorporate modalities. These modalities are possible with personhood and impossible with objects. Hence modal logics, personhood, and conceivability of the inconceivable are intricately tied.

Observers' experiences constitute their knowledge, which can also be represented in language, art, and music which means that these expressions must inherit all the non-dualistic properties of knowledge. Due to this inherent non-dualism, we can say that books, art, and music inherit personalism.

The Falsehood of Material Inertness

The difference between a book and an author is that the book is static while the author is not. This fact has been used to call matter inert. This claim, however, falls apart when we analyze the distinction between inertness and consciousness—every property of the one can exist in the other.

- Everyone becomes inert while sleeping. Even during waking, we can keep our body inactive and thereby remain inert. So, why can't we call matter a sleeping or inactive consciousness?
- A yogi becomes inert by fixing his consciousness, although he is fully awake. Yogis are able to stay fixed and conscious for long. So, why can't we call matter a fixed consciousness?
- Factually, matter is not always inert. Even this world changes, which means that matter is not totally inert. Rather, it exhibits activities just like the activities of other consciousness.
- If we say that matter exhibits lawful order while living entities are lawless, the distinction could be attributed to self-control in matter and its relative absence in other living entities.
- If by order we mean periodicity, then many people follow a strict daily routine due to which their consciousness can be called periodic, depending on how strict their routine is.

Therefore, all claims about inertness and non-consciousness about matter are begging for distinction from sleeping, fixed, active, self-controlled, or self-disciplined consciousness. If the world was static, then we could call it a consciousness that is either inactive due to sleep or inactive due to fixity. If it moves lawfully, we can call it self-controlled consciousness. If it moves periodically, we could call it a self-disciplined consciousness. Where is the distinction between matter and consciousness?

In fact, people have been training themselves for eons on how to remain inert, alert but fixed, self-controlled, and self-regulated—the properties of matter! All these aspirants are thus trying to attain the state of perfection already in matter, and therefore, matter must be a more advanced consciousness than ordinary living entities. We should eliminate the distinctions that we cannot justify.

The Nature of Material Persons

Once we discard the artificial, unjustified, and prejudiced distinctions between consciousness and matter, then we can say that books, art, and music don't just inherit the non-dualism of persons due to being created by them, but they are in themselves persons. However, they could be sleeping persons, awake but fixed persons, lawful due to self-control persons, or periodic due to self-disciplined persons. Thereby, matter is not uniform or just of one type. Rather, different material objects are different kinds of persons.

For example, land and stones can be sleeping persons, trees and mountains can be awake but fixed persons, rivers and seas can be lawful due to self-control persons, and planets can be periodic due to self-discipline persons. If we don't find a personal template for something we consider inert, the correct question would be whether and how consciousness itself could exhibit such behaviors.

This idea is not as outrageous as might seem at first sight. Practically all nationalists talk about their motherland or fatherland and worship them as if they were persons. Plants and animals have been repeatedly demonstrated to have feelings and cognitions. Ecosystems are known to be self-preserving and self-sustaining quite like ordinary organisms. Most of us have a hard time personalizing stones and mountains because they remain static for long. But this problem would go away if we practiced fixing our consciousness to make our bodies and minds motionless for long durations.

Person and Personality

Once we understand how inanimate or inert objects are also persons, and we know that ordinary persons can produce or manifest art, music, and books, then this process of creativity can be modeled as one person giving "birth" to another, and these two persons can be related as "parent" and "child".

It is not uncommon, for instance, for people to call their musical, artistic, and literary creations their "babies". It is not rare for nations to call their founders "fathers" or "mothers" of the nation. It is not infrequent that new organizations are "born", startup founders undergo "birthing pangs", and startups "grow up" after some years. In many religions, sacred books are worshipped like deities and divinities.

What is of particular interest to us here is that all these created persons carry the *personalities* of their creative fathers and/or mothers. The sacred books, being the word of God, are considered embodiments of God. Likewise, the author's persona is in their books, the musician's character in their music, and the artist's emotions in their paintings. An organization mimics the values of its founders, a nation the virtues and ideals of those who struggled to carve it different from other nations.

This is not difficult to understand if we note that the parents transmit parts of their nature into their children, see their children as extensions of their own personalities, and vicariously live through the youth of their children in their old age. The same principle upholds for all creations. The author wishes to see his books continue even after his death. The musician hopes to travel to places far and wide through his music. The artist hopes to be remembered long after he is gone. The founders of nations hope that they will continue to live through the citizens in the form of values they give them.

The personality of the parent is present in the children to varying extents, because the parents pass their genes, ideas, beliefs, culture, morals, values, ideals, and religions, to their children. The parents feel disheartened and betrayed if their children relinquish what their parents bequeathed them. This indicates two things. First, the children inherit the personalities of their parents in part. Second, the parents wish to live through their children. Even materialists agree that the biological entities have a great purpose of passing on their genes and ensuring the survival of their species and race.

The Problem of Parental Immanence

Thus far, we have established four things. First, reality must be modeled as persons to avoid logical contradictions. Second, the mind vs. matter distinction is not just logically incoherent, but prejudiced without justification; all seeming material objects are also persons. Third, so-called inanimate things are treated as children and parents—a book is an author's child, and some land is the author's mother. Fourth, the child inherits the parental properties, and parental personality lives through their children.

At this juncture, we can draw a distinction between a person and their personality. Obviously, a person has a personality. That same personality becomes immanent in their children, including artistic creations. However, that personality may not be *fixed*. In this world, people change their personalities. When a person dies, the person is disconnected from their personality and gets a new one. However, if that person is alive, their personality is unchanged, and that personality is immanent in their child creations, and we tend to say that the person lives *in* and *through* their children. If, however, the child dies, or discards the parental personality, then the parent is not automatically supposed to be dead.

The parent is immanent by his personality, and transcendent as a person. The person is outside the child, and yet, inside the child through the personality. If the parent dies or changes his personality, then the children are disconnected from the parent, although they have their former parental personality.

Now, let's suppose that (a) the parent is eternal, (b) their personality is eternally unchanged, and (c) their children can never completely disconnect themselves from the parental personality. In such cases, the parent would be said to be eternally living in the children, although the parent is still distinct from the child in the sense that if the child died, the parent would not be automatically deceased.

Such rare forms of immanence arise in cases of spiritual personalities who continue to live through their disciples, books, and other creations, because (a) the person and personality are eternal, (b) the connection between the person and personality never changes, and (c) the personality is so unique that we cannot attach the children to any other personality other than falsifying them as children. I will return to this eternally immanent and yet transcendent person-personality in a short while.

Personalism and Non-Dualism

We can put all these conclusions together by noting that *everything is a person*. There are no objects. Objects cannot be both inside and outside, or neither inside and outside. But persons can be. Therefore, there is no contradiction in saying that the person is transcendent and immanent. The difficulties we find in such a conception are due to dualistic object thinking. The person thinking is non-dualistic.

The difference between a person and an object is that the *person can exist in logically contradictory states* falsifying the principle of identity (A is A). An object is always in a single state. Therefore, when we use a word to refer to that person, that word has many meanings, corresponding to the different logically contradictory states of the person, such that if the word is treated like an object rather than a person, logical contradictions are created. We have seen examples of such words in the Liar's Paradox and the Barber's Paradox. They are resolved by giving the words multiple meanings or treating them as persons. At the least, we have to give up dualistic logical thinking to avoid paradoxes.

To elaborate further using the word "I" that involves self-awareness, the self is at once observer, observed, and observing, but in each of these modes, it is *not* the other modes, falsifying the identity principle. That is not a self-contradiction because the self is not an observer and observing in the observed state, not observing in the observer and observed states, and not observed in the observer and observing states. This requires that the self be *one* and yet *three* different things. Those three different things are the *modes of the self*. Each mode is not separate from the other modes and not identical to them. This peculiar idea is noted as the Bhedābheda doctrine of Vedānta. Bhedābheda is inconceivable under dualistic logic and conceivable under non-dualistic logic.

Demystifying the Problem of Modes

Most people struggle with the breakdown of all these logical principles, especially that of identity. Demystifying it requires what I call the *principle of underdetermination*, which in simple terms means that each modality determines what the other mode *cannot be* but does not determine what *it is*.

A classic example is an underdetermination between percepts and concepts. Each percept tells us what the concept cannot be, although it doesn't tell us what it will be. For example, if you see something red and round, you can be sure that it is not a banana, but you can't be sure if it is an apple or a nectarine. Similarly, each concept tells us what the percept cannot be, although it doesn't fix the percept. For example, if we call something a chair, you can be sure that it is not a fluid, but you can't say if it has four or six legs, whether or not it has a hand rest and backrest, whether it is high or low, and so forth.

Yet another easy example is the underdetermination between the answers to six questions—what, why, how, who, where, and when. By fixing the answer to one question, numerous alternative answers to the other five questions are preempted. But that doesn't fix the answers to those five questions. Since one mode decides what the other modes can't be, therefore, the modes are not *independent*. However, since each mode doesn't decide what the other modes will be, therefore, they are not *dependent*.

This is how we get seemingly contradictory conclusions like neither identical nor separate. They are self-contradictory in dualistic logic, but not so in non-dualistic logic. This is how the inconceivable becomes conceivable—it is inconceivable as objects and conceivable as underdetermining modalities.

The Personification of Knowledge

Since logic always applies to knowledge, therefore, knowledge can be viewed as a person or an object. When knowledge is governed by dualistic logic, then it is modeled as objects, and when it is governed by non-dualistic logic, then it is modeled as persons. This idea is seen in Vedic texts when Saraswati is called the personification of knowledge. Whatever we call "knowledge" in this world is therefore not an idea in a Platonic world, nor is it confined to books, nor is it our interpretation. Rather, there is a person called Saraswati, who embodies that knowledge. In simple words, knowledge is a person, not an object.

Similarly, the Absolute Truth is called *jñānam advayam* (SB 1.2.11) or non-dual knowledge known in three modes of Bhagavan, Paramātma, and Brahman, which are neither separate nor identical. Of these, Bhagavan is the author, Paramātma is the part of the author's persona visible in the book, and Brahman is the book. In general, being the author is itself one of the aspects of the full person, due to which the author is a part of the person, and a part of the author is visible in the books.

In the material creation, for example, Kāraṇodakaśāyī Viṣṇu is the person, Garbhodakaśāyi Viṣṇu is the person in the author mode (and hence a part of Kāraṇodakaśāyī Viṣṇu), while Kṣīrodakaśāyī Viṣṇu is the part of the author mode visible in the book (and hence a part of Garbhodakaśāyi Viṣṇu). This situation is simplified by referring to Garbhodakaśāyi Viṣṇu as Bhagavan and Kṣīrodakaśāyī Viṣṇu as Paramātma. Context determines the meaning of these words as Bhagavan and Paramātma can be interchanged because the child of a creator can again become a creator and produce further children. For example, the demigods are the children of Paramātma, and in that regard, He is referred to as Bhagavan.

Three Modalities of Knowledge

To fully appreciate the tripartite division of personalities, we have to understand that knowledge exists in three modalities—individual, universal, and contextual. Take an ordinary concept like a man. There is an ideal personification of man called Manu present in a heavenly planet, due to which "man" is not a Platonic idea, but a person. Manu is the ideal man, and hence the universal. Different descendants of Manu constitute the human population, and they are individuals. However, in between Manu and the human population is a ruler or a king, who implements the Laws of Manu while governing humans. These laws are not universals. They are contextually prescribed for a local population. Thereby, the localized and contextualized ruler of the population constitutes the contextual but is still a person.

Now, if every man voluntarily follows the Laws of Manu, we could say that Manu's laws are immanent in each man. But if they sometimes disobey the laws and the king corrects them, then we could say that Manu's laws are transcendent to ordinary men, because they are reposed in the king. However, if most men are disobedient, but they follow the Laws of Manu out of fear of the king, then we could say that they are obeying out of fear of the king and hence the king is immanent in the population. Likewise, the population could also follow all the laws out of love of the king—he is our king, and we love him, so we do as he says.

Thus, there is no contradiction in saying four things: (a) the laws are immanent, (b) the laws are transcendent, (c) the king is transcendent, and (d) the king is immanent. The laws are immanent if the population is aware of the laws and voluntarily obedient. The laws are transcendent if they are forced upon the population due to their ignorance and/or disobedience of the laws. The king is transcendent if the population is generally disobedient, and follows the laws only out of fear of the king. And the king is immanent if the population follows the laws out of love of the king.

The Nature of Immanence

The Paramātma is the ruler of the material world and prescribes the *laws of nature*. These laws are impersonalized in modern science because nature obeys laws like a voluntarily obedient person, and Paramātma, therefore, has no need to interfere in nature's work. However, if the soul doesn't follow the laws, then Paramātma punishes them. But if we remember Paramātma, then He is immanent, and we follow the laws perfectly due to that remembrance. The question is: What happens if we don't remember Paramātma? Is He immanent or not? This is when we have to recall our foregoing discussion that an eternal creator is eternally immanent, although we may not be *aware* of that immanence.

The meaning of Paramātma's immanence is that each person has an *innate idea* of God, namely that there is order in nature due to a supreme being, who rewards and punishes and can lead us to salvation from this world. People call this "a higher power", "a perfect being", "God" and so forth. Every person has a conscience in them due to which they tend to avoid sinful actions. Atheists too innately believe that nature has rational order. Descartes, Kant, and Jung have all relied on innate idea paradigms. Therefore, the idea is always immanent. However, the idea can be more or less *manifest*. Due to that, some people are more or less conscionable. Some believe in God more than others. And some may believe in natural order, natural justice, karma, and retribution, to varying levels of conviction.

There are deeper issues of causality involved here noted in Satkāryavāda due to which we never *learn* anything new because everything is already innately present. We only *remember* and *forget* things. The soul's fall in the world, for example, is attributed to forgetfulness and liberation to remembrance. What is present, and yet can be forgotten, is described in Bhagavad-Gita as *avyakta mūrti* or an unmanifest form. This unmanifest form is the innate idea of Paramātma which manifests to different levels in different persons. It manifests more when one suffers and less when one is enjoying life.

The Genesis of the Impersonal

When a person is understood *partially*, then the impersonal is created. This impersonal includes ideas, objects, numbers, equations, processes, vibrations, force, etc. Simply by revealing or hiding different aspects of His personhood, the Paramātma can manifest different ontologies to a person. Thus, when Paramātma manifests more, slowly a person becomes more conscionable and personalist. For instance, he might start treating other people as he would like to be treated himself. When Paramātma is manifest even more, then nature is progressively personalized. Finally, if Paramātma is fully manifest, then the whole universe is seen as being governed by a person rather than impersonal laws.

Modern science is a byproduct of a near-complete ignorance of Paramātma, under which scientists believe that there is regularity and order in nature, but it is mathematical laws rather than a person. They also assume that natural laws are not normative or moral in nature. And they have slowly become accustomed to the idea that they themselves are not persons; they are merely complex objects.

Materialism is nothing but the objectification of persons, due to which the world is "outside", each thing is separated from the other things, and the idea that something could be "inside" terrifies people. In one sense, since everything is inside and outside, and yet, neither inside nor outside, therefore, everything in materialism and modern science is false. There is not a shred of truth in it. And yet, this science works because nature is still ordered and lawful due to Paramātma.

We can observe this order and capture it in mathematical equations quite like we can capture the order in train arrival and departure at train stations using a mathematical equation although trains are not arriving and departing because of that equation—they are working orderly because of dutiful train drivers and administrators in a command center. If the train administration works well, then trains will continue to arrive and depart on time, and the mathematical equations will continue to predict correctly.

Reverting to Personalism

The problem is that you cannot capture many observations using such equations. When predictive failures appear, science resorts to formulating predictive probabilities. When those probabilities prove inadequate, it talks about the dynamical evolution of probabilities. When that fails, arbitrary variables and constants are inserted, modifying equations for computing the dynamical evolution of probabilities. When that fails, then extra dimensions are postulated. When that fails, then extra dimensions curving around other dimensions are postulated. Modern science is a factory for manufacturing equations.

This is why we have to go to fundamental questions about logic. If logic is dualistic, then reality is objects. When reality is objects, then it can be quantified due to the separation of objects. When it is quantified, then it has to be modeled using mathematical equations. Nobody can question this process because everything logically follows from the fundamental assumption of dualistic logic.

The challenge to science is the problem of observation due to which dualistic logic is broken. The solution to that problem is that reality is persons rather than objects, and needs non-dualistic logic. Factually, objects have no reality. This means there is nothing called idea, thing, number, equation, process, vibration, force, etc. All these are produced by *hiding* different aspects of a person. When sufficient aspects of a person are obscured from our vision, then the person is reduced to an object, process, equation, vibration, force, and number.

To conquer this ignorance, one has to revert to personalism and ask ourselves how a person is both inside and outside the other persons. Dualistic logic is the biggest hurdle in this process. By discarding it, we wipe the slate clean of everything that modernity has created in the name of knowledge.

We now begin with a new idea, namely, that *knowledge is a person*. Thereby, we are inside knowledge and we are outside knowledge. Similarly, knowledge is inside us, and knowledge is outside us.

Inside knowledge means that each of us is some partial knowledge. Outside knowledge means that there is complete knowledge available for knowing. Knowledge inside means that complete knowledge can be known. And knowledge outside means that complete knowledge is not our creation. These simple ideas about knowledge are accepted by everyone. But they are not so simple. Just realizing them involves overturning thousands of years of false object-based dualistic logical thinking.

The "God Has Many Names" Problem

Names as Descriptions of a Person

There are many ways to demonstrate the problems of logic, set theory, and Gödel's incompleteness. They are all different ways to look at the problem, to become convinced that there is a problem. One such way is the statement "God has many names". These names are not *synonymous*. By assigning various names to God, we describe Him in many non-synonymous ways. We don't equate one name to another, and we don't reject any of the names.

This is contrary to logic, in which one thing can be only one thing. To preserve logic, we can discard all but one name, and then, we will know God incompletely. To keep all the names, and know God completely, we have to discard logic. "God has many names" leads to inconsistency vs. incompleteness. In this post, I will summarize the paradoxes that arise in logic, set theory, and number theory, before discussing how the same problem appears when God is called by many names. We will discuss the solution to the problem, and its pervasiveness.

Three Formulations of Incompleteness

Gödel proved two incompleteness theorems. We can call them 1T and 2T for brevity. 1T states: "All systems of arithmetic are incomplete—i.e., they cannot prove or disprove all the statements within the purview of that arithmetic system". 2T states: "No system of arithmetic can prove its consistency". These two statements are constructed cleverly by using the phrase "cannot prove or disprove". How do you prove that you cannot prove or disprove? The answer is—by using the method of proof by contradiction. You *assume* that you can prove or disprove, and show that the assumption leads to a contradiction.

Some people say: Proof by contradiction isn't proof. To prove something, we must construct a step-by-step procedure to prove it. These objections suppose that there is something wrong with logic—the principle of excluded middle—X must either be true or false, not neither. Hence, on the off chance that someone might say: You haven't proved anything by constructing a proof by contradiction, Gödel's theorems are phrased as "you cannot prove or disprove" rather than "the arithmetic system, if complete, is inconsistent". But before incompleteness, Gödel had proved the consistency and completeness of formal logic—that logical statements are true by virtue of their *structure* rather than *meaning*. Thereby, objections to proof by contradiction are rejected.

If we combine two facts—(a) logic is consistent and complete, (b) assuming consistency and completeness for arithmetic leads to a contradiction—then we can say "an arithmetic system is either inconsistent or incomplete". This simpler statement combines three theorems—logic's consistency and completeness, 1T, and 2T—and is generally used, although it is not a theorem that Gödel "proved" in the historical and academic sense of published papers. Let's call this theorem 3T. We can rephrase it as follows: "Assuming that logic isn't broken, arithmetic is either inconsistent or incomplete".

The Fundamental Problem of Logic

We have to remember what logic is—statements true by virtue of structure rather than meaning. For instance, "A is A" must be true for *all* A. It cannot be true for some A and false for other A, depending on what the word A *means*. It also entails that we have to distinguish between A and its meaning.

"A is A" can be "God is God", a useless tautology. To make the identity principle useful, we have to say "God is omnipotent" and identity will imply that "Omnipotent is God". If we now say that "God is omniscient", then by identity, we will conclude "Omniscience is Omnipotence" because we are relying on the truth conclusion by virtue of sentence structure rather than word-meaning.

To eliminate such outcomes, Aristotle limited logic to those words that either have only one meaning or all alternative meanings are *synonymous.* Thereby, "God is omnipotent" and "God is omniscient" are not permissible in logic because God has two non-synonymous meanings—omniscient and omnipotent.

Hence, when we say that logic is consistent and complete, we are relying on every word having only one meaning. Since one of the above two statements about God is forbidden by logic, therefore, one of these statements—"God is omnipotent" or "God is omniscient"—must be rejected within logic.

The Fundamental Problem of Set Theory

20th-century philosophers and mathematicians tried to solve this problem by set theory and ran into paradoxes. For instance, we can form two sets—Omniscient := {God} and Omnipotent := {God}—and then we have a well-defined notion of "is": X is Y if X is a member of Y. However, with set theory, a new problem concerning "is not" is created. For instance, by the above definition of "is", the definition of "is not" would be that something is not a member of a set. Then, "Omniscience is not Omnipotence" must mean that some member of either of these sets is not a member of the other set. Since there is only one member in both sets, therefore, to sustain the difference between Omniscient and Omnipotent, we must remove God from one of the two sets. Thereby, God cannot be simultaneously Omniscient and Omnipotent, due to set theory!

If we insist that God is both Omniscient and Omnipotent, then we get a contradiction. The system of reasoning is either inconsistent (God is a member of mutually exclusive sets creating a logical contradiction) or incomplete (God cannot be both omnipotent or omniscient, so one of the above two claims must be rejected). Anyone who claims that God is both Omnipotent and Omniscient is now *irrational* because he has broken the principles of logic and set theory.

Multiple Forms of the Problem

The problem of logic, the problem of set theory, and the problem of Gödel's incompleteness are the *same* problem in different *forms*. Incompleteness simply means that logic will not allow multiple meanings of the same word—e.g., "God is omniscient" and "God is omnipotent". If we try to evade that problem by redefining "is" as membership of a set, then we will get a problem with "is not". We can state the problem in many different ways—(a) one word has only one meaning, (b) sentences that use different meanings of the same word must be rejected, (c) any system that tries to include words with multiple meanings leads to contradictions, thereby rendering the logical system self-inconsistent. It takes a while to get convinced about this problem. You have to try different formulations, and you will find that each leads to a new problem.

Let's suppose we try to define God as a set {Omniscient, Omnipotent}. Since we are using a set-theoretic language, hence, we must define the members of the above set as follows—Omniscient:= {God}, and Omnipotent:= {God}. By substitution, God := {{God}, {God}}, which means that I must assume God to define God. Let's now try to define "is not God". We can have two definitions—(a) some of the attributes of God are missing, or (b) all of the attributes of God are absent. By the first, we can remove either Omniscient or Omnipotent, and get not-God := {{God}}, which means "God is not God". By the second, not-God := {}, which means nothing is not God (since not-God is an empty set). Hence, either God is a self-contradictory concept (God is not God) or everyone is God. Depending on your creativity, you can create infinite additional problems.

The Theological Form of the Problem

The Vedas state that God has infinite names. God is *Svarāt* or independent. God is infallible or *Acyuta*. God is the supreme truth or *Satyam-Param*. God is endless or *Ananta*. God's stomach is bound by a rope; hence one of His infinite names is *Dāmodar*. These names do not refer to different *gods*. They refer to one God with many names. But those names are not *synonymous*. Viṣṇu Sahastranāma notes one thousand non-synonymous names of Lord Viṣṇu as He is all those qualities.

We cannot use infinite non-synonymous names of God in logic, because due to contradictions—e.g., "the endless is bound by a rope". To be consistent, we have to remove either "endless" or "bound by a rope". Thereby, what is permitted by logic must also become an incomplete truth by eliminating some truth about God. Thus, we get a theological form of Gödel's Incompleteness: The use of infinite non-synonymous names of God is inconsistent; however, if we restrict ourselves to only one name of God, then it is incomplete. This is why religion is logically contradictory: The word "God" has many non-synonymous meanings.

In Christianity, God is omnipotent, omniscient, and omnibenevolent. The use of three words leads to a contradiction of the problem of evil (since I'm suffering, therefore, either God doesn't know that I'm suffering, or He isn't powerful enough to cure my suffering, or He doesn't love me to cure my suffering). But if limit God to only one of the three words, then He is described incompletely.

My Realization of Incompleteness

I struggled for 15 years with this problem. Every subject I studied revealed that "one thing is not one thing". It is actually many things. One word doesn't have one meaning. It actually has many meanings. I traced this problem back to Aristotle, and then the historical legacies of Socrates and Plato. Socratic debates were conducted on the principle that any word with one definition is flawed. If you say that man is a two-legged animal, then a man who lost one leg in a war is no longer a man. Similarly, the definition of man as a two-legged animal includes penguins. Whatever definition we use, is either too broad or too narrow. But if we permit many definitions then we also get contradictions.

Plato then misled many generations of Greeks into believing that our inability to provide one complete definition is merely *our* flaw. In reality, there is an ideal world in which everything has one definition. Obviously, to be logically consistent, that ideal thing in the ideal world must not have contradictory definitions. For instance, the ideal man in the ideal world must either be kind or cruel. He cannot be sometimes kind and sometimes cruel. Platonic eternity meant everything was fixed, static, unmoving, and unchanging.

Aristotle then misled hundreds of generations by saying that we can restrict ourselves to those words which have one meaning. He thought that numbers are such words that have only one meaning. But Gödel disproved Aristotle when he showed that even numbers can be used in many ways—e.g., as names and things—and all such ways are necessary to complete mathematics.

At the end of my struggle, I wrote *Gödel's Mistake—The Role of Meaning in Mathematics*, tracing the origins of paradoxes in set theory, number theory, and computational theory. Digits like 1 and 0, for instance, are used in three distinct ways in computers—(a) data, (b) instruction, and (c) truth values. A program is 1s and 0s—because a program is instructions. A picture file is 1s and 0s—because a file is data. And you can pass a data file to a program to print a truth value—true or false. But since we cannot reconcile three different meanings of 1 and 0, hence, we have to compartmentalize them into three separate memories—data memory, instruction memory, and truth value memory. A computer compartmentalizes these three types of number interpretations.

The result is *incompleteness*. When you pass a program file to a compiler, the compiler treats it as *data* rather than *instructions*. It can at most check if the program has a correct *syntax* and not what the program *does* on being executed because it is parsing data rather than instructions. The compiler cannot know if the program is malicious. All problems of computer security are rooted in the inability to interpret numbers alternately as data and instruction.

Origins of the Problem in Reality

Identifying the problem is different from solving it, although part of identifying it is knowing that "one thing is not one thing". The solution is found in Vedic philosophy—one thing is many things. Everything originates in one thing—God—who is infinite things at once. This is why there are infinite names of God that describe the various things that He is. Those infinite things include mutually *opposite* things—e.g., that He is endless, and yet He is bound by a rope.

The things that originate from God are *fewer* things at once. So, it is possible to look at the simplest thing around us—which has expanded from more complex things to be fewer things at once—and say "one thing is only one thing". This is an oversimplification of reality but if it works in some cases, people get addicted to oversimplifying everything in order to study it. Logic, or "one thing is only one thing" is the embodiment of that tendency to oversimplify.

The solution to the problem requires *aspects*. The opposite things that God is are His aspects. We can liken these crudely to the six faces of a cube. Left and right, top and bottom, front and back, are logical opposites, but they are aspects of the cube. If you see one aspect, you don't see the others. Hence, all aspects are potentials that can be realized by a choice, and at the point of choosing, the whole can be equated to the aspect by using the connector *is*. In another case, however, we can equate the whole to the opposite aspect by using the connector *is*. Contexts are not *simultaneous*. Thus, the left side and right side, the top side and the bottom side, and the front side and the back side, are the cube, but not simultaneously. The problem of logic is *universalizing* the opposite claims.

Realizing the Problem in Reality

This problem reached its pinnacle in quantum mechanics where one macroscopic thing is many *orthogonal* microscopic things—like the faces of an infinite-faced dice—but you can never measure them simultaneously. This is why frustrated with the problem, Einstein claimed that "God does not play dice". The problem went even further into the properties of a particle. For instance, position and momentum cannot be measured simultaneously. Niels Bohr then devised the term "complementarity" to describe atomic reality.

However, nobody had the foresight to rethink what "complementarity" meant in the case of the "simplest" things—if the simplest thing is not one thing, but many things, then logic fails because logic was formulated based on the assumption that at least the simplest things are just one thing.

If atomic particles are the numerous "faces" of an object, then table and chair are the multiple faces of a room; the many rooms are the many faces of a house; the house is one of the many faces of the city, and each citizen of a country is one of the many faces of the country. If someone changes their citizenship, they change to become the face of another country. Thereby, "motion" is not uniform because the moving thing changes in the very process of becoming the face of something else. If a chair is moved from the kitchen to the bedroom, it changes imperceptibly because it is now a face of the bedroom instead of the kitchen. If we go to a holy place, we change because we are now the face of the holy place. To go to another planet, we must have the capacity to become the face of something that we are currently not. This also requires us to construct an inverted tree that converges from many *things* to many *faces* of one thing.

Nobody wants to go down that path, because they want to think of many things rather than many faces of one thing. The many things are separate from each other. The many faces are inseparable. Quantum entanglement would be trivially easy if we said that many particles are just many faces of one thing, and hence while they seem distinct, they are actually inseparable. To avoid these conclusions, quantum physicists created a "measurement problem"—a "collapse" by which one thing which is actually many things, "collapses" into one thing—just to preserve the idea that one thing is only one thing as far as our everyday world is concerned and atomic reality is an exception.

The problem of quantum mechanics is also the problem of logic—the false idea that "one thing is only one thing". If empirical evidence shows that one thing is many things, scientists create interpretations of that evidence that helps them preserve the false idea that "one thing is only one thing" because that is the lens through which science has always interpreted and perceived reality. They cannot think in any other way because rejecting that false idea requires them to start from scratch from the time that Aristotle had gone wrong.

The Absolute Necessity of Semanticism

This idea of aspectism—as seen through the six faces of a cube—however, proves inadequate when we realize that we are talking about a "cube" separate from its "faces". In quantum mechanical language, there is something called a "wavefunction" akin to a cube, which collapses into the observation of one of the faces. When it collapses, you can say "this face is the cube", but otherwise, "the cube is not just the face". This is also a violation of the principle of identity in logic, because sometimes "X is Y" but at other times "Y is not X".

Therefore, aspectism alone doesn't solve the problem, because there is a deeper problem of logic. We cannot superimpose the ideology that "one thing is many things" upon the logic that claims "one thing is only one thing". We also need to be able to say that when we see one of the faces, we are seeing the cube. However, the cube is distinct from these faces. Thus, "seeing one of the faces is also seeing the cube", but, "the cube is not reducible to any of those faces".

This problem can only be solved by *semanticism*, in which the "cube" is a *concept* and the six faces of the "cube" are its *conceptual* aspects. This is just like "black is color" but "color is not black". We have to treat the cube just as we treat color, and each of its faces just as we treat the various shades. Set theory does the opposite—it treats color as a set of shades, and reduces a cube to a set of its faces. If we cannot see all the faces simultaneously or if one face is logically non-synonymous to others or if one non-synonymous face is logically opposed to another face (e.g., top and bottom) then we run into many problems.

Intension and Extension

This problem is discussed in linguistic philosophy by using two terms—*intension* and *extension*. The word "color" means something, which is its *intension*. The set of "shades" is the *extension* of that intension. We cannot equate the intension to the extension, which means "color" has two non-synonymous meanings. These two meanings, while distinct, cannot be separated from one another because the extension is a part of the intension, and intension is a part of extension. For instance, when we say that "black is a color", the intension (color) is a part of extension (black). But since color includes black, therefore, the extension (black) is a part of intension (color). Thus, we cannot separate the intension and extension and we cannot equate these non-synonymous meanings.

The problem of non-synonymous meanings of a word being mutually inseparable is called Bhedābheda in Vedic philosophy. We can extend this to a cube. The six faces of a cube are non-synonymous meanings of the word "cube", not separable from the cube, and hence each other. Now, we can talk about how the same thing is many things without creating logical contradictions.

The simple statement that God has infinite names is not so simple, because the names are non-synonymous, and when the same thing is two different things, then logically speaking those two different things must be synonymous, giving us a contradiction. All the extra complexity comes from trying to resolve that contradiction to say how one thing is many things. We need to say that each thing has many aspects, and that thing and its aspects are meanings.

The Philosophy of Word and Meaning

This problem is seen in two distinct uses of the Sanskrit term *pada*. A *pada* is a word. But because that word has many meanings, those meanings are *aspects* of the word. Hence, *sampada* means "along with the aspects". But *padārtha* represents the "meaning of a word". Thereby, when the five elements of Sāñkhya, namely, earth, water, fire, air, and ether are called *padārtha*, we have to ask: What is the *pada*? That *pada* is the concept in the mind (such as a table) and it is expanded in five ways as sound, touch, sight, taste, and smell into a sense-perceivable object. Thus, what is within the mind can be called *sampada*—"along with the aspects". But what is perceived by the senses is called *padārtha*—the "sense-perceivable meaning of the concept residing in the mind".

The "word" in the mind is not the sound we hear. But if we think of the concept, its presence in the mind has an effect on the sense of hearing, due to which the sound is also triggered by the thought. Hence, the thought "table" and the sound "table" are not identical and not separable. The thought "table" can be called by another name, but since it is called in a particular linguistic context by one specific name, therefore, in that context, the name is one of the faces of the concept. However, we can strip all these faces from the concept and add a different set of faces because the thing is distinct from the faces, and yet, in a certain context, that thing is identified by using one of its many faces.

Therefore, we have to talk about the cube and its six faces as concepts. The cube is the *sampada* or intension, while its six faces are the *padārtha* or the extension. The *sampada* and *padārtha* are non-synonymous meanings of the word "cube"—because sometimes the word refers to my thought and at other times to the thing being seen. Both meanings are required but they are non-synonymous.

The additional problem is that just as thought gives rise to the object, similarly, the object gives rise to the thought. Thereby, the thought of "cube" is *sampada* with the *padārtha* of five sense-perceivable properties of the six distinct faces, and the five sense-perceivable properties of the six different faces are the *sampada* with the *padārtha* of the thought "cube". This problem is called *inside* and *outside.* The cube is inside all the faces, and the faces are inside the cube. This problem is noted succinctly by stating that the five elements of Sāñkhya are inside and outside each other. For instance, everything is in ether and comes out of it. And everything that comes out of ether has ether within it.

Since the mental concept is present in the sense-perceivable reality, therefore, we can acquire the concept by observing that reality, provided we also use the mind along with the senses. When the mind is used along with the senses, the mind is called the "sixth sense". It is that sense which perceives the concept *in* the sense-perceivable reality. However, the sense-perceivable reality is produced from the mental reality. Thus, we can produce a world out of thought, and we can perceive the world to know the thought that produced it. Thereby, the world is in the thought, and the thought is in the world. They are non-synonymous, inseparable, and necessary aspects of each other.

We can apply this principle to mind and body. The mind is in the body, and the body is in the mind. If the mind wasn't in the body, then hurting the body would not hurt the mind. If the mind wasn't outside the body, then the death of the body would mean the death of the mind. Therefore, we need two opposite claims for life and death. The materialist gets away by saying "the mind is in the body" because he is only talking about life. He needs the opposite claim while talking about death. Given the contradiction between the two claims, we can never solve the mind-body problem *logically*. Instead, we need a semantic way of thinking in which the cube is in the faces and faces are in the cube.

This philosophy is essential to explain how we can know God by chanting His names. That is because all the names of God are *in* God and God is *in* all His names. This is because those names of God are His many faces, and when we see one face, we are seeing Him. The ability to know God through many names entails that each name is one face of God, and He can be known through all the faces. Similarly, God has many forms—which are partial aspects of God akin to His faces—and God can be known from those many forms.

Implications for Theology

The many forms and faces of God are not monotheism in the classical sense—because one thing is many things. The many forms and faces of God are not polytheism in the classical sense—because those many things are one thing. This is not just the philosophy of God. Rather, it is the philosophy of everything. God just happens to be that thing with the greatest number of faces. But even a quantum particle has multiple faces. By increasing or decreasing the number of faces, we don't change the fundamental principles of reality.

This idea was first articulated by Sri Ramanujāchārya through the Viśiṣṭādvaita philosophy. The "Advaita" is that one thing called the cube, and the many faces of the cube are the details, specifics, or Viśiṣṭa of the cube. The problem is that in this cube-face philosophy, the cube was not separate from the faces. Hence, if the soul was one of the faces of the cube, then when the soul suffers, then God must be suffering. Sri Mādhavāchārya then revised the philosophy into Dvaita where the cube and the faces are separate. This led to the problem of how God could be the cause of the soul—and the cause of all causes—if the soul was eternally separate from God. Then the philosophy of Śuddhādvaita was given by Viṣṇu Swami to say that soul and God are just like a drop and an ocean—same in quality and different in quantity. This led to the problem that if the drop is removed from the ocean, then the ocean must reduce. Hence, Nimbārkachārya created the philosophy called Bhedābheda in which the ocean and the drop are one and different such that the part is in the whole and the whole is in the part. We could not visualize how these contradictory claims could be reconciled in logic, hence Sri Chaitanya formulated the term Achintya Bhedābheda to say that all these things might be logically inconceivable, however, they are true.

The problem is that Vedānta applies not just to God, but to everything, including the material world. The cube-face philosophy is a truth about God—as the thing with the greatest number of faces. And it is a truth about the quantum particle—the thing with the least number of faces. So, if the doctrine of God is inconceivable then the doctrine of atomic particles is also inconceivable. That—of course—is a fact now: Nobody can conceive how an atomic object can be in many places at the same time, be an individual thing and yet remain inseparable from other things, or how it can be described both as a wave or particle alternately. So, it is wrong to say that religion is inconceivable and science is conceivable. Both are equally inconceivable. In fact, if we understand the nature of the two problems, they are inconceivable in the same way.

However, if we can solve the problem of quantum objects—or any subject that is inconceivable due to each word having many meanings—then we have solved the problem caused by Achintya in the philosophy of Bhedābheda. This is the beauty of Vedānta or the "conclusion of knowledge". It gives us one word, that summarizes everything from God to atoms. This one word—Bhedābheda—is the theory of everything, if we can explain what it means. What it means is simple—a cube-face philosophy of aspects with everything defined as meaning.

When we talk about the many names of God, such as infallible, independent, or endless, we are talking about the *extension* rather than the *intension*. These different extensions are like the many faces of a cube, but the cube is the intension. One face is not the other face, hence, infallible is non-synonymous with endless. And yet, because there is an intension, hence, they are all different names *of* God. The simple statement that "God has many names" is a very complicated problem of logic, set theory, Gödel's

Incompleteness, and linguistics—"one thing is factually many things". If we don't understand why the problem is this complicated, then we also don't understand the statement.

When that one thing expands into many things, the intension expands into extension. However, by that expansion, the intension doesn't cease to exist. It exists like a cube distinct from its six faces. If we cannot distinguish between the extension and the intension, or the intension being many extensions, then we will run into contradictions. Those contradictions are not unique to religion; they exist in all subjects because each word or *sampada* has many expansions called its *padārtha.* The same contradictions appear within religion when God is called by many non-synonymous names. Therefore, the problems associated with religion can also be discussed in the context of every other subject.

Four Causes of Incompleteness

Now we can talk about the four ways in which incompleteness manifests—(a) the whole is not reducible to its aspects, (b) each aspect is not equivalent or identical to the other aspects, (c) the parts are not separable from the whole although the whole can be spoken of separately from the parts, and (d) the aspects of the whole, while distinct, cannot be separated from each other.

The Whole is Not Reducible to Its Parts

In physical theories, the properties of macroscopic objects are not reducible to the properties of the microscopic. The microscopic properties are the various extensions of the macroscopic intension. However, they are organized in a specific manner, rather than randomly, just like the six faces of the cube have to be organized in a specific manner to construct a cubic structure.

In principle, we can cut the six faces of a cube and align them into a rectangle. We cannot reduce the cube to its six faces because those faces can also be organized into a rectangle. The cubic nature of the whole is responsible for organizing the faces in a structure, which means that the presence of the cube—the whole—creates additional properties absent from its parts.

Each Part is Not Equivalent to Other Parts

The six faces of the cube may seem *indistinguishable*, but they are not identical. If we could color these faces with different shades, then we can also distinguish them. Even otherwise, if we examined these faces microscopically, we will find them non-equivalent. Non-equivalence of the faces also involves a distinction between "face" and its "parts". All the parts are not identical and hence the face is organized as a square instead of being aligned in a straight line.

The thing we consider "invisible" as a whole, has a visible effect: It organizes the parts in a specific. The parts alone cannot determine that organization. Hence, there is an observable effect, and yet, we don't seem to perceive the cause that causes that effect. This is because that effect is akin to the concept in the mind different from sense perceivable effects. The thing we call a "cube" or "rectangle" is due to a mental perception rather than sense perception.

Parts Cannot be Separated from the Whole

In principle, we can break the cube into smaller pieces. However, all those pieces will be *different* from when they were part of the cube. This is just like we can cut an elephant into pieces and all the pieces would then be "dead"—i.e., they will lack the property of being leg, trunk, tail, ear, and stomach.

Reductionism is predicated on the premise that joining two things keeps those things unchanged. That is contradicted by what we now call "quantum entanglement" of the parts. The parts get entangled and acquire properties that they would not if they were non-entangled. The entanglement requires the concept of an "ensemble"—the whole that combines the parts into an entangled structure. If you try to remove the "ensemble", then the entanglement breaks, and the parts are also mutually different. Hence, while the parts are in the ensemble, we cannot talk about them as if the ensemble doesn't exist.

Parts Cannot be Separated from Each Other

The nature of entanglement is that we cannot define the parts independently of each other. Something would not be a tail unless there was also a trunk, ear, stomach, and leg. Every part requires the other parts to be defined as that part. Hence, we can only define all the parts collectively and mutually or not at all. Given the problem of circularity arising from this mutual definition, we define the parts in relation to the whole rather than in relation to other parts. This requires the whole to exist logically prior to the parts—i.e., as the intension that precedes the expansion of that intension into its extension.

Each extended part bears a different but unique relation to the intension. By this relation between intension and extension, the different extensions are also mutually defined and inseparable. Thereby we can say that the parts are not separable from the whole, and cannot be separable from other parts.

The Nature of Vedic Philosophy

Vedic philosophy can be summarized in one word—Bhedābheda. The simple requirement is cube-face philosophy with cube and faces being meanings. The rest of the discussion is simply what the different kinds of meanings are and how one meaning is the cube and other meanings are faces, and how those faces in turn are treated as cubes to expand more faces.

- There are many non-synonymous expressions of this philosophy:
- Holism instead of individualism or reductionism
- Unification instead of fragmentation
- Aspects instead of "one thing is only one thing"
- Personhood instead of objectivity
- Semanticism instead of physicalism
- Qualities instead of quantities
- Completeness and consistency instead of either/or
- Hierarchical reality instead of one-tier reality
- Non-binary logic instead of binary logic
- Higher and lower truth instead of true vs. false

Non-synonymous doesn't mean a *different thing*. It means a different *face* of a thing. Every non-synonymous description is turning the cube to see a different face, just like the ideology of "one thing is only one thing" is a cube that produces many different problems of logic, set theory, number theory, computational theory, causal indeterminism, and probabilistic descriptions.

If we formulate Bhedābheda in the context of scientific problems or describe it in new ways unknown before, we are motivating the same philosophy in such a way that even those who don't like to discuss God but would like to discuss the material world can learn about God. The doctor gives a sweet-tasting medicine so that children will accept them like candies. We can do that too.

The Drop in the Ocean Argument

Bhedābheda and Physical Analogies

All physical analogies fail to correctly describe Bhedābheda philosophy. One such analogy is a drop in an ocean. The Bhedābheda proponent says: The drop is distinct from the ocean and yet one with it. The reductionist's counter to that claim is that if you remove all the drops, there will be no ocean; hence the ocean is a fictional construct *reducible* to drops.

The impersonalist's counter is that there is only an ocean and dividing it into drops is a temporary illusion; hence the drops are a fictional construct produced from and *reducible* to the ocean. Due to these counters, it is impossible to say that both drops and ocean are real, and Bhedābheda becomes Achintya or inconceivable.

Person vs. the Body Distinction

To understand Bhedābheda, we have to define the "Pacific Ocean" independent of the drops in it. Adding drops to the Pacific Ocean will not make it something other than the Pacific Ocean. Removing drops from the Pacific Ocean will not make it something other than the Pacific Ocean. This is achieved if we treat the Pacific Ocean as a person—if a person gains or loses weight, he doesn't become a different person. If losing some weight doesn't reduce the person, then, in the limiting case, the person exists even without a body. But if there is a fat or lean body, then you can point to it saying—"this is the same person". Thus, the "person" is unchanged with a fat body, a lean body, or no body.

The distinction between the body and the person is inconceivable in logic because the person is defined as a set of things. For example, we can say that "natural number" *is* the set S := {1, 2, 3, ...}. Thus, "X is a natural number" is equivalent to "there exists an X such that X is a member of S". If you remove some elements from the set S, then it can no longer be called S. It must be called S′ or something else. The *identity* of a set is not preserved when we add and remove elements from a set. But the identity of a person is preserved when a person gains or loses weight. If identity preservation was allowed even with sets, then the set formed after removing odd numbers from natural numbers would still be called "natural number", and that will naturally lead to logical contradiction because "natural number" now equals "even number".

The Logics of Persons and Bodies

Most people cannot see how the logic of *things* is not the logic of *persons*. This is because, in common parlance, we treat most so-called things—e.g., the Pacific Ocean—as persons. How we talk in ordinary language is not logical. And yet, most people cannot see the fact that we preserve the identity of the Pacific Ocean even though it gains and loses drops every day. That is absolutely the antithesis of logic. The Aristotelian dictum "A is A" is falsified if the Pacific Ocean remains the Pacific Ocean despite the addition or removal of drops.

Bhedābheda is inconceivable when we use logic because logic is meant to be used only for *things* (sets of things are also things). Bhedābheda is conceivable if we reject binary logic and treat everything as a person. If we have trouble thinking in terms of person and body, then we can think in terms of mind and thought. The mind doesn't reduce to the thoughts because the same mind can think different thoughts one after another. And yet, at the point of thought, the mind is the thought. That is just like a person is a fat or lean body and yet the fat or lean body is not the person. Under Bhedābheda, we can say "the ocean is the drops, and yet, the drops are not the ocean". This is how we refute both materialism and impersonalism—both ocean and drops are real; the ocean doesn't reduce to the drops, and the drops don't reduce to the ocean.

Correct and Incorrect Analogies

The ocean and drops analogy is poorly used if we *quantify* the ocean as many drops. The same analogy is used correctly if we treat the ocean and drops as *qualities*. With the quantity description, the ocean ceases to exist if all the drops have dried up. With the quality description, the ocean exists as a distinct quality even if all the drops have dried up.

The Saraswati River dried up a few thousand years ago. But the personality of Saraswati still exists. Saraswati is the knowledge of karma-kānda rituals. Those rituals ended as the Saraswati River dried up, destroying with it the Indus (also called the Mohenjo-Daro and Harappan) Civilization. But Saraswati as the knowledge of karma-kānda rituals still exists.

Saraswati is the person, and the Saraswati River was her body. Even if the body ceases to exist, the person still exists. How Saraswati exists even when there are no drops in the Saraswati River requires personalist non-binary logic contrary to the objectivist binary logical thinking. Such existence is beyond the imagination of materialism and impersonalism.

Descriptions of Oceans in Vedic Texts

When Lord Rāma wanted to attack Lanka, He waited patiently for three days "praying" to the ocean to give way for His armies to cross. However, the ocean did not provide a way. Then Lord Rāma took His bow and arrow and was about to launch a weapon, by which the ocean would be dried to make way for His army, when the ocean *personified* appeared before Him begging for forgiveness and provided the following solution: "If your army drops a rock into the ocean with your name written on it, then those rocks will float on the water". The ocean did not part to make way for the army, as Lord Rāma had originally intended. Instead, a bridge was constructed *over* the ocean to allow for Lord Rāma's army to cross, by following the proposal given by the ocean personified. The ocean was not trillions of drops; it was one person.

During the creation of the material world, a primordial *kāraṇa* or the "causal ocean" is expanded from the body of Kāraṇodakaśāyī

Viṣṇu as His sweat. Each drop in the ocean becomes a universe. Kāraṇodakaśāyī comprises kāraṇa (cause), udaka (water), and śāyī (resting), due to which the water was previously in Kāraṇodakaśāyī, it came out of Kāraṇodakaśāyī, and He lay in it resting. Thereby, Kāraṇodakaśāyī is the original cause, and a secondary cause is produced from Him, but Kāraṇodakaśāyī "rests" in that secondary cause, appearing to be causally inert. That *kāraṇa* or cause of creation is the guna, karma, and chitta of the individual soul.

Kāraṇodakaśāyī then "enters" each drop as Garbhodakaśāyi Viṣṇu, to produce the universe. Garbhodakaśāyi comprises garbha (womb), udaka (water), and śāyī (resting). In this case, Garbhodakaśāyi is the soul in the womb. By His presence, the womb becomes a body. Finally, Kṣīrodakaśāyī Viṣṇu "enters" each part of the body—the atoms of the universe—to become the soul resting in each atom. Kṣīrodakaśāyī comprises kṣīra (milk), udaka (water), and śāyī (resting). By His presence, each atom "sees" other atoms in the universe, and that vision is also a universe in each atom comprising *pictures* of other atoms. Even an atom is a person.

The universe *has* infinite atoms, and each atom *is* a universe. The universe is outside and inside the atom. The "outside" is the terrain, and the "inside" is a map of that terrain. The map is not the terrain, but by knowing the map, we can know the terrain. If we know one atom completely, then we know the entire universe, because that atom is an ocean of information. If we dive into the ocean, then the atom is many things. If we stay outside the ocean, then it is one thing. That one thing is a mind in which the entire universe is compressed as knowledge due to Kṣīrodakaśāyī Viṣṇu. To study atoms, we must think of minds and meanings.

The Three Stages of Experience

These three Viṣṇu forms represent the deep sleep, dreaming, and waking stages of experience. The deep sleep stage is an unconscious realm of guna, karma, and chitta, which becomes the cause of dreaming and waking experiences when its parts are mixed by time. The dream is a self-created experience, with no corresponding external reality. The waking experience is correlated to an external reality. Thus, the information in an atom has a corresponding external reality, like waking. The information in a universe has no corresponding external reality, like dreaming. And the information in the causal ocean is not experienced, like deep sleep.

These three stages of experience are called māyā, which means what God is *not*. God is a master with no desire for mastery. Instead, māyā is God's power with a desire for mastery. When a soul loses self-satisfaction and develops the desire for mastery, then he comes under the control of māyā. The creation is the result of God's interplay with His power.

In the spiritual creation, māyā dominates God to increase Him, and God submits to that domination. In material creation, māyā dominates God to decrease Him, and God defeats that domination. Hence, the spiritual world is a place of cooperative harmony, and the material world is of competitive conflict. The fact is that every person has the power to improve or degrade themselves. They can accept the power of improvement and reject the power of degradation. But in the material world, almost everyone is enamored by the power of degradation and almost always averse to the power of improvement.

The Three Meanings of Ocean

The atom-body-ocean-universe can be described in three ways—knower, known, and knowing (it may be worth noting that this is not the only triad; there are six distinct types of triads for self, cognition, conation, emotion, intention, and relation). The person is the knower, the different individual parts of this person correspond to some known (because they are the pictorial representations of the external reality), and the parts are organized in a certain *structure* by the activity of knowing to construct the knowledge as the result of combining the knower, known, and knowing. We can describe these three as *sets*, *objects*, and *structures*—if we wish to use a set-theoretic metaphor.

If we consider all universes, atoms, bodies, or oceans, then everything is inside and outside everything else. Since everything contains a picture of everything else, they are in some sense *equivalent*.

But the *structure* inside each universe, atom, body, or ocean is *different* because they constitute different *perspectives* on the same reality. Each atom is a perspective on the whole of reality and it is a part of reality. However, *one* of these perspectives is the *original* perspective by which the various atoms were created, which constitutes the *absolute reference frame.* All subsequent perspectives are relativized versions of the original reference frame. Hence, all the perspectives are not identical. Each perspective is different, and many perspectives are produced from an original perspective. But relativized reference frames do not refute an absolute reference frame.

We can explain this difference again with a set-theoretic analogy of a bag with infinite balls in it. The balls in the bag can be drawn out of the bag in many orders or sequences. By sequencing the balls, we assign them different *numbers.* If there are just three balls—red, green, and blue—we can assign each ball a different number—1, 2, or 3—thereby sequencing them in different orders. The problem of sequencing objects in a set is called the Axiom of Choice in set theory because many such sequencing orders can be constructed as a *choice.* All these choices are *equivalent* in one sense, and yet, they are not *identical.*

Set theory doesn't delve into how these choices are created, because the *knower* is disregarded, and the set is just a collection. Ordering the set is not the set's own choice. These choices appear in the paradox of Buridan's Ass, who has a pile of hay and a bucket of water in front but cannot decide whether to drink or eat first. The paradox says that since both alternatives are *equivalent,* hence the ass cannot make a choice and dies of hunger and thirst. The answer to that paradox is that the ass has a *personality* due to which it will either prioritize drinking or eating, and one of the alternatives will be chosen. The personality of the ass, therefore, determines the sequence or how the hay and water are sequenced and labeled by numbers as *first* and *second.* Even the ass must be treated as a person with the capacity for choice to resolve this problem.

Thereby, set theory speaks about three things—sets, objects, and structures—but due to the problem of choice in ordering the objects into a structure, we must replace that set with a person. In the context of an ocean, the ocean is primarily a person. Then there are drops—the objects in a set. And there is a structure by which the drops are arranged in some way although they can be arranged in another way. Typically, the drops in an ocean are not in a fixed structure due to ocean waves. The drops move around, changing the structure between the drops. That can only be explained if we say that the ocean has many drops, but the structure is not *fixed* because there is a choice to reorganize the drops in many structures. That reorganization of the drops—i.e., ocean waves—is the Axiom of Choice in action. At each moment, the ocean can make a new choice, reorganizing the parts in a new way, because the ocean is a person.

While these arrangements are *equivalent*, they are not *identical*, if the drops in the ocean are like differently colored balls—red, blue, and green. If all the drops were all like white balls, then no matter how you rearrange them, they will look the same and remain *indistinguishable*. Then it would be impossible to choose one arrangement over another because they will be like two identical buckets of water or two identical piles of hay instead of a pile of hay and a bucket of water. When a choice cannot be made, then postulating a person for reordering elements is an unnecessary addendum. When a choice can be made, but it hasn't been made, then the set is simply a *potentiality* for creating many orders.

The Significance of Three Meanings

If the atoms are like white colored balls, then they can be organized in any way. But if the atoms are distinguishable in some way, such as red, blue, and green colors, then some choices are *better* than others and the choices can therefore be *judged*. Since these balls are pictures of external reality, hence, some arrangements of the balls are "true" if they correspond to the external reality. We can change that order in different situations and call that arrangement "right" if it is more suited to the specific context. Finally, we can say that some arrangement is "good" because I prefer to see things in a certain way. Thus, the choices can be judged as good based on individual preferences, as right based on contextual appropriateness, and as true based on universal reality.

This helps us recognize additional features of the set, object, and structure. The objects have to be qualitatively unique in some sense for us to distinguish them. There should be a possibility to choose one of the many structures. And there has to be rationality—i.e., a method to judge whether a choice is true, right, or good—based on universal, contextual, and individual natures.

We can now say that a set is a person, who makes choices. Those choices operate on qualitatively distinct parts. And those choices can be judged to be true, right, and good. We transform set theory into a theory of personhood, knowledge, choices, and rationality for making better or worse choices.

In this theory, each drop in the ocean is not identical to the other drops; the drops are not white-colored balls, because if that were the case, there would be no rational way of organizing the drops in any order. Rather, each drop is a different colored ball—i.e., qualitatively different from other drops—to construct different orders and then choose one of those orders as better or worse. The ocean that organizes these drops makes a choice, so it is a person. And the ocean's choices are judged. This is a complete answer to the problem of choice.

Thus, we transform impersonal thinking into personalism—(a) the set is a person, (b) the parts of that person are qualities, (c) those qualities constitute a picture of reality organized based upon the nature of reality, personal preferences on how to visualize reality, and contextual appropriateness of some vision over another, and (d) the choices of the person organizing this vision are judged as better (true, right, and good) or worse (false, wrong, and bad). Now, we speak about the *consequences* of those rational judgments by which different balls are added to the bag or removed from the bag, to construct a theory of the *evolution of the bag*—a metaphor for the evolution of conscious experience in which different things (balls) go in and out of our consciousness (the bag) due to a judgment (rationality). This would be the theory of experience in which a person evolves lawfully due to the judgments of their choices.

Two Uses of the Ocean Analogy

Advaita impersonalists transformed the above personalist analogy into impersonalism in three steps—(a) the red, blue, and green balls are separated aspects of whiteness, (b) the distinction between the balls as separated things is an illusion, and (c) the choice of one ball over another is a false idea. This transformation is affected by postulating two categories—called Brahman and māyā—in which Brahman is an undivided white ocean, which is divided into separated red, green, and blue balls by māyā, and if we merge red, blue, and green colors, then we recover the undivided whiteness in the ocean.

The materialists instead say that only the drops are real and the "ocean" is an emergent property of the drops. There is factually no such thing as an ocean because only the drops of the ocean are reality. The ocean can be *reduced* to drops, and it is merely a word that refers to the collection of drops.

Thus, in the impersonalist use of the drop in the ocean analogy, the ocean is real and the drops are an illusion. But in the materialist use of the drop in the ocean analogy, the drops are real and the ocean is an illusion. They can be contrasted as the oneness of the ocean vs. the multitude of the drops. The analogy of the ocean in the drop is thereby reduced either to the ocean or the drops, eliminating one of them. We can no longer talk both about the ocean and the drops so the questions about their oneness and difference do not arise.

The impersonalist accepts that all the drops are qualitatively different—e.g., red, green, and blue balls. Thereby, there is a possibility of judging which order is better. But since all these distinctions are false, the judgment of a better choice is rooted in the ideology of dividing white into red, green, and blue. If we collapse that distinction, then the divisions, choices, and judgments disappear.

The materialist claims that all the drops are qualitatively identical—e.g., as white balls. The result is *indeterminism*—we can arrange the white balls in infinite sequences none of which can be preferred over the others. Since no choice of rearranging the balls is preferred over the others, therefore, there is no rational way to choose. Without choices, there is no person who makes a choice, no person who is judged, and no law of consequences of choices.

The Third Use of the Ocean Analogy

There is yet another use of the ocean analogy employed by personalists in which ocean and drops are *separately* real—i.e., neither ocean nor drops are reduced to the other. It is also accepted that the ocean is a person, from whom the drops have manifested. It is also recognized that the drops manifested from one kind of ocean are qualitatively different from the drops manifested from another ocean. For example, there can be oceans of milk, water, honey, yogurt, butter, etc. whose drops are qualitatively different from each other's. Then, a partially correct analogy of the ocean and drops is created in which the drops are qualitatively similar to each other and the ocean is quantitatively big.

The fact is that if all the drops were qualitatively identical, then there would be no way to sequence them or organize them into a structure, and the choices of these organizations would be indistinguishable. When you cannot tell how one choice is different from another, you can reject choices and persons. Therefore, the drops can never be qualitatively identical within an ocean. The drops in a water ocean can just be more similar to each other compared to the drops in the milk ocean. That similarity of the drops is relative to the drops in other kinds of oceans, not a factually qualitative equivalence. Likewise, the quantitative bigness of the ocean relative to the drops is also relative to the quantitative bigness of other kinds of oceans and drops. The ocean is not qualitatively identical to the drops, because the ocean organizes all the drops within itself.

The different shades of color are similar to each other because color is present within red, green, and blue. Since color is not *confined* to either red, green, or blue, therefore, it is beyond each shade. Since color includes red, green, and blue, hence every shade is in color. The qualitative similarity arises because color is *in* each shade, and yet, (a) red, green, and blue are not qualitatively identical, and (b) the shades of color are not qualitatively identical to color itself. However, if we contrast the set of colors to the set of smells, then we can say that color is qualitatively similar to the shades and different from the various flavors of smell and smell itself. That qualitative similarity between color and shades is a *contextual* rather than a *universal* claim. If we universalize that contextual claim, then we get the erroneous idea that (a) all shades are qualitatively identical, and (b) they are qualitatively identical to color, which is nothing more than the bigger quantitative collection of all the shades.

The correct universal claim is that each drop in the water ocean is qualitatively different from the other drops and the ocean is qualitatively different from each drop. But in contrast to the milk ocean, each drop in the water ocean is qualitatively *similar* to the other drops and *similar* to the water ocean. That similarity between the water ocean and the water drops in contrast to the milk ocean and the milk drops is not a universal fact. It is just a contextual claim similar to saying that the president of a country is similar to the people of that country and different from the presidents and people of other countries. This analogy is employed only when there are numerous countries and their respective citizens and presidents. The analogy becomes totally false and misleading if it is treated as a statement about one universal country.

The fact is that if the quantitative analogy is used all the way, then either there is an ocean without drops, or drops without the ocean because ocean and drops cannot exist as *distinct realities*. That distinctness between ocean and drops requires the use of qualities such as color and shades or smell and flavors.

Nuances In the Ocean Analogy

The soul is a part of God, like shades are part of color and flavors are part of smell. However, there are many forms of God, akin to the difference between color and smell. Then, there is a complete form of God, of which color and smell are simply two aspects. The soul that is like a shade of color is part of both color and the complete form, just like the soul that is a flavor of smell is a part of both smell and the complete form.

The claim that "the soul is a part of God" can be interpreted in three ways—(a) the soul is a shade of color, (b) a flavor of smell, and (c) a part of the complete form that includes color and smell. These three claims are not mutually equivalent.

Factually, different souls have a different svarūpa due to which they can be parts either of different partial forms or a complete form. Someone who looks at this big picture of reality can say that "the souls are qualitatively similar to each other and quantitatively smaller than God" because they are comparing a soul to the specific form of God that they are part of. This contextual claim is contingent on the fact that there are many partial forms of God and one complete form of God. But in English, "God" means one form. With this assumption, we get the false idea that all souls are qualitatively similar and God is quantitatively bigger because the contextual claim has been universalized by removing diversity.

The fact is that the legs and hands—as part of the body—are not equal to the head. But if there is love, then each part gets to play its role in the body without trying to equate the hands to the legs or head. There is an ideology of egalitarian respect even in Vedic philosophy in which souls of different natures respect each other, but they do not mix closely. But in the ideology of loving devotion, a soul with one nature lives with other souls of a contrasting nature.

The emancipation of egalitarian respect is called *mukti*, and that of loving devotion is called *bhakti*. The diversity of bhakti is orders of magnitude higher than the diversity of mukti. Factually, there is no contradiction in saying that a shade is a part of color and a part of the complete form. But whether we see the similarity between colors, or see the differences between colors and smells is up to us. The pleasure of the diverse experience is greater but loving others with a different nature is harder. Hence, bhakti and mukti are not identical.

The Misuse of the Ocean Analogy

The ocean analogy is misused in three ways—(a) by the impersonalists when they say that the ocean is real while the drops are unreal, (b) by the materialists when they say that the drops are real and the ocean is unreal, and (c) by the mukti proponents when they equate the parthood of a shade within a color with the parthood of color and smell in the complete form of the bhakti proponent.

Acharyas have contextually used the analogy of drop and ocean, referring to the qualitative similarity of the parts and the quantitative magnitude of the whole. But if this quantitative analogy is universalized, then we will end up either with an ocean without drops, drops without the ocean, or the inability to organize drops within the ocean because all the drops are now indistinguishable. All these positions are incorrect. The correct usage is that the drops are not qualitatively identical to each other or to the ocean. The ocean is not just quantitatively bigger, but also qualitatively different than each drop.

Physical analogies are imperfect because reality is not quantities. The correct analogy is that of mind and thought. All the thoughts are semantically different from each other and the mind as a summary of the thoughts is semantically different from the thoughts. Since some thoughts can summarize other thoughts, therefore, some thoughts can be superior to other thoughts.

The problems with the ocean-and-drop analogy disappear when it is replaced by the mind-and-thought analogy, and this is also the correct analogy because the ocean is a *person*, distinct from the drops manifested from him. The ocean exists even when the drops have dried up, the ocean does not decrease if the drops are manifest, and the ocean does not decrease with the drops merging into the ocean. All these are best illustrated by the *kārana* ocean, manifested from Kāraṇodakaśāyī Viṣṇu at the time of creation and merged into Kāraṇodakaśāyī Viṣṇu at the time of annihilation. They are also illustrated by the pastimes of Lord Ramachandra where the ocean personified appears before Him. The fact is that the ocean is a person, distinct from the drops that make up the manifest ocean. If we don't preserve the distinction between the person and the collection of drops then our analogies would always be mistaken.

Statements from Brahma-Saṁhitā

The complete form of God is described in many ways in Brahma Saṁhitā, of which I will examine two distinct descriptions to further illustrate how soul and God are distinct and similar—(a) sac-cid-ānanda-vigrahaḥ, and (b) ānanda-cinmaya-sad-ujjvala-vigrahasya. We will examine them one after another.

Let's begin with the term "vigraha" used in both statements. The term "graha" means a house; it is often used as a substitute for planets, although a person lives *in a house*, but a person lives *on a planet*. A planet is not equivalent to graha, although this equivalence is used in dictionaries without noting the differences. The "graha" denotes a region of space in which the soul can roam, just like a person under house arrest can roam from one room to another, but cannot escape the house. A person, however, can leave a planet at any time.

Thus, when "graha" is translated as "planet", a problem in cosmology is created where a soul is under house arrest in a graha, but he can leave a planet. The graha signifies the soul's bondage while a planet signifies its freedom. This distinction lies at the root of the famous "moon landing" controversies where according to Vedic cosmology a soul can never leave the present graha to go to another graha and hence there is no way to go to another graha using a rocket.

However, remember that each atom is also a universe. What is inside that atom is a picture of the universe, because that atom is a mind, and pictures of the universe are thoughts in the mind. The first thought in the mind is that of the *self*. Everything else is a secondary thought. There are thoughts "closer" to the self-thought, and "farther" from the self-thought.

When the soul is confined to a graha, its consciousness is confined to the graha and it can roam to various parts of the graha. The soul itself is not bound to a graha. In the case of the earth graha, what we call the round earth is akin to the self-thought in the mind. If you sit in a rocket and travel outward for a trillion years, you are still in the earth graha. However, you have left behind the self-thought to roam to other thoughts. This is not going to other planets, but seeing their *pictures* closely. That picture is an earthly representation of the graha, not the graha. Looking closely at the earthly picture of the graha is not looking closely at the graha. So, "going" to the moon inside the earth graha is not going to the moon graha.

The term "vi" means separation with reciprocity. For example, if a friend comes to your house, the process is called saṃyoga and when the friend goes back to his house the process is called viyoga. The friendship is not broken if the friend returns to his house. The relationship continues but the friend is still separated. Hence, the term "vi" means departure without a separation. When "vi" is prefixed to "graha" in "vigraha", there is a departure without a separation. This process can be understood as the mind manifesting a thought and then remaining connected to the thought. The thought is in the mind like a person in a house, and yet, the mind is separate from the thought. However, when the thought is manifest from the mind, the mind *becomes* that very thought.

Thereby, sac-cid-ānanda-vigrahaḥ means all the emotions, intentions, cognitions, conations, and relations that are in the house and yet not the house. The mind is the graha, and all its contents are vigraha. Since those contents are produced from the mind, hence there is a distinction between the fully manifest and the fully unmanifest states of the mind. The fully unmanifest state is the sleeping state and the fully manifest state is the awake state. Hence, vigraha denotes the awake state of God. But in this awake state, the mind *is the thought*. God's wakefulness is His complete self-awareness. We don't call it awareness *of* the self, because we cannot separate the self from its awareness.

The situation changes when we use vigrahasya because "asya" means "of". Now, there is awareness *of* sad-ujjvala or the six self-effulgent qualities described as knowledge, beauty, power, wealth, fame, and renunciation. These six properties of the self-thought or self-image are distinct from the self that was earlier described as vigrahaḥ. The vigrahaḥ is the self-aware mind, and sad-ujjvala-vigrahasya is the self-thought or self-image produced from the mind as the first thought. We can say that God is self-aware, and His self-thought or self-image is the combination of six qualities. These qualities are ānanda (pleasing) and cinmaya (eternal), so when God thinks of Himself, He is not deluding Himself since all these qualities are eternal and He is not suffering by this self-image because these qualities are pleasing.

Moreover, these qualities are ujjvala or self-effulgent. Just like a light source expands into light rays, similarly, each of the six qualities self-expands to construct a world springing out of self-thought that remains in His mind as a *picture* that could be externalized.

When the world is externalized by God's power—akin to His power of speaking—then the picture of the world (which was previously inside, in which God had pictured Himself as part of a world), becomes a world. The world emerges from God due to His power of expression and is connected to Him in exactly the way that He had previously envisioned an eternally pleasing (ānanda-chinmaya) self-image (sad-ujjvala-vigrahasya) connected to a world in His mind.

The Ocean of Six Pleasing Qualities

These things are important when we speak about the ocean and its drops because the ocean is not the post-facto manifest world in which the soul is one of the parts. It is rather the person from which the ocean has sprung out in the process of realizing His self-image like a painter visualizing who he is, and then articulating that self-image into a portrait distinct from himself.

When the ocean is a person, then He is the source of the post-facto ocean, the cause that produced the post-facto ocean from Himself, controller of the post-facto ocean, and yet a part of the post-facto ocean. Then, we speak of the ocean in three ways—the pre-facto ocean, the structure of the post-facto ocean, and the drops in the post-facto ocean structure. The pre-facto ocean is God, the structure that controls and organizes the drops in the ocean is His power, and the drops controlled by His power are the souls. The ocean can thus be described in three ways—God, His power, and the various souls.

The impersonalist says that there is no God nor is there any power. There is simply an ocean of souls, which are illusioned to think they are separate from each other. The impersonalist transforms the ocean of drops into the pre-facto ocean. The materialist says that there is no ocean other than the drops. And some personalists equate a soul to other souls and sometimes partly to God.

The ocean and drops analogies are dangerous because they can be, and have been, misinterpreted. But they are used because they are easily understood. That ease is deceptive because the pre-facto ocean is the sum total of eternally pleasing six qualities which are divided into parts in the post-facto ocean to create distinct drops but we cannot equate the various drops to each other, nor can we say that each drop has all the qualities in small amounts and the whole is just the greatest amount of all the qualities. That claim will convert all the drops into white balls, and the collection of the drops into an infinite white ocean. All the diversity in the world will disappear by that quantitative claim.

As qualities are combined, new irreducible qualities are produced which exist only in the combination and never in the parts. For example, when beauty and knowledge are combined, then there is knowledge of beauty and beauty of knowledge. The power to understand beauty and produce beautiful knowledge doesn't exist if beauty and knowledge are separated. Then, a knowledgeable person can speak the truth, but not beautifully, and an artist can only produce beautiful lies. However, to the extent that a person can speak more truths, we can say that there is a quantitative increase in the number of truths. However, the additional truths are not qualitatively identical to other truths.

Bigger Man vs. Better Man

All quantitative conceptions of truth are false because no two things in the world are exactly alike. But we can count them after ignoring their differences. For example, we can count grains of rice although no two grains are identical. The differences between the grains of rice may be small and neglectable in one case but not in another. Thereby, quantitative claims are useful in some cases and useless in others. However, even when they seem to be useful, they are merely approximations obtained by a process of simplification.

Under the process of simplification, we can say that God is a bigger man. But that is not the whole truth because God is also a better man. In fact, He is bigger because He is better. But since most people may not understand a "better man", while they understand a "bigger man", therefore, one might simplify the understanding of God to say that "God is the biggest man" (i.e., an ocean) while we are "small men" (i.e., drops).

Generally, when a society degrades morally and spiritually, then people cannot understand the meaning of "better man". They can only understand the meaning of "bigger man". Then, we loosely talk about God as the biggest man. But if society advances morally and spiritually, and develops discrimination between better and worse, then we start talking about "better" more than "bigger". The material universe is big, but it is not better. God is not big, but He is the best. When the mind is underdeveloped, then we impress a person by talking about quantitative bigness. When the mind is developed, we impress them by talking about qualitative betterness.

In the ultimate analysis, God is the best man. In the love of His devotees, He becomes a small man, a child, or a puppet, dominated and conquered by their love. He is still the best man, but He is no longer the biggest. Exceptions to God's bigness exist but exceptions to God's betterness do not. Since everyone cannot understand how something small can also be the best, and in their imagination bigger is more important than better, hence the Acharyas describe God as the biggest man rather than the best man. That is not always true, it is certainly not the whole truth, and it is definitely not the most important consideration in understanding God. But it is used because it works on most people.

TRUTH, RIGHT, AND GOOD ARE MUTUALLY DEFINED

Alternative Conceptions of Truth

Truth in Vedic philosophy is defined quite differently than in Western philosophy. While Western philosophy talks about empirical and rational proofs of truth, Vedic philosophy gives the following peculiar conception of truth. If you reject the truth, then you will commit bad deeds; due to those bad deeds, you will suffer; when you suffer, then you will change what you call truth. Conversely, if you accept the truth, then you will commit good deeds; due to those good deeds, you will become happy; and then, you don't need to change your idea of truth.

While giving an empirical or rational definition, truth is separated from the righteousness of action and the happiness of feeling. But the definition of truth is intimately tied to the right and good in Vedic philosophy: Truth is also morality and happiness.

Truth is Symptomatized by Eternity

By the above definition, everyone is free to choose whatever truth they want. The laws of nature will then take them through suffering if their conception of truth isn't true. Thus, change, instability, and oscillation are hallmarks of falsity while eternity, stability, and constancy are the hallmarks of truth. Based on these traits, we don't have to perform a complete and exhaustive rational and empirical analysis of the truth claims. We just look for eternity, stability, and constancy and we can conclude that it is true. If we find their opposites, we know it is false.

Hence, the truth can be known from its *longevity*. It is not rational proof based on logic and axioms because axioms and logic can be changed. It is not empirical proof by instrument measurement because the measured objects and measuring instruments can be changed. As we change the axioms, logic, measured objects, and measuring instruments, we arrive at new ideas of truth. These may not be long-lived, let alone eternal. Whatever is changing is not true. Truth and eternity thus become identical although they are not synonymous.

Contrast to Western Notions of Truth

Is truth rational? Yes, it is. But it means that not seeking one's happiness is irrational. Since that happiness comes from moral action, therefore, deciding what moral action is, is also rationality. Rationality based on axioms and logic is universal, but rationality for moral action is contextual, and rationality for a happy life is individual. Right and wrong change from one time, place, and role to another, and happiness is different for each individual.

Is truth empirical? Yes, it is. But empiricism is extended to righteous action and happy life, not limited to sense perception or merely instrument measurements. Is truth both rational and empirical? Yes, if we use the collective definition of truth, right, and good. Is truth neither rational nor empirical? Yes, if we are rejecting the notions of axioms, logic, and proofs as the sole definition of rationality, and object-instrument measurements as the sole definition of empiricism.

Separation of Truth, Right, and Good

Since the time of the Greeks, the notions of truth, right, and good have been separated in Western philosophy. The Greeks called them logos, ethos, pathos, and sometimes truth, justice, and beauty. Vedic philosophy also accepts these three categories and calls them *chit*, *sat*, and *ānanda*. The difference is that Greeks tried to define truth, justice, and beauty independently of each other while Vedic philosophy defines them mutually—falsity leads to immorality which then leads to suffering; truth leads to morality which then leads to happiness.

Conversely, Aristotle divided all Platonic forms into two categories—theoretical and practical. The theoretical forms include just truth, while the practical forms include justice and beauty. Hence, you use mathematical reasoning to arrive at truth; you use democracy to arrive at justice; and you are free to define your idea of beauty as you like. Truth, right, and good is thus separated.

Separation Results in Relativism

As time passes, the personal idea of beauty is extended to a personal idea of justice leading to constant changes to social norms. The personal ideas of beauty and justice are also extended to truth leading to constant changes to what is true. We can still use mathematical reasoning, but our axioms and logic are no longer the same. Instead, mathematicians can define ever-new domains of mathematics based on a new set of objects and operators on those objects. Since there is no limit to how varied these theories can be, hence, there is no limit to how varied truth can be. Each believer in a different truth only needs to assert their personal belief in some axioms and logic over others. They can use a different set of observations or facts to justify or empirically prove their personal axioms and logic.

We cannot escape this relativism of truth, right, and good without defining them mutually. The escape involves the rejection of empirical and rational verification as sole measures of truth. After all, both painful and pleasurable experiences can validate a theory. But nobody wants eternal pain. Hence, only a subset of experiences that give happiness are marks of the truth. Likewise, both just and unjust experiences can validate a theory but nobody wants eternal injustice. Hence, a subset of experiences that deliver justice are marks of the truth.

Injustice and Suffering are Irrational

When suffering and injustice are rejected as valid experiences to determine the truth, then mere empirical verification cannot be called truth. Likewise, when suffering and injustice are rejected as valid rationalities, then mere rational proofs based on arbitrarily chosen axioms and logic cannot be called truth. A subset of rational proofs and empirical observations—that deliver happiness and justice—must now be designated as markers of truth. Current ideas of empirical verification and rational proof as marks of truth are replaced by a subset of theories and experiences that are also just and happy.

If we separate the definitions of truth, right, and good, then we will create a painful and unjust world. Since nobody likes suffering and injustice, therefore, they will change the truth until it leads to happiness and justice. Thereby, all empirically and rationally proven theories will keep changing because empiricism and rationality are not limited to truth; they also extend to the right and good. When the truth keeps changing, then it cannot be called truth. Whatever we call truth today will be called falsity tomorrow because nobody wants an unhappy or unjust truth. We search for a truth that is also right and good. This is the meaning of collectively defining truth, right, and good.

Complementary Aspects of the Self

This search is related to the theory of consciousness comprising three aspects as noted above. These aspects are not identical, and hence, truth, right, and good are not identical considerations. These aspects are not separate from each other, and hence, the considerations of truth, right, and good cannot be separated. In the Greek separation of logos, ethos, and pathos, a single person is fragmented into three—the first that seeks the truth, the second that seeks justice, and the third that seeks beauty. Once you fragment a single person into three separate proclivities, then they keep fighting with each other.

This fight leads to an inner conflict under which the truth, right, and good is never reconciled with each other. Rather, one aspect becomes dominant for some time, while the other aspects are subordinated. Then the other aspects become dominant for some time, while the previously dominant aspect is subordinated. Thereby, the truth, right, and good notions keep changing.

In India, this triad is called satyam-shivam-sundaram. Satya is the truth; Shiva is justice; and Sundaram is beauty. This triad constitutes reality, which means that if we reject the truth, then we will be forced into "injustice" and "ugliness", to change our notions of truth. That "injustice" and "ugliness" is not truly injustice and ugliness because it forces a correction on us. It is like a bitter medicine or a painful surgery mandated by nature to correct our false conceptions of reality. Doctors, surgeons, medicines, and treatments are not considered evil because they cure illnesses. The ugliness and injustices that we see superficially are well-intentioned and morally justified.

The History of Successive Separations

Aristotle called these three *modes of persuasion,* which means that there are three ways to convince a person. But he could never integrate them. In fact, he separated them into theoretical and practical forms, and the practical forms were divided into a subjective notion of beauty and an intersubjective idea of justice while objectivity was restricted to the truth. Thereafter, the epistemology of truth was separated from the epistemology of beauty and justice.

Immanuel Kant, for instance, claimed that justice is non-ontological (his theory of morality is called deontology). Thereby, nature has no justice. If you escape a ruler's justice, you escaped justice. Shakespeare similarly wrote: "beauty lies in the eyes of the beholder". Thus, science evolved independent of the considerations of right and good. Some people complain that science is devoid of value judgments; they are talking about the inability to define right and good based on scientific considerations. But the problem is not limited to science. It is as old as Western civilization itself, going back to Aristotle if not much before.

When Christianity adopted Aristotle's fragmented system to construct "apologetics", the truth, right, and good were never reconciled. Christianity axiomatized God as good, which led to the problem of evil when it should merely have been called God's justice. Then, justice was axiomatized as commandments and dictates of messiahs, but since there was no way to reason about them, all these religious dictates were constantly manipulated by empires and emperors.

During Enlightenment, the considerations of right and good were relegated to contracts and private opinions, while the study of nature through the use of reason and observation was deemed "scientific truth". By definition, this fragmented "science" is incapable of dealing with questions of justice and beauty because justice is defined to be something intersubjective while beauty is defined to be subjective, while science is called objectivity.

Fragmentation of Reality Into Subjects

We cannot neglect or ignore objectivity, subjectivity, or intersubjectivity. We cannot reduce or equate one to the other. And we cannot reconcile them in a system of reasoning restricted to the truth. This is why the separation of these three leads to cycling dualities and never-resolving contradictions.

There is a new focus on studying consciousness at present. But in this study, consciousness is the study of the objective truth, rather than right and good. Objective truth is itself reduced to the *existence* of physical properties rather than to the perception of qualities, the assimilation of meaning, and the attribution of truth to the meaning. Thereby, truth is equated to existence. If you can measure something's existence, then it is true. By that measure, the existence of a fictional book and the false propagandas on television must also mean that they are true. After all, you can measure their existence, the world has no meaning, therefore, their existence itself implies their truth.

These problems are so old in Western thinking that people have forgotten about the time when they started. Since they started at least 2,500 years ago, and everything since then has been a progressive compounding of one mistake by another, it is impossible for people to accept that their thinking has been flawed from the very beginning. Everything in religion, philosophy, and science has been fragmented over and over due to the original fragmentation of truth, right, and good. When every subject has become so fragmented over time, it is impossible to find the complete truth unless we go back to the origin of the problem and rethink the unsolved problems from the beginning.

The Principle of Inseparability

That rethink is not very hard to understand. It simply means that truth, right, and good are mutually defined. They are not identical, and they are not separable. This is the Bhedābheda principle. It changes epistemology because all experiences and rationalities are not true—that which leads to suffering and injustice will be rejected over time. It changes our conception of reality as something in three *modes*. They are described in various ways as *modes of nature*, *modes of consciousness*, and *modes of God*. They are aspects of the whole, parts of the whole, but not separable from each other and the whole.

If anyone understands the basics of Vedic philosophy, namely, that truth, justice, and beauty are mutually defined then they will easily reject all forms of scientific epistemology as flawed ideas. If they further understand that truth, right, and good are judgments applied to some meaning, then they will easily reject a conception of reality devoid of meaning. To understand why these flawed notions exist today, we can trace all the problems of modern thinking back to Aristotle's separation between truth, right, and good, and show how everything else follows from it, just as a corollary of that separation.

The course correction involves conceiving reality in terms of three modes that are distinct and yet inseparable. It involves a different epistemology, ethics, and aesthetics. It involves a reformulation of reasoning as something that involves truth, right, and good. It involves a reformulation of experience as something truthful, just, and happy as opposed to false, unjust, and unhappy. The false, unjust, and unhappy also exists, but only as a rational and empirical method to lead a person to the truth. Hence, if you cherry-pick axioms, logic, and data to concoct your truth, then nature will force injustice and suffering on you. Then you will naturally say: This unhappy and unjust truth must be false.

Alternative Conceptions of Science

The modern scientific method of reason and observation is known to be incomplete because (a) an observation can be described by various axioms and logics, and (b) all the observations that could validate or invalidate a theory are not accessible for all places, times, situations, and persons. Nobody can guarantee that the scientific method converges. Scientists just claim that it is better than faith and belief. That is because of the separation of truth, right, and good. When they are combined, then the reformulated rational and empirical process converges because it pushes a person away from falsity toward the truth by forcing "injustice" and "misery" on them. The reformulated rationality and observation make the reasoning and observing process convergent.

These reformulated rationalities and observations constitute a science. But they are not modern science. These reformulated rationalities and experiences constitute a religion. But they are not what most people call religion, namely, something based on blind faith, separated from the study of reality, devoid of reason and experience, and endlessly manipulated over the ages by empires and emperors. Ideally, we must not use the words "science" and "religion" to describe Vedic philosophy because these words are culturally contaminated by the problems of religion, science, and philosophy as practiced for 2,500 years in the West. But we use them only because the alternative words do not exist.

The Conception of God in Vaiṣṇavism

Vaiṣṇavism and Non-Dualism

Vaiṣṇavism presents a conception of God that doesn't fit into well-known categories such as monotheism, polytheism, monism, pantheism, panentheism, henotheism, deism, and others. This is because Vaiṣṇavism accepts all their assertions and rejects all their negations.

For example, the monotheistic claim that "God is one" doesn't negate the polytheistic claim—i.e., "God is many". Likewise, the panentheistic claim that "the world is inside God" doesn't negate the claim of deism—i.e., "the world is outside God". These oppositions arise in *quantitative* conceptions of reality as separable, mutually exclusive, and non-contradictory entities but not in a *qualitative* conception of reality as distinct but inseparable entities.

The latter is also called Bhedābheda. It is inconceivable in quantitative conceptions of reality and conceivable in qualitative conceptions of reality. I will use this article to discuss the foundations of the Bhedābheda doctrine, and then use it to demonstrate how it accepts all theistic doctrines in one sense and rejects all of them in a different sense.

God and the World

The easiest place to start discussing the nature of God is with the distinction between the speaker, speech, and speaking. Before speaking, the speech is inside the speaker. After speaking, the speech is outside the speaker. The speaker can be known from the speech; hence he is also within the speech.

Analogously, the world is God's speech. Prior to being spoken, the world was inside God. After being spoken, the world is outside God. God is known from the world because the speaker is in the speech. This tripartite distinction is essential to establish the twin conditions of causality—necessity and sufficiency. God is a sufficient cause of the world if He can express the world as His speech. But God will be a necessary cause of the world if and only if we can establish that nothing else caused the world. That is possible only if we can prove that the cause is present within the effect. Necessity is established based on God's immanence in the world—the speaker being known from the speech.

(Immanence is absent in modern scientific causality, and hence, no scientific doctrine provides causal necessity. The main result of the absence of causal necessity is that all scientific theories must become indeterministic.)

The speaker doesn't become ignorant after expressing his thoughts. Hence, even when the speaker has spoken, and the speech is outside the speaker, it hasn't ceased to exist inside the speaker. Thereby there is no contradiction in saying that the world is inside *and* outside God—it is inside like the speaker doesn't lose his ideas by speaking and it is outside like the speaker expresses his thoughts as speech. Likewise, there is no contradiction in saying that God is inside *and* outside the world—it is like the speaker can be known from the speech, but the speaker is not exclusively confined to an utterance.

Semantic Conceptions of Reality

All these claims rest upon a semantic conception of reality—speaker, speaking, and speech—which are sometimes described as manas (mind—the speaker), prāṇa (activity—of speaking), and vāk (effect—the speech) in Sāñkhya philosophy. The thought exists as *one* of the potentials in the mind. When it manifests, it can remain in the mind as the awareness of the thought. But it can also be instantiated into a copy of the thought and separated from the mind as speech. Speaking is that copy instantiation created by a person's prāṇa.

The mind-body problem is resolved by connecting the speaker to the speech through speaking. The act of speaking copies the idea into an instance of that idea. The copy-instance is a different individuality but the idea is the same universality as in the speaker's mind. The universality in the copy-instance is similar to the individuality of the speaker such that you can identify the speaker from the speech—each sentence has some unique characteristics of the speaker that uniquely identify the speaker—although the speech is not the speaker.

The world is no longer *things*. It is symbols of meaning comprising six aspects: (a) how the speaker views himself, (b) the mood of the speaker, (c) the intended effect of the speech, (d) the concept expressed, (e) the reference of the concept, and (f) the power to create an effect. For instance, if you say "darkness engulfed me in the alley", then you are using a metaphor to remember a time when darkness had entered your life, the tone of your utterance indicates if you are still in that experience or out of it, you intend to share your experience to a listener, the sentence uses concepts like alley and darkness, it references a real event, and it has the power to give the listener the same experience.

All the meanings are in the sound, although some sound encodings are better suited to recreate a meaning than others. If that encoding is recited attentively, then it can recreate an image of the author, their mood, their intentions, their concepts, and their references, simply from the power to create an effect. We don't need to know dictionaries. The sound is sufficient to recreate everything.

Materialism, however, accepts one of the six aspects (the power to create an effect) and discards the other five—the speaker, their mood, purpose, concepts, and references. By neglecting five out of the six aspects, a symbol is reduced to an object or a quantum of energy. The result of converting a symbol to an object is causal incompleteness, or the inability to explain and predict effects.

Present-day linguists disregard the author's personality, the author's mood, and the author's purposes while interpreting texts. They disregard their metaphors as poetry, rather than telling them about the author. The concepts and references are provided by an interpreter based on dictionaries (although the dictionaries permit many possible meanings of words). The text that was composed to be recited attentively is interpreted without knowing the effects of its recitation. Thus, linguistics inherits the problem of materialism—e.g., the inability to explain and predict the effects of recitation. It assigns meanings discordant with the meaning that appears upon recitation, without a dictionary.

Problems of Binary Logic

Semantic conceptions of reality violate binary logic (identity, mutual exclusion, and non-contradiction) because the six aspects of a symbol are neither separable nor identical to each other. Each of the six aspects *underdetermines* the other five. Since they determine the other five partially, therefore, they cannot be identical. And yet, because they do determine the other five—even if partially—they cannot be independent. This is yet another reason to say that the six aspects are distinct and yet not independently separable.

For example, knowledge is not beauty, but knowledge is beautiful. Romance is not friendship, but romance is friendly. A parent is not a servant of the child, but a parent serves the child. These claims arise because a word can be a noun, adjective, or verb. Knowledge is not beauty because they are distinct as nouns. But knowledge is beautiful because beautiful is an adjective that describes knowledge; we cannot separate beautifulness from knowledge. Servant and parent are distinct as nouns. But the parent serves the child because serving is a verb that describes parenthood. Romance and friendship are distinct as nouns. But romance is friendly because friendliness is an adjective. The contradiction disappears due to figures of speech. Two words are distinct in one figure of speech and inseparable in another. They are forms of the same word, but two different forms. Hence, they are at once distinct and inseparable.

Non-binary conditions are necessary for consciousness because the observed is inside the observer (as their experience) and yet outside the observer (because the observed is not limited to one observer's experience). The observer is inside the observed (exclusively focused on observing one thing at a moment) and yet outside it (because he can focus on something else at the next moment).

This general problem of meaning is termed *modalities*—figures of speech are examples. There are many such modal conditions that are impossible to cover here, but they are all summarized in the philosophy of Bhedābheda—distinctness with inseparability. All seeming contradictions in Bhedābheda can be resolved using modalities. For instance, speech is inside the speaker in the universal modality and outside the speaker in the individual modality. The speaker is inside the speech in the universal modality and outside the speech in the individual modality. Thus, if you print a million copies of a book, the author is not replicated. However, each book inherits the author's personality. The readers of that book can know the author simply from the book.

Physical conceptions of reality do not permit or require modalities. Hence, binary logic works for them. Under this logic, either two things are identical or they are separate. And if they are separate, then they cannot be inseparable. Binary logic is tied to things, described using numbers or quantities. Non-binary logic is necessary for grasping persons, described using distinct but inseparable qualities. Bhedābheda is inconceivable under binary reality. It is conceivable under modal conceptions of reality. Bhedābheda is incompatible with quantities, but it is compatible and necessary with qualities.

The conflict between modern science and Vedic religion is between quantities and qualities. This conflict is deep: (a) things, binary logic, and quantities vs. (b) persons, non-binary logic, and qualities. But it is not a conflict between this world vs. the other world, because both worlds are described in terms of qualities. It is also not a conflict between faith vs. reason and experience, because even matter is described using a different system of reasoning (non-binary or modal reasoning) and observation (quality perception).

Manifest and Unmanifest Realities

The system of qualities expands into subsidiary qualities like a root expands into trunks, branches, twigs, and leaves. The tree is *inverted* because the cause is higher than the effect. For example, we can construct an inverted tree of perceptual qualities—maroon is a shade of red, which is a hue of color, which is an aspect of seeing, which is one of the five sense perceivable property categories of an object concept (e.g., a table), which—depending on the context—can either be judged as true, good, and right or false, bad, and wrong.

Accordingly, an Absolute Truth is that which is simultaneously true, right, and good, and a Relative Truth is that which may be partially true, right, or good, or some of these in combination. The Relative Truths expand from the Absolute Truth—like a tree expands from a root—and they are neither the Absolute Truth (i.e., at once true, right, and good) nor are they completely false, wrong, or bad. They are true, right, and good to varying extents (or they can be true, right, and good in another time, place, situation, or for a different person).

For example, a criminal has to be punished for his wrong acts. That punishment is truthful (that a crime was committed and should be punished), righteous (proportionate punishment for a crime), and good (the criminal is corrected by proportionate punishment). However, the punishment may not be judged good by the criminal because he doesn't see his own good in that punishment.

This inability to perceive what actually exists is called *avyakta* or unmanifest. It is not factually absent, and yet, it is not visible to everyone. Like a criminal may not see the good in his punishment, although the good is present, similarly, lots of *deeper realities* remain hidden from our vision. Like a reader may not discern the nature of the author, their mood, intentions, concepts, or references, and yet, those things are present for others, similarly, many realities can remain hidden from our vision. Due to the absence of perception of what is present, we may fail to understand their true nature or misunderstand what they actually represent. Accordingly, we might designate them as bad, wrong, or false.

This principle is employed in Nyāya to discuss the relationship between language and reality. When you see a cow, you can infer—it is not a horse. How do you know? You haven't seen a horse, and the absence of evidence of a horse is not the evidence of the absence of a horse. Nyāya explains that the horse is present in the cow as an absence. We perceive that absence, and that's how we know that a cow is not a horse. Likewise, we know that the cow is a mammal—because the concept mammal is present in the cow although as an absence. If we don't perceive the things that are present, then we create binary logical dualisms—e.g., that hot and cold are separated—when the fact is that hot exists in cold and vice versa, which is why we connect them into logical opposites instead of contrasting hotness to fluidity. That logical contrast between hot and cold is non-dualism because it mutually defines two concepts. We cannot separately or independently define hot and cold, horse and cow, etc.

Duality and Non-Duality

The material world is called *duality* because the non-perception of what is present creates the illusion that it is factually absent. In short, the absence of evidence is equated to the evidence of absence. If those realities are perceived correctly, then the same world is called *non-duality*. Under duality, we think that two things are independent of each other. Under non-duality, we see that they are entangled, inseparable, and mutually defined. Everything is inside and outside everything else. This makes matter just like consciousness—the thing within is an idea of the world outside. Everything carries a *model* of reality (which may be partial), and it acts rationally based on that model.

All reality is non-dual, but some of that non-dual reality is seen as a duality. This is because we cannot perceive how the thing outside is also inside—e.g., as a model of reality within itself. This transforms a consciousness-like reality into a thing-like reality in modern science. The postulate of separate things, which justifies the use of mutual exclusion and non-contradiction, then facilitates their counting, and finally rationalizes the use of mathematical equations to describe quantitative measurements on them, is entirely an illusion.

Reality is distinct but inseparable things but the reason they are inseparable involves a modality that lies hidden, quite like the goodness in punishment, or knowledge of reality inside a thing, or the contrast to hot within cold, or the commonality between cow and horse as mammals within both. There are many such kinds of inseparability, all summarized under the name Bhedābheda.

As a noun, good is a pleasure. But as an adjective, good is the intention to correct. If a good intention underlies a punishment, it can remain hidden from a criminal's vision but can be visible to the punisher. This is how "evil" is created from good. It is not evil, but we *perceive* it as evil because we don't perceive the good intention which lies hidden in a different modality within the same thing. Goodwill exists as an adjective within the punishment noun. We might perceive the noun and not the adjective. The non-perception of such hidden realities leads to the conclusion that the world is evil when it is not.

Of course, the non-duality of the material world (e.g., goodwill punishment) is *inferior* to the non-duality of the spiritual world (e.g., goodwill reward). Both material and spiritual worlds are non-dual. But the material world is inferior because one modality (e.g., punishment) obfuscates another (e.g., goodwill). The spiritual world is superior because each modality (e.g., reward) reveals the other modalities (e.g., goodwill). Nothing is hidden, because all the adjectives and verbs are visible in every noun. This is called *vyakta* or manifest.

Dominant and Subordinate

The material world is sometimes called duality because some modalities are suppressed by others in a mode combination—like punishment suppresses the perception of goodwill. Since that suppressed reality is still objectively present, the material world is non-dual, and yet *non-ideal*, although still *perfect*. This requires highly nuanced considerations. For instance, war is not ideal. Ideally, one must resolve a conflict with a negotiation. But if negotiations fail, and war is the only option left for self-defense, then war is perfect. Likewise, when nature creates situations that lead to a war, the underlying intention is good—e.g., to teach arrogant people humility—which is why nature is not evil, although most people will not be able to perceive goodwill in the painful punishment.

A sick man may have to be given bitter medicine, but the doctor is not evil. Of course, a bitter medicine is not ideal. Ideally, a sweet medicine would be better. If possible, it is preferred over bitter medicine. But if the sweet medicine would worsen the illness, then the doctor prescribing the bitter medicine is not evil.

Qualities can be combined in many ways, but some combinations enhance each other (e.g., goodwill reward) while others suppress each other (e.g., goodwill punishment). The latter scenarios in which modalities are suppressed and remain hidden constitute the material world. In this world, one modality goes dominant and subordinates the others. The dominant mode becomes the noun, and the subordinate mode becomes the adjective or the verb. The subordination of one modality by another hides the subordinated modality, leading to the illusion of duality. In contrast, in the spiritual world, the dominant modality enhances the subordinated modality, making both modalities visible.

This is why the material world is inferior to the spiritual world and is called *duality* although it is non-dual. The seeming duality is an illusion. It is like bitter medicine that must be ingested for our good. But God and nature are not evil doctors prescribing them. And yet, an ignorant child will hate the doctor for forcing a bitter medicine, although the knowledgeable adults know better.

The Vaiṣṇava Conception of God

The distinctions between binary vs. non-binary logic, qualities vs. quantities, manifest vs. unmanifest, duality vs. non-duality, how duality is created from non-duality as an illusion, and the distinction between the speaker, speech, and speaking that reconciles the illusion with reality and resolves many seeming logical contradictions, are the essential and fundamental conceptual backgrounds required to understand everything else in Vedic philosophy. They are essential to understanding the Vaiṣṇava descriptions of God as well.

This is because: (1) the complete form of God is the most ideal and the source of other partial forms, (2) the partial aspects of the whole form are less than most ideal, although still perfect in different contexts, (3) these distinct but partial aspects are both inside and outside the complete form like speech and speaker, (4) they cannot be separated from each other due to the use of qualities and non-binary modal reasoning, and (5) the complete form can be known from each form quite like the author can be understood from his speech.

Every part of the complete form of God—known as Kṛṣṇa—is capable of the function of every other part. This is because every part exists within every other part as an adjective and verb, but it also exists outside that part as a noun. For instance, Kṛṣṇa doesn't just see with His eyes; He can also hold things in their place by gazing at them, He can bring anything close to Him by looking at it, He can move it away by changing His glance, He can impregnate by His glance, He can taste food by glancing at it, and He can communicate with anyone by moving His eyes. This is because the verbs (holding, moving, tasting, smelling, hearing, etc.) exist inside the noun eye and can become manifest.

The capacity to display all qualities and activities is reduced to varying extents in everything other than Kṛṣṇa, including other partial forms of God. That capacity is most constrained in ordinary material objects, leading to conclusions of duality. Even as every quality and activity exists in a hidden form in everything else, most of these qualities are necessarily *avyakta* or unmanifest to varying extents in everything other than Kṛṣṇa. They can all be *vyakta* or manifest in Kṛṣṇa. The parts of Kṛṣṇa are thus Kṛṣṇa, and yet not Him.

Kṛṣṇa can display everything in the material and spiritual creations within His mouth. He can also display every other partial form of God within His complete form. All the universes are within His stomach, and yet, a rope that is within one of the universes is also outside Kṛṣṇa and binds His stomach. Kṛṣṇa's eyes, hands, tongue, legs, skin, etc. are distinct from each other as nouns, and yet, each part is *inseparable* from the other parts as adjectives and verbs. Therefore, we cannot say that Kṛṣṇa's eyes are *not* His legs, hands, tongue, ears, skin, etc. and we cannot equate Kṛṣṇa's legs, hands, tongue, ears, skin, etc. to His eyes.

Contrasts to Other Philosophies

Contrast to Varied Forms of Theism

Monotheism is true if it claims one complete form of God. But monotheism is false if it denies the possibility of knowing God partially. God has many partial forms and one complete form. The partial forms are inside the complete form (like speech exists in the speaker) and the complete form is present inside the partial forms (like the speaker exists in the speech).

Polytheism is true in the sense that there are many partial forms of God. But polytheism is false if it denies the existence of a single complete form of God, or equates all the forms. It is also false when it says that these are separate gods that don't lead to a common understanding of God.

Pantheism is true because the speaker exists in his speech. The material world is God's speech. Hence, God exists in all atoms in the material world—if we study these atoms like speech—because He is the author within the speech. However, pantheism is false if everything is equated to God. Speech does not equate to the speaker.

Panentheism is true in the sense that speech exists in the speaker, even after its utterance. But panentheism is false if it is taken to mean that because the speech exists in the speaker, therefore, it can be equated to the speaker.

Monism is true in the sense that there is only one source that caused diversity and represents its unity. But monism is false if it is treated as the dissolution of individual identities.

Henotheism is true in the sense that different people and religions can worship God in different ways and forms, without negating the other forms. But henotheism is false if it claims that all these forms of God are equivalent—i.e., that no form is more ideal than the others, and there isn't a complete form.

Deism is true in the sense that the speaker stands apart from the speech. But deism is false if it means that the speaker cannot be known from the speech, and is only known by faith. God is outside the world, and yet, God is inside everything.

Unitarianism is true in the sense that the thing with many aspects is a single thing. But it is false if it claims that many aspects of a thing do not exist, or everyone knows all aspects. The aspects of God are either known simultaneously by different persons, or they can be known alternately by the same person.

Contrast to Varied Ideas of Reality

Realism is true if it claims that a Supreme Person who caused everything else exists. However, realism is false if it claims that there is only one understanding of that Supreme Person.

Idealism is true if it claims that the same Supreme Person exists within each person (like the author in the speech). But it is false if it claims that the Supreme Person is merely our creation, that He has no existence outside our consciousness, or that God has no objective reality.

Nominalism is true if it says that God is a name, and there are many names of God. But it is false if it says that God has no existence if those names are not uttered or known to others.

Platonism is true if it says that God is a transcendent ideal form in a transcendent world, who has partial expressions (not completely ideal). But it is false if it says that the ideal form of God cannot appear in this world because everything in this world must be non-ideal.

Liberalism is true if it says that God can be known in many forms. But it is false if it claims that every personal conception of God must be real given our freedom. The freedom of religion extends to many real forms of God, but not to arbitrary concocted notions of God.

Dualism is true if it says that the speaker is distinct from the speech. But it is false if it claims that speaker and speech are two different substances, and matter has no meaning because those meanings only reside in the mind, and are arbitrary conventions of society.

Contrast to Non-Theistic Religions

Impersonalism is true if it says that this world is non-ideal, illusory, and the self transcends the world. However, impersonalism is false if it equates this self to other selves or to God. Impersonalism is also false when it calls the material world inert or unconscious.

Voidism is true if it says that the conscious being can enter a state of deep sleep and dissolve all experience and identity. But it becomes false when it calls this state permanent. Time indeed passes even when we are in deep sleep although we remain unaware of passing time.

Contrast to Vedānta Interpretations

Advaita is true in the sense that the soul can take on the mood and role of God, and God can take on the mood and role of the soul. However, it is false if it says that the soul and God are identical, because God is the original cause, including of the soul, but the soul is not the cause of God. The soul doesn't become omniscient or omnipotent by taking on God's mood and role. Likewise, God doesn't lose His omniscience or omnipotence by taking on the soul's mood and role.

Viśiṣṭādvaita is true in the sense that every soul is a quality of God. However, it is incorrect to say that if the soul suffers then God must also suffer because the soul is tied to God through an object-quality relation. When the soul forgets its godly qualities and identifies with material qualities, then the soul-quality is dissociated from the object of that quality—God. The soul is now like a prosthetic arm that can be removed from the body to repair the arm.

Śuddhādvaita is true in the sense that the soul and God have the same potential for cognition, emotion, and relation. Everything that God can know, feel, or do, the soul can know, feel, and do in principle. But it is incorrect to equate the soul to God by this because God can do all of those things simultaneously while the soul can only do those things one by one.

Dvaita is true in the sense that the speech is separate from the speaker. But it is incorrect to say that the speech is eternally separate from the speaker because it exists in the speaker even after being spoken. And it was spoken by God which is why God is the cause of all other causes.

Bhedābheda is true in the sense that everything is at once different and inseparable. However, it becomes false if that difference and inseparability are considered fixed. God and the soul are different and inseparable in one way in the material world and in another way in the spiritual world. The difference with inseparability is always true, but not always true in the same sense.

Achintya Bhedābheda is true in the sense that difference with inseparability is inconceivable in binary logic. But it is false to say that it is inconceivable per se, or that because it is called inconceivable therefore there is no point in trying to understand or know anything.

Contrast to Anti-Theistic Ideologies

Atheism is correct in the sense that we should not accept anything based on blind faith, without reason and experience. But it is incorrect to say that religion must conform to the current ideas of reason and observation and there cannot be alternate rationalities and experiences.

Materialism is correct in the sense that matter, space, time, causality, and laws are real. However, it is false to say that all these things can be understood consistently and completely using quantitative notions of reality—as materialism is defined in science at present.

Agnosticism is correct in the sense that God may or may not exist, and we don't know for sure. But agnosticism is false when it claims that we can never know whether God exists. There are many paths to knowing God, but we cannot know God without following one of those paths.

Skepticism is correct in the sense that we should entertain radical doubts about any truth claims. But a doubter can reject all sensations, thoughts, judgments, intentions, and morals as doubtful and he will find a pure self-awareness even after all these rejections. Now he can ask: Who am I—after I have stripped away all potentially doubtful externalities? Skepticism fails because skeptics do not want to strip themselves of all doubtful positions. They want to believe in something, and they use skepticism to challenge only that which they don't like. Skepticism with a predetermined agenda is a self-contradiction and cannot be called skepticism.

Rationalism is correct in the sense that reality is governed by some system of reasoning. But reasoning cannot work without axioms. Rationalism axiomatizes separability, binary logic, and the uniformity of reality across all space and time, and confines itself to mathematical inference, even when this model is well-known to be inadequate due to Gödel's incompleteness.

Empiricism is correct in the sense that the truth must be observable. It becomes false when observation is reduced to measurement. We can measure the height, weight, and speed of a book, but that is not going to tell us anything about what the book means. To know what the book means, we have to broaden empiricism to include mental intuitions—decoding an author's persona from the text, understanding his intentions, grasping his mood, understanding the concepts he employs, and how those concepts could refer to things that we may not have seen. Then we can read the world like a book, instead of trying to measure it through instruments. Reading the world like a book is also empiricism, but not the empiricism of instrument measurement.

The Nature of Bhedābheda

The rejection of binary logic doesn't mean "anything goes". We can clearly demarcate what the non-binary position accepts and rejects. Every position is accepted in one sense and rejected in another. Those senses are not arbitrary.

Vaiṣṇavism is devotionally simple but philosophically sophisticated. This is a virtue. By its simplicity, everyone can practice Vaiṣṇavism, as it appeals to the simple mind looking for peace and love. And yet, it is not simplistic. It challenges and satisfies the most sophisticated mind that ponders the hardest questions of mankind that have either been answered piecemeal or not at all.

However, it cannot be slotted into any existing category, nor is it completely opposed to any existing category. All these categories are partially true, and yet not the complete truth. There is some grain of truth in them. But the complete truth is that which reconciles all the other strains of partial truths.

The Fallacy of the Idol Worship Argument

The Problem of Sacred Objects

Some religions argue against the Vedic system that its followers worship "idols". An "idol", or a deity, as the Vedic traditionalists call it, is a symbol of God. It communicates meanings just like symbols in a book. If we burn a book, we don't burn the ideas denoted by the book; we only remove one way of accessing those ideas. Conversely, if you we the book respectfully, then we gain knowledge from the book. Likewise, if someone breaks the deity, they don't destroy the person symbolized by it. They just lose access to the person symbolized by that deity.

Even those who argue against idol worship, sometimes called iconoclasts, happily read books. Religions consider their scriptures sacred objects. But they don't extend that same level of sacredness to other objects. Different religions consider different symbols, icons, and pictures sacred. But there is no philosophical justification why sacredness must be extended to some and not other objects. In this article, I will try to discuss the reasons for sacredness.

All sacredness comes from the meaning depicted by an object. The books and deities represent and communicate meaning. The distinction between a book and a deity is therefore artificial and unjustified. We can either have sacred books and deities or nothing would be sacred.

The Symbolic View of Reality

This requires us to understand that *everything is an instance of an idea,* including God. God is the most primordial idea called non-dual *knowledge*. He is also the original instance of non-dual knowledge. When the original idea is also the instance of that idea, then the idea becomes a person. The same idea, however, can also be instantiated in subsequent instances. Those instances can books and deities. Creating subsequent instances of the original idea neither changes the original idea nor creates anything new. It just makes the idea accessible to more people. A book is published and a deity is installed simply to communicate that idea.

All material objects are also instances of ideas, with the pure idea also being an original instance. A material object is not "stuff" as most people currently think. It is also the instance of an idea, and it may comprise instances of other ideas. A table is an incarnation of the idea of a table, a symbol of that idea that communicates the idea. Material objects are also *text* and so the world is a book to be read. Since all these things are not straightforward for most people, I will discuss them briefly in this post for those who might not have encountered them.

All followers of all religions are therefore idol worshippers because all of them revere some book. There is no fundamental difference between books and idols as they are both symbols of meaning. Those meanings, however, may be sacred or unsacred, which makes the symbol also sacred or unsacred. Therefore, if deity worship is an abomination, then by the same measure, reverence for any religious text is also an abomination. If an idol is simply stone, wood, or metal, then by the same measure, a book is nothing more than paper and ink.

The philosophy of religion is coextensive with the philosophy of language. You can either say that symbols represent meaning or not. Those symbols can be carved out of wood or stone, cast into metal forms, or drawn on paper, with or without colors. There is no fundamental difference between the shapes of linguistic squiggles drawn on paper and the shapes of deities formed out of metal, wood, or stone. There is also no basis for drawing a distinction between deities and books, or at least, not a rational and consistent one.

The Platonic Theory of Forms

Plato conceived of a world of pure and ideal forms, of which the present world was but a poor imitation. The imperfect forms were created by a combination of substance and form, where substances include things like air, fire, water, and earth. Thereby, the trees, humans, and tigers of this world were imperfect reflections of the pure form of a tree, human, and tiger. By looking at these imperfect worldly forms, we could get an inkling of what the pure forms were, although we could not know them perfectly. Perfect knowledge was impossible.

The Platonic theory of forms is symbolism in a primitive form, in which the form is the meaning represented by substances such as ink, paper, metal, wood, or stone. The problem with Platonism is that whatever Plato called substance is also a collection of forms. For instance, a stone has the properties of shape, color, hardness, heaviness, etc. each of which is a form. The forms are also subdivided into other forms; for instance, color can be white, black, and gray; the shape can be square, circle, or triangle; and so on. Therefore, whatever we call a stone or wood is not a substance; it is also many distinct forms.

The form vs. substance distinction is false. There is only form. But there are *whole* vs. *part* forms. For instance, a human form is a whole form, while hand and leg forms are part forms. The variation between hand and leg forms—e.g., in a human vs. animal body—has to be solved from a theory of whole and part forms, although no such theory has been developed in Western philosophy.

Symbolism of Ordinary Objects

Due to the form-substance dualism in Western philosophy, and because nobody knew how to study forms, all scientific thinking after Plato (i.e., beginning with Aristotle) focused only on the substance. Descartes called the mind "the thinking substance" and matter "the extended substance". Thereby, all mind-like properties (e.g., meaning) were removed from matter, and matter was reduced to just one property, i.e., extension. Even if we measure temperature or speed, we are measuring the movement of a pointer on the dial of an instrument, which means that we are always measuring length. We just change the instrument that measures length to arrive at a different kind of length. We give a *form* to the instrument by calling it the instrument that measures speed, temperature, pressure, weight, etc., to strip the measured object of form.

We now denote the properties of an object as a tuple {5T, 3M, 6S} where T is temperature, M is mass, and S is speed (for instance). The material object is thus denoted by symbols like T, M, and S, but science does not talk about forms. If you ask: "What do we mean by T, M, and S?" then you will be pointed to measuring instruments. But the instrument is not *contained* in the measured object. So, how can the property be contained in the measured object?

Philosophers of science have not been able to answer this question because they always think in terms of substances. If a clock defines time, and time is not a form, then to say that time passes in my body, that clock must be present in my body. That clock must be present in every single body because it is the definition of time. If instead, it is simply a measure of time, then there must be something called time as a pure form, that transcends all things, and yet, is immanent in all things. Both answers are problematic for science. Therefore, we should not assume that scientific materialism is a good idea even in the study of matter. Factually, each scientific property is an incoherent idea.

The correct answer is that there is only form. The measuring instrument is one instance of the form and the measured object is another. These two are immanent renditions of the transcendent form. They are also combined with other forms, which is why we cannot say that the instrument is contained inside the measured object, although we can say that the same form exists in all places. Both measured and measuring instruments are symbols of forms.

The Vedic Theory of Forms

When we take the problem of forms seriously, then we have to consider whole and part forms, and the whole form must be both immanent and transcendent to the part form. An example is a body and its parts like hands and legs. Human legs are different than tiger legs because the hand or leg forms are modified by the immanence of human or tiger form in them. The modified hand and leg forms are then combined into the tiger or human form by the transcendent form. Otherwise, leg-form and hand-form have an original *pure* existence, in God's body. His body defines the meaning of pure leg and hand forms.

Contrast this to Platonism where the hand and leg forms are separated things in the Platonic world, along with shape, size, color, and so on. In fact, opposites like hot and cold, bitter and sweet, black and white, must be separated forms. But in Vedic philosophy, all these forms are combined into God's form. This is why God's form is the whole, pure, and complete form. Shape, size, color, sweetness, etc. are part forms. The whole form, if symbolized by some part forms is a symbol of the whole form, called a deity. Since the whole form is transcendent, hence, breaking the deity doesn't destroy God. Since He is immanent, hence, worshipping the deity is worshipping the whole form.

This is similar to how humanness is immanent in every part of the human body. If you remove one of the human body parts, the whole humanness still exists, although an aspect of that humanness is unmanifest. For instance, the voting rights of a war veteran with amputated legs are not reduced, because even with amputated legs, the veteran is a full human. That humanness is a transcendent form, which is why it is not reduced even if some parts are removed. Of course, the veteran cannot go to war because full humanness is not manifest.

This theory of forms is responsible for what people call "biological evolution" in which some transcendent forms are manifest or unmanifest over time. Their bodily structures can also seem to change simply due to the manifestation or unmanifestation of some of the eternal forms. But since all forms are eternal, hence, all species are eternal. And yet, they are not eternally manifest.

The Theory of Linguistic Forms

When a form begins manifesting into something perceivable, the first step is a sound that gives the form a *name*. This name is not an arbitrary man-made linguistic label like the word "human" assigned to the human form in English. It is rather a sound that if heard perfectly evokes the human form in the mind. The sound we hear is an effect of the mental form, and the mental form created upon hearing is the effect of the heard sound. The sound emerges from the form, and the form emerges from the sound. This problem has been studied in neurolinguistics through what is called the Bouba-Kiki effect. The sound "bouba" produces the mental effect of something round and bulbous, while the sound "kiki" produces the mental effect of something sharp and angular. Individually, these sounds have no dictionary meanings in English.

The process of chanting the names of the Lord is based on the same principle as the Bouba-Kiki effect. The forms are immanent in the names, and by chanting, these forms can manifest in all the senses. God can therefore be perceived by chanting because the form of God is immanent in the sound. Hence, the names of the Lord are also sometimes called the deity incarnations of the Lord.

Once the name manifests from a form, a structure manifests from the name, quite like the word "cube" can be expanded into a cubic structure. This structure cannot be seen but its effects can be perceived as push and pull, hot and cold, inertia and force. This structure is called vāyu or "air". Since force, heat, and inertia can be perceived as the touch sensation, hence "air" is perceived as touch. It corresponds to what modern science calls "dark matter" and "dark energy". It is also responsible for geometrical effects like the curvature of space in relativistic theories. We cannot see the curvature of space, hence it is dark. But it exerts force, inertia, and heat; hence it exists.

Then when this structure is filled by visible properties, or what we call quanta in modern physics, we say that a visible object has emerged. The so-called quantum-gravity problem involves two tiers of reality, namely, "air" and "fire". The "air" is an invisible structure and "fire" is the visible atoms in that structure. The space of modern science is not the "ether" of Sāñkhya. Instead, the space of modern science is "air" expanded from words. Like a chapter title expands into a section structure, which is then filled with paragraphs, similarly, "ether" is the chapter title, "air" is the section structure, and "fire" is the visible paragraphs. We can say that a word expands into a structure that is then occupied by words.

The Expansion of Meaning Forms

In set theory, we use three concepts of set, objects, and structure to describe this process. The cube is a set, with many objects (points), and a structure on the set and in between the points. If those points could themselves be considered sets, then there will be another structure, with another set of objects within it. This process is employed recursively to describe the perceptual and conceptual apparatus in Sāñkhya. For instance, the mind is like a set, prāṇa is like a structure, and the ideas in the mind are like objects. The appearance of different ideas in the mind (called "thinking") is due to the prāṇa focusing the mind on different parts of its structure (like vertices of a cube).

One such idea is "my body". This object expands into another set, structure, and object. The second-order set is the sense of hearing, the second-order structure is places of words (i.e., figures of speech and the grammatical structure), and the second-order object is words. From these words expand yet another set, structure, and object which is called the sense of touch, the places of touch, and the objects of touch. Similarly, the objects of touch then expand into the sets, structures, and objects of sight, taste, and smell, recursively. Since the set, structure, and object are the three modes of the same thing, hence, we use modal logic to avoid the contradictions of one word having three meanings. But these three meanings constitute the process of expansion by which the mental idea transforms into a sense-perceivable object. It is a symbol of the mental idea, it communicates that idea, and it has been produced from that idea.

Modern physics is a partial study of the visible portion of sense perception using physical properties like energy, momentum, mass, charge, etc. There is no physical theory of smell and taste, dark energy and dark matter, or of sound's effects on other sense perceptions and the mind. One out of the five "gross material elements" of Sāñkhya is studied in current physics improperly and the other four elements are simply beyond the scope of current physics.

The five sense-perceivable properties of sound, touch, sight, taste, and smell contain the original form, which means that the form can be evoked in the mind by sense perception. For instance, just by the smell of a mango, the taste of the mango, the picture of the mango, the softness of the mango, and the sound of the name mango can be created along with the idea that this smell corresponds to a mango. This is because the idea of mango is in the smell. Thereby, all sense percepts are *symbols* of the meaning form, and the meaning form is immanent in and transcendent to the sense perceivable qualities.

Religious Implications of Forms

Everything has expanded from God and God is immanent in everything. But that immanent form is realized better through some sense perceivable objects than others. This is just like an author can be known better from his personal diaries than from non-fiction works. The author is immanent even in the other works, but he is manifested more in the personal diary. These diaries of God are religious symbols. God can be known by chanting some names, touching His deity, offering the deity food, clothes, and flowers, eating and drinking sanctified food, and smelling the odors of flowers and clothes offered to the deity far better than His other manifestations. This is because the transcendent is also immanent and manifest. If we worship the deity, then the transcendent is known through its immanence. However, if we break the deity, then the transcendent is not destroyed. It ceases to be immanent; we lose access to the transcendent and make it harder to access the transcendent in the future.

The primary difference between Western and Vedic philosophies is that the meaning of the symbol is *in* the symbol in Vedic philosophy, while the meaning is *in* our minds in Western philosophy. Factually, even a religious book—e.g., Quran, Bible, or Torah—is not sacred under the Western theory of meaning. It is paper and ink that we *consider sacred* because there is no objective difference between a religious text and a book of pure fiction. If we like, we can assign some arbitrary books a sacred status, and that assignment of sacredness would merely be someone's personal belief. This is how religion becomes a matter of personal belief, rather than a scientific fact about a book or activity.

If we want to escape this conclusion and designate some things as sacred, then we have to say that there is a transcendent reality immanent in things. That conclusion, however, will not just be limited to the book. It can be extended to anything, including incantations, rituals, deities, food, clothes, places, and practices if there is manifest immanence of transcendence in them.

Hypocritical Rejection of Deities

The same theory of symbolism that makes a book sacred also makes a deity sacred. Both are symbols of meaning, the meaning is immanent in the symbol, and whatever is immanent has a perceivable effect. If we cannot perceive what is immanent, then we can measure its presence by its effects because the immanent reality may be dark to our vision, but its effects are not dark.

These conclusions, however, cannot be understood without a theory of meaning. Plato's theory of forms remained unsustainable due to the form vs. substance distinction. By eliminating the presence of pure forms in this world, the possibility of knowing the perfect truth was also eliminated. Christianity claims that God is transcendent but never immanent. So, how can anything in this world be sacred? How can God be present in a book or place of worship if He is always transcendent and never immanent? Modern science then separated the study of matter from the study of meaning and purpose in the mind. Thereby, every object in this world is meaningless and purposeless, including sacred texts, places of worship, deities, and so forth. For any religion to claim that some things are sacred while other things are not is now a matter of pure faith that can never be justified based on any rational principle.

The rejection of "idol worship" is hypocritical because they cannot establish why their own chosen religious symbols are sacred. For them to say that deities are not religious symbols begs the question of how a Cross, Star, or Crescent is sacred. Without a theory of meaning and the immanence of that meaning in things, nothing can ever be considered sacred. However, if that meaning's immanence is recognized, then there are rational criteria for sacredness.

Objective Measures of Sacredness

In principle, we can say that God may exist in different houses (temples, churches, mosques, and synagogues), books (Gita, Bible, Koran, and Torah), rituals, foods, and clothes. However, before we can make such claims, we have to test God's immanence in these things through objective criteria:

- Do we get scientific knowledge of the world around us that we can confirm by observation?
- Do we get a comprehensive understanding of moral action to produce a moral society?
- Is our mind purified of anger, lust, hatred, greed, egotism, and fear by religious practice?
- Does the form of God spring in our minds by the perception of religious symbols?

If the answer to these questions is yes, then the religion that uses such symbols for the purification of a person is true, right, and good and God's immanence is manifest in the symbols. If not, God is hidden in things that we have designated sacred. The measure of sacredness is not blind faith in scriptures, messiahs, or even God's existence. It has to be decided by the effects of associating with the sacred objects. By such association, we must get verifiable truth, a moral society, happy people, and ultimately the direct perception of God.

Everything can give us the truth, right, and good because God is immanent in everything. However, God's presence is not equally *manifest* in everything. Thus, associating with a table, chair, or bed is not the same as associating with a truthful book, deity, mantra, or sanctified food. Thus, we do not call everything a sacred symbol. We designate those things as sacred symbols whose association manifests sacredness in us. Of course, one who has attained perfection sees God's presence in everything and what is unmanifest to others is manifest to him. Thereby, everything is sacred for a person who has attained perfection. But for one who is following the path toward perfection, God's presence in some things is emphasized through some sacred symbols because by associating with them sacredness will be manifest within us.

The empirical test of sacredness is the change in the hearts, minds, and lives of religious practitioners. The heart is the emotional reality, the mind is the cognitive and conative reality, and life is the relational reality. By the purity of emotions, cognitions, conations, and relations, we get an enlightened, moral, and happy person and society. By applying this objective measure of sacredness, we can know which religion is sacred to which extent simply by observing the hearts, minds, and lives of the people practicing the religion.

Observation and Inference

It is sometimes said—*phalena parichyate*—we can know if something is true, right, and good by the results it produces. There are two well-known methods of knowledge called *pratyakṣa* or observation and *anumāna* or inference. Seeing God is *pratyakṣa*. But even if we cannot see God, we can still perceive the change in the hearts, minds, and lives of people who associate with sacred symbols. By those effects, we can *infer* God's presence, because there is no other way to explain the appearance of knowledge, morality, and happiness in them.

This is not to say that God cannot be perceived directly. It is rather to say that direct perception follows three stages—(a) perfect knowledge, (b) moral action and organization, and (c) peaceful and pleasant emotions. The appearance of these symptoms cannot be explained in any way other than God's immanence in the sacred symbols. But because we haven't yet perceived God directly, therefore, these fall into the category of *inference* rather than *observation* (*anumāna* instead of *pratyakṣa*). Further progress yields observation too.

Religions devoid of sacredness in their symbols define their success in terms of materialistic achievements—e.g., military conquests—instead of knowledge, morality, and peacefulness. But as their power reduces, they do not infer their defeats as God's anger toward them. Instead, they become nihilistic. For them, God exists to serve our needs. If our need isn't served, then God does not exist.

Correct and Incorrect Inferences

The symptom of false inferences is that they transform into their opposites over time. The symptom of true inferences is that they get stronger over time. The truth is therefore called *non-reducing*. If we aren't convinced that knowledge, morality, and peacefulness are the correct symptoms of sacredness, then we can take any other symptoms of sacredness we like and we will always find those symptoms disappearing over time and the assumptions about sacredness would be replaced by their opposites—such as atheism or nihilism.

Sacredness, therefore, isn't just a personal belief. It is an objective truth. It is measured by objective criteria. But if we invent criteria for sacredness, then the religion that invented it once will have to reinvent it, again and again, until the sacred has been completely transformed into the originally profane.

Those who adhere to the objective criteria of sacredness will affirm the sacredness because they have accepted the correct symptoms of sacredness. The deity is such a sacred symbol. If we worship the deity, then we will progressively get knowledge, morality, and peacefulness. Over time, we will also see God directly. This is the scientific principle of sacredness—the whole truth is immanent in every partial truth, but some partial truths reveal the whole truth more. If we associate with that sacred symbol, then we can find the whole truth.

Personalism vs. Monotheism vs. Impersonalism

Personalism is Not Monotheism

Many people at present see similarities between Abrahamic monotheism and Vedic personalism and contrast these two philosophies to impersonalism and voidism.

Personalism is similar to monotheism in some superficial ways but different from it in essential ways. Likewise, personalism is different from impersonalism in one way—accepting or rejecting an eternal personality of a person—but in many other ways, personalism is similar to impersonalism. The differences between monotheism and personalism are bigger but those between personalism and impersonalism are smaller.

In this article, I will discuss many nuances to help clarify the respective positions of these philosophies.

A Brief Survey of Comparisons

Personalism vs. Impersonalism

Vedānta Sutra begins with *athātho brahma jigyāysa* or "now, therefore, let us inquire into brahman". All Vedānta interpretations accept that brahman is the *whole truth*, including the material and spiritual worlds. All interpretations accept that some part of brahman is "I am" while other parts of brahman are "I am X". The debate is about whether "X" is eternal or temporary. The "I am" is a person and "X" is a personality. All personalities are ideas, meanings, or qualities. Hence, even the material world is an idea, meaning, or quality. The question boils down to the debate between whether some idea, meaning, or quality is an eternal personality or whether they are always temporary.

Shankaracharya summarized impersonalism in four sentences: (a) brahman is truth, (b) the world is false, (c) the soul is brahman, and (d) there is nothing beyond. Personalists agree with the first three claims and disagree with the fourth. Personalism is thus 3/4th impersonalism. The difference is that the "X" of "I am" can also spring out of "I am" in personalism and it is always an external addition to "I am" in impersonalism. Impersonalists say that we must negate the choice of X, and personalists insist on making a good choice.

We can describe this difference by two words—color and shade. All shades—white, black, yellow, red, and blue—are colors. Brahman is color. When color becomes a shade, then we get "color is yellow" kinds of statements. Of these, "color is white" is a complete shade, because it includes all other shades, while "color is yellow" is incomplete. The distinction between God and soul, in personalism, is the distinction between "color is white" and "color is yellow". The impersonalist says that we must drop all "X" to just have instances of color—which are still individual things—but without the shades attached to these instances, we would not be able to *tell the difference* between them. This is the essence of Shankaracharya's third statement above—"the soul is Brahman".

The souls *do not merge* into one Brahman even in Shankaracharya's philosophy. They just become indistinguishable from one another. This is the meaning of Advaita—non-dual or non-different, rather than "oneness". These are not the same. Non-duality, in this case, refers to the epistemic indistinguishability of persons. Oneness would instead refer to the ontological identity of all persons.

In personalism, each person is like a fountain that can spout dirty water, pure water, or no water. When it spouts a different colored water, then we can tell the difference between fountains. If it stops spouting water, then we cannot say which fountain is better or worse. Without the ability to distinguish fountains, we cannot *order* or *sequence* them. Indistinguishable fountains cannot be called first, second, or third fountains. And yet, they are individual fountains. Similarly, impersonalism is the indistinguishability of distinct persons.

Personalism vs. Monotheism

The superficial similarity between personalism and monotheism is that there is one Supreme Person. The fundamental dissimilarity between them is that this Supreme Person has infinite personalities in personalism, that are ranked from highest to lowest, and named differently, but this Supreme Person has only one personality in monotheism. The highest personality of the Supreme Person is called Śyāmasundar in personalism because the Supreme Person identifies with this personality the most. Other personalities, including Viṣṇu, Shiva, or Durga, are lower, in the view of the Supreme Person (not due to our belief). The Supreme Person loves to think that "I am Śyāmasundar" the most. He likes to think that "I am Viṣṇu", "I am Shiva", and "I am Durga" progressively lesser.

The Supreme Person is Kṛṣṇa, or all-attractive. Even if one is attracted to Viṣṇu, Shiva, or Durga, the *reasons* for their attraction are a subset of reasons for attraction to Kṛṣṇa. Even if one is attracted to a house, country, man, or woman, the *reasons* for their attraction are a subset of the reasons that one can be attracted to Kṛṣṇa. As this attraction grows, one is progressively more attracted to Śyāmasundar. But Kṛṣṇa is the Supreme Person, and Śyāmasundar is the Supreme Personality. Since Kṛṣṇa most identifies with the Śyāmasundar personality, therefore, He is Śyāmasundar the most. But it doesn't mean that He is not Viṣṇu, Shiva, Durga, or others, with a subset of attractions in Kṛṣṇa.

Under monotheism, the Supreme Person has only one personality and all others are false. Monotheism universalizes one personality, while personalism accepts infinite personalities, that are seen by different individuals with compatible personalities. Seeing one personality of a person is about compatibility between the seer and the seen personalities. Before we equate monotheism to personalism, we should try to understand how one person can have many personalities, but all personalities are not revealed unless the seer is a compatible personality. The universalism of personality is a false idea even in the case of ordinary humans. Nobody reveals the same personality to everyone. The number of personality types revealed to different individuals must increase with the Supreme Person. Instead, monotheism reduces those personalities to one, just next to impersonalism which removes all personalities from God.

Equating monotheism to personalism, while contrasting monotheism against impersonalism, is seeing a lot of similarity between one and infinity while seeing a lot of difference between one and zero. The fact is that monotheism is almost completely impersonalism in contrast to personalism. Monochromatic universalism destroys all variety and diversity is therefore designated nirviśesa.

One vs. Many Philosophical Problem

The Katha Upaniśad states: *ekam satyam vipra bahudha vadanti,* which means "there is one truth, *spoken* of by the sages in many ways". That *speaking* is calling the Supreme Person by many non-synonymous names (see earlier article "God Has Many Names" Problem). Each person can have a different name for the Supreme Person that *describes* the personality and *refers* to the Supreme Person. The description and reference are not identical. We can say "this is a tree" where "this" is a reference and "tree" is its description. If there are no other trees in the current context, then we can replace "this" with "tree". But that substitution is not universal. Someone else can say "this is a mango tree" and substitute "this" with "mango tree". Similarly, the Supreme Person is called by many names but described differently in those calls.

The Chāndogya Upaniśad states: *sarvam idam khalu brahma,* which means "all this (world) is certainly brahman". The debate is about whether brahman has an eternal personality. In both personalism and impersonalism, the soul is a part of the whole truth, although that whole truth has a personality in personalism but not in impersonalism. Impersonalists have to accept the distinction between brahman and Param Brahman, as noted in the Upaniśads. And yet, they liken Param Brahman to an ocean in which the soul is a drop.

The ocean supposedly has no personality (which is also ultimately a false idea, as explained in the earlier article The Drop in the Ocean Argument). Once all personalities are stripped, it is impossible to tell the difference between the supreme and non-supreme persons. The personalists make that difference clear by describing the non-supreme personality as an *aspect* of the complete personality of the Supreme Person. For instance, personalists would describe Param Brahman as white color rather than an ocean because the white color is also an ocean of partial shades although it has a specific form, just as all partial shades have a form and are yet color. There is nothing wrong is calling both white and yellow colors, without equating them. Thus, in both personalism and impersonalism, the material world is modeled as a person and an idea-like personality. The debate is only about whether the personality is eternal or not. The impersonalist says that matter is not an eternal personality, whereas the personalist says that even matter is an eternal personality called Durga.

If we combine the statements from Katha and Chāndogya Upaniśad, we get the following (a) there is one truth, (b) which is described in many ways, (c) even the material world is one description of the same truth, and (d) the material *description* of the truth is erroneous and temporary. This is just like a fountain spouting dirty water, or one of the shades of color being black. We think that the fountain is dirty, or the color is black, but that *description* of the fountain or color is erroneous, as indicated by the fact that this equivalence of fountain and water, or color and shade, is temporary. However, that equivalence is not universally temporary. In some cases, the equivalence is eternal.

This is the resolution of the one-vs.-many philosophical paradox (how the same thing is one and many): The one is like the sun, and the many are the rays of the sun. Each ray describes the sun—even if the description is blue, its reference is the sun. When we say "this is a tree", the term "this" refers to a soul, but it is being called a "tree". That designation is temporary, but the reference is eternal. Similarly, even if someone says that the sun is blue, the description of the sun is false, but the reference to the sun is true. Each soul is a ray of the Kṛṣṇa-sun. When that ray becomes blue, it also becomes a false description of the reference; however, if it becomes yellow, then it becomes true. Since it can still become truthful, hence, the falsehood is temporary, and eternity is the truth.

Contrast this to monotheism where each individual is a *separate* person. They are like many suns rather than one sun and many rays of the sun. Even the material world is not a ray of the sun, but a sun. Hence, if you study matter, you don't know God under monotheism, because matter is a thing-in-itself separate from God. This leads to many kinds of dualisms—God vs. the soul, God vs. the world, and the soul vs. the world. Monotheism is fundamentally dualistic, while both personalism and impersonalism are non-dualistic. These dualities are bound together in monotheism via contracts, covenants, and laws, which are negotiable, modifiable, and upgradeable precisely because there is nothing eternally connecting or binding two fundamentally different dualities. In contrast, in personalism, every part is eternally bound to the whole in some unchangeable manner whether or not the part recognizes that connection.

This difference appears when people "convert" to a monotheistic religion by accepting a covenant. There is no "conversion" in personalism since the connection between the whole and the part is eternal. It has been forgotten and by spiritual practice, it is remembered. It is like a son who forgot his father. The father-son relationship is fixed at birth and cannot be created or revoked by our agreement or disagreement. However, the son can forget about the father, or he can remember the father. Conversion and deconversion in monotheistic religions create and revoke a connection because that connection is not eternal due to the soul-God dualism. In personalism, the whole and the part are eternally connected. Personalism rejects conversion due to non-dualism.

In all personalist philosophies, people can keep calling themselves Christian, Muslim, Jew, Buddhist, Jain, Sikh, or even Hindu. It doesn't matter what you call yourself because that is not an eternal thing. After you die and are reborn, that sectarian identity may change. So, why hurry to change it? Let it be whatever it is. It doesn't matter. Just try to revive the eternal connection to the Supreme Lord. This non-sectarian philosophy has been given the sectarian name of "Hinduism" by sectarian people. But that is not the name that this philosophy calls itself. It calls itself knowledge and truth, not yet another sect.

The Problem of Comparisons

One of the problems of comparisons is that two things that look similar are often drastically dissimilar. We can illustrate this problem through the discussion of the four qualities of sattva, rajas, tamas, and transcendence. A person in tamas is lazy, a person in rajas is ambitious, and a person in sattva is dutiful. To the ambitious person, the dutiful person seems lazy. To the lazy person, the dutiful person seems ambitious. Thus, the person in rajas thinks that the person in sattva is in tamas whereas the person in tamas thinks that the person in sattva is in rajas. This is the first problem of misdiagnosing one type of quality as another—we call sattva either rajas or tamas, not sattva.

Similarly, people under three qualities do not understand the transcendent person because he is like all three qualities and not like any of them. Since a transcendent person is lazy in their materialistic life, hence, we can liken him to a person in tamas. Since he is ambitious in the Lord's service, therefore, we can liken him to a person in rajas. Since he is dutiful, consequently, we can liken him to a person in sattva. And yet, the transcendent person is in neither sattva, nor rajas, nor tamas. Those in sattva, rajas, and tamas see one aspect of his personality and compare it to themselves to conclude that he is like them.

Misperception and mischaracterization are the norms rather than the exceptions because we are used to thinking in terms of binary opposites and mutual exclusions and not in terms of three qualities that are similar to other qualities in one way and dissimilar to other qualities in another way. Those things that look similar in some way, but are dissimilar in other ways, can belong to completely different classes. If we don't understand the fundamental distinction and rely on similarity, then we get erroneous conclusions.

Direct and Inverted Reflections

Everything in Vedic philosophy is constructed from qualities. The material world is the conflictual state of qualities, voidism is the separated state of qualities, impersonalism is the merged state of qualities, and the spiritual world is the cooperative state of qualities. But all these are qualities *of a person.* This is the magic of qualities—they can be conflictual, separated, merged, and cooperative. The same thing can enter a different state, and it becomes completely different from the previous state. But it is always a person entering a different state. Some state of a person is better than other states of the person.

The material world is a direct bodily reflection of the spiritual world. But the material world is an inverted mental reflection of the spiritual world. Due to direct and inverted reflections, the topmost tip of reality looks very similar to the bottommost tip of the reflection from a bodily view. Thus, Śyāmasundar, the topmost reality, is blue, which is also the color of tamas, the bottommost reality. Tamas is frivolity, hedonism, and immorality along with disregard for industry, ambition, duty, and responsibility. These traits of tamas are similar to those in Śyāmasundar—He looks immoral, hedonistic, and frivolous, and He looks not ambitious, dutiful, responsible, and industrious. But this similarity is only with regard to the body. Mentally speaking, tamas is ignorance, arrogance, and selfishness, but Śyāmasundar has none of these mentally toxic traits. Quite in contrast, He is fully knowledgeable, most humble, and utterly selfless.

If we see bodily similarities and the mental differences, we might say: The two are similar in some ways and dissimilar in other ways. That would not be partially true. It would be completely false because they are dissimilar in all essential ways, like an apple and its plastic replica. We cannot get partial nutrition by chewing a plastic apple. Instead of gaining health, we will get sick by chewing on a plastic apple. Similarly, the topmost reality looks like the bottommost reflection, but the latter is also most different from the former.

Śyāmasundar is beautifully and desirably twisted in three ways (*tribhanga lalitam*), just as tamas is disagreeably and hideously twisted in three ways. The twisting in tamas is ignorance, immorality, and laziness. The twisting in Śyāmasundar is rejection of knowledge, morality, and endeavor. Rejection of knowledge is not ignorance; rejection of morality is not immorality; rejection of endeavor is not laziness. Śyāmasundar doesn't think science and philosophy, but He is not ignorant. Śyāmasundar doesn't honor social norms or boundaries, but He is not immoral. Śyāmasundar doesn't work, but He is not lazy.

For many centuries, ignorant and unscrupulous people in India have called Śyāmasundar an immoral, irresponsible, selfish, hedonistic, ignorant, and naïve villager, because they see His body and behavior, but not His mind and emotions. When the best can be compared to the worst, because the best looks just like the worst, we should not shy away from asking: Are we inadvertently equating the best to the worst? We have to always keep the inversion of the mind and the imitation of the body in our view. The similarity between bodies is irrelevant. The difference in mentality is of the greatest consequence.

The equivalence between monotheism and personalism is based on a body count—God is one. That is a negative idea of God—God is not many, He is not absent, and He is not silent. Materialism is about many bodies. Voidism is about emptiness. Impersonalism is about silence. Saying that God is not many bodies, not absent, and not silent is not saying what God is. An infinite number of possibilities about what God is, remain possible after we have said what God is not. Among these possibilities are those that have a bodily semblance but a mental difference. Additionally, saying that God is not many, God is not absent, and God is not silent, is a false claim because He is also those things. A person can go to sleep to become absent; He can enter a waking thoughtless state to become impersonal; He can relate to many people where He shows different personalities to each one of them while still being just one person.

Thus, making a monotheistic claim is not sufficient—because infinite alternatives are still open after that claim has been made. Similarly, making a monotheistic claim is not necessary—because all that has been claimed to not exist factually exists in God. Monotheism, polytheism, monism, henotheism, pantheism, panentheism, unitarianism, impersonalism, and voidism are all true in some respect and false in other respects. We have to make that claim which makes all claims true while not universalizing any of these. If our claim rejects other claims implicitly, then it must be considered false. If something is not so nuanced and broadly encompassing, then it is necessarily false.

Dualistic and Non-Dualistic Philosophies

Four Doctrines of Cosmic Origins

God appears in every religion through a doctrine of creation. Given that the universe is infinite (or extremely large, close to infinite, as far as we can tell), and we want to talk about the creation of this universe (because whatever exists must have had an origin), religious differences appear through different creation doctrines—the source of the universe can be finite, infinite, or nothing. Each of these three doctrines has an origin in the Vedic philosophical idea that the world comprises *duality*, or opposites like hot and cold, bitter and sweet, heavy and light, black and white, big and small, so the origin of the world must reconcile these opposites and the result of reconciliation will be *non-duality*.

The proponent of nothingness says that when opposites combine, they cancel each other. Hence, the infinite must emerge from nothingness where neither opposite exists, but because language always uses mutually opposed words, therefore, nothingness cannot be spoken of. Nothingness can only be known through silence. This idea is called *Pratītyasamutpāda* or co-dependent arising of opposites. The opposites are also *appearances* (rather than reality) while their combination cancels the opposites, so reality is ultimately nothing.

The impersonalist rejoinder to this conclusion is that something cannot come out of nothing. But the thing that causes an infinite universe also cannot be finite. The cause of the universe must itself be infinite. There are at least two fundamental ways in which the infinite universe can emerge out of an infinite cause, which can be modeled as "infinite body" and "infinite mind". In the "infinite body" case, there is an infinite energy that takes a *form* to become worldly objects and their dynamics. But when the form becomes formless, then the energy exists but is unperceivable. In the "infinite mind" case, the world is like a thought in the mind, and when the thought subsides, the mind remains thoughtless. Present-day impersonalists lean toward the "infinite mind" case while present-day scientists lean toward the "infinite body" case. While both are impersonalism, for the sake of our present discussion, I will call the "infinite mind" case *impersonalism* and the "infinite body" case *materialism*. Materialism can also be called *depersonalization* in the sense that the body is fundamental and the mind is emergent. Impersonalists, however, say that the mind is fundamental whereas the body is emergent. By restricting impersonalism to "infinite mind" and materialism to "infinite body" we can make things clearer.

The personalist rejoinder to these two forms of impersonalism is that it does not provide a method by which the formless becomes form, and vice versa. We cannot call these transformations accidents. Personalists also disagree with the idea that the infinite cannot come out of the finite; that restriction applies to the body but not to the mind which can produce infinite ideas. To produce any idea, the mind must choose, which necessitates a personality. That personality makes a mind finite because it excludes other personalities. But the capacity of the mind to produce ideas even under a personality is infinite. Since the mind can produce mutually opposite ideas, hence, opposites do not cancel each other.

We may not (and we do not) experience the opposites simultaneously. But because they can be created successively, hence, they must coexist in the mind even when one or none of them is experienced. The arguments for materialism, nothingness, and impersonalism are rejected by personalists for different reasons—(a) the finite can produce the infinite, (b) the opposites don't cancel each other, (c) the finite that produces the infinite is like the mind that creates thought and not smaller and bigger bodies, and (d) the mind has a personality.

The Monotheistic Doctrine of Creation

Monotheism speaks of *ex nihilo* creation, which is something out of nothing. There is also a rejection of the existence of opposites in God evidenced by the famous problem of evil in which if God is good, then evil must not exist in God, begging the question: If it was not present in God, then where did it come from? Finally, it treats the material world as inert stuff—that we can liken to the body—rather than as thoughts (which we liken to the mind) to solve all of the above problems. Monotheism doesn't address basic questions: (a) How does the infinite come out of the finite? (b) Why opposites don't cancel each other? The existence of opposites is rejected and the problem of infinity is ignored.

The ex nihilo doctrine of creation led to the Big Bang, proposed by Georges Lemaître—a Catholic priest—consistent with the ex nihilo thesis. God solves the problem of materialism, namely, how formless energy takes forms of subatomic particles, atoms, molecules, planets, cells, living bodies, societies, and so on, through the Intelligent Design Argument under which God injects *form* into energy. This takes us back to the Greek substance-form dualism in which energy is substance and form comes from God, and the combination of the two produces a world. This is just another formulation of the mind-body problem. Neither substance-form nor mind-body dualism is a solvable problem.

The equivalence between personalism with monotheism hides all the fundamental and essential tenets of personalism—(a) the world is idea-like, (b) it emerged out of a mind, (c) it disappears into a mind, (d) the ideas are eternal, (e) but they are not always seen, (f) the mind creates both true and false ideas, (g) false ideas are dreaming fantasies, (h) true ideas are wakeful knowledge, (i) truth and falsity coexist as the ability for dreaming and waking (j) the mind that enters dreaming or waking knows the state it is in, (j) hence, dreaming is known to be false speculation, imagination, or fantasy, rather than truth, (k) there is no substance because one form produces many forms, (l) the form appears to be finite but it produces infinite forms, and (m) hence, the infinite comes out of the finite because both the infinite and the finite are forms.

The Four Stages of Experience

Personalism is dangerously close to impersonalism because the material world is like thought in the mind, and when the thought subsides, the mind remains thoughtless. The difference is that the mind has a persona in personalism while it doesn't have a persona in impersonalism. The thoughtful state of the mind is dreaming and the thoughtless state of the mind is deep sleep. Quite apart from these, is the waking state of the mind, which is neither dreaming nor deep sleep. The impersonalist who postulates "infinite mind" as the cause of the material world is correct in the sense that his theories of worldly illusion and freedom from that worldly illusion pertain to dreaming and waking thoughtless states of the mind. He is incorrect only in the sense that the same mind could also be thoughtfully awake, just as it could be thoughtlessly asleep.

The mind is capable of three things—(a) truthful thoughts, (b) fantasy thoughts, and (c) thoughtlessness. Thoughtlessness is better than fantasy, but truthful thought is better than thoughtlessness. Therefore, the personalist schools do not reject thoughtless states, but don't consider it the final destination. They are different from impersonalists who claim that "infinite mind" implies the absence of form because impersonalists cannot explain how the mind produces thought except by postulating the existence of will; the existence of will necessitates the existence of personhood—due to which the will leans one way or another—which then necessitates a form. The mind always has a form. A mind with form, though finite, can produce infinite thoughts. They do not include all possible thoughts, but they can be infinite. The same mind can dream, or be thoughtlessly asleep, just as it is can be thoughtfully awake.

Personalism, impersonalism, voidism, and materialism are all *non-dualistic* because they postulate only one category—(a) mind with choice in personalism, (b) mind without choice in impersonalism, (c) choice without mind in materialism, and (d) no mind and no choice in voidism. Dualisms—such as mind vs. body, form vs. substance, spirit vs. matter, and God vs. soul—are unique to Western philosophy. They have never existed in Indian philosophy.

Philosophies that arose in India were always non-dualistic, a point that eludes many people today. The debate was only about which type of non-dualism is correct, and the personalist conclusion is that all forms of non-dualism are correct as the self that can be waking thought (spiritual world), thoughtless waking (impersonalism), thoughtless sleeping (voidism), and dreaming thought (material world). After recognizing all the states as different states of a person, personalists conclude that waking thought is the best. The preference is based on *better* and *worse* states, rather than *existent* and *non-existent* states.

Mind-Based Reality is Not Solipsism

It is thus inappropriate to equate or limit the philosophy of personalism to the spiritual world because it is also a philosophy of the material world in which the world is the dreaming thought of the Supreme Person. When people hear about the description of the material world as a dream reality, they think not in terms of the dream of the Supreme Person but in terms of *their* dream, to conclude that we must be talking about solipsism. We are not talking about solipsism, because the world is not *our* dream. Realism only means that there is something that I cannot control, and I call that the "world". If we extend this idea to God, then realism from God's perspective would mean that the world is out of God's control. Thus, when we talk about the material world as God's dream we are implicitly implying: The material world is completely in God's control.

Confusions about realism and solipsism arise because the correct definition of realism (as something that I cannot control) is replaced by numerous false definitions of realism (an extended substance, the stuff that exists even when nobody knows about it, something that is known by everyone, quantifiable through measurements, etc.). It will take us a long time to refute all these false conceptions of realism, so I won't get into it. I can only summarize the problem: There are numerous false conceptions of realism that have never been substantiated, and yet, they remain popular in the common imagination.

These false notions arose in Western thinking due to the monotheistic idea that God created the world, relinquished control over the world, and gave man *dominion* over the world. The correct definition of realism under which the world is different from I because I don't have control over the world is rejected by monotheistic doctrines. Alternate definitions of realism are postulated to maintain the idea that man has dominion over the world. In contrast, the personalist concept of realism is that God has control over the world and we do not. Thereby, the world is a part of God, however, the world is not our part.

Conflict with false ideas of realism is not a problem that I can solve. I can only say that there is one correct definition of realism—as something that I cannot control—and matter is real by that definition. And yet, matter is a dream for God because He can control matter. Hence, we model the material world from God's perspective as ideas and adapt *our* realism to idea-like reality. Idealism is true for God, but realism is true for us. However, when idealism is true for God, then the realism true for us is not substance, objectivity, or numbers. It is like ideas and pictures in a dream. The quantitative, objective, mathematical, exploitative, inertial, and substantive modeling of material reality is hence a falsehood.

Epistemic vs. Ontological Dualism

The term "dualism" is also used in personalism, although restricted to the *perception* of duality without an *objective* duality. This perceived duality—when there is no duality—is an *illusion*. Even as we perceive opposites like hot vs. cold, bitter vs. sweet, black vs. white, or heavy vs. light, in an idea-like world, neither side can be *defined* without the other. Opposites are like two sides of a coin, which requires a third entity—akin to a coin—that reconciles these opposites.

The definition of a coin head necessitates the existence of a coin and a coin tail. And yet, the head is not the tail and not equal to the coin. In some cases, when we see the head, we can say "it is a coin", which is just like saying that "yellow is a color". That doesn't equate yellow to color, because color includes other shades too. This problem is easily demonstrated by saying that even as yellow is a color, color is not yellow. Color is now akin to a mind in which shades are different thoughts. While thinking, the mind becomes the thought, and yet, the thought is not the mind because the mind can think other thoughts—including thoughts contradictory to previous thoughts. Thus, the duality of head and tail is perceived by the mutual exclusion of opposites even as opposites are mutually defined and factually co-existent. Duality is the perceived mutual exclusion.

We can call the perceived duality *epistemic dualism* while reality is *ontological non-dualism*. Since perception is dualistic while reality is non-dualistic, hence, perception is an illusion. This illusion of dualism is the dreaming state of the mind in which when we see something, we do not see the opposite thing. This perceptual dualism can be corrected if we mentally imagine a head and coin while seeing the tail, a tail and a head while seeing the coin, and a head and a coin while seeing a tail. We don't have to see only with our five senses; we can also see with our mind. That mental perception involves "seeing" two other things (e.g., head and a coin) when we see only one thing (e.g., a tail).

When we can "see" things that we are not seeing with five senses, epistemic dualism disappears and ontological non-dualism is reinstated as the correct notion of reality. That epistemic non-duality is the waking state of the mind in which the mind can see everything that the senses cannot. Finally, if duality and non-duality disappear to dissolve the head, tail, and the coin, then the thoughtless state of the mind is its deep sleep state, which is also called non-duality because the perception of duality (i.e., the mutual exclusion of head and tail in sense perception) has disappeared by dissolving thought. Since there are four different kinds of non-dualisms—personalism, impersonalism, voidism, and materialism—hence, we don't need to (a) equate one non-dualism to another, (b) reject a non-dualism, or (c) universalize one non-dualism.

The Theory of Smaller and Bigger Minds

Clean and Unclean Mirror Analogies

The term non-duality in personalism means that we can see everything within everything else because everything is like a mirror that can reflect everything else. But when it reflects only itself and excludes everything else, then we are compelled to say that one thing is *separate* from another thing. This separated state is likened to a mirror covered with dirt which blocks every other reflection, and when we look at such a mirror, we cannot see anything other than the mirror covered with dirt. A mirror capable of reflecting everything, but covered by dirt, becomes a *thing-in-itself.* If the same mirror is cleaned, then it starts reflecting everything and becomes a *thing-for-everything-else.*

The thing-in-itself is an illusion produced by covering the mirror with dirt. Duality—or the separateness of things—appears as the result of dirt covering the mirror, and is called *māyā,* which means "that which is not true", which is also called an illusion. Thus, many terms are used to describe the same situation—dualism, illusion, dirt, falsehood, and separation. This is epistemic dualism rather than ontological dualism. Ontological dualism would be true if there was no mirror, and dirt was the only reality. Ontological dualism is false because the mirror is the primary reality, the dirt is a temporary covering of that reality, and by removing the covering, ontological non-dualism as well as epistemic non-dualism are established as the ability to see everything reflected in the mirror.

Nuanced Acceptance of Dualism

The dirt covering the mirror is sometimes considered different from the mirror—because it covers and obscures the mirror—but even that dirt is a mind that *absorbs* information about other things. If dirt was transparent and did not absorb the light incident on the mirror, or reflected by the mirror, then we would be able to see everything reflected in the mirror. The dirt is problematic only because it absorbs the light incident on the mirror and/or reflected by the mirror. That absorption converts a mirror into a thing-in-itself.

There is a sense in which there is mind-matter dualism, likened to a mirror and dirt. And yet, that dirt is also a mirror that absorbs information about other things, rather than passing it transparently. This requires us to understand the nature of the dirt—i.e., matter—covering the mirror more deeply.

Matter is a medium of communication between minds, but that medium can be likened to a post office that deletes or redacts the letters between the minds. Due to this deletion or redaction, each mind becomes a thing-in-itself because everything that is in one mind is not transparently reflected in another mind. The further problem is that each mind prefers message redaction and deletion to create a "private" world separate from a "public" world because each mind wants to separate itself from other minds and focus exclusively on itself.

People have conjured a "right to privacy" to hide what they truly are from other minds. They are not interested in knowing other minds. Their preference to hide from others and to remain disinterested in others is the desire to separate themselves from everyone else. Separation is not just because material nature deletes and redacts messages between minds but also what each mind *wants*. The material nature deletes and redacts messages between different minds only to fulfill the desire in each mind to separate itself from other minds.

Individualism Causes Dualism

The desire for privacy is individualism, by which each mind is separated from other minds. It is a desire in the mind, but it is fulfilled by matter when it redacts and deletes messages. If that desire ends, then individualism disappears, and we can see a person transparently, provided the seer mind is interested in seeing the seen mind and willing to communicate transparently. Thus, the dirt that covers the mirror is called *egotism* in each mind. It makes the mind individualistic and creates a "right to privacy", which is fulfilled by the material nature obscuring all other minds. What we called dualism, illusion, dirt, falsehood, separation, and māyā earlier, is thus also called egotism.

The ability of matter to redact and delete messages between minds is the reason that matter covering the mind is considered separate from the mind. But matter covers the mind only if the mind wants privacy, prefers individualism, and is disinterested in knowing other minds. Obsessed with itself and disinterested in everyone else, the mind takes shelter of the material energy to redact and delete what is in the mind. Thus, the mind, which was not originally a private entity, becomes private due to individualism. Then we cannot see the thoughts, feelings, and intentions of other minds although we can see the redacted and deleted version of the meaning in the mind which we call the body.

Now, people start doubting the existence of the mind because they can only see the body. They can only see the body because the mind is imbued with egotism and has become disinterested in knowing other minds. An egotistic mind cannot see other minds. A humble mind easily perceives all other minds.

The distinction between matter and spirit is that between two media of communication—in the former, the meaning in the mind is redacted and deleted while in the latter the meaning is transmitted without redaction or deletion. Both are meant for communication. But matter is meant for communication between selfish minds while spirit is meant for communication between selfless minds. Each mind can also be selfish or selfless. Hence, this distinction is simplified into a binary difference between spirit and matter, selfish and selfless, individualistic and personalistic, mind and body, and so on. This binary difference looks like dualism but it is only because the medium of communication is also a mind that selectively transmits and receives some messages while it redacts and deletes other messages. Spirit vs. matter dualism is not about two kinds of substances, but about two kinds of minds.

Smaller vs. Bigger Mind Distinction

The distinction between sender, receiver, and medium is not hard and fast, because they are all minds. And yet, a distinction between the three is drawn because they are *distinct* minds. The sender and receiver are *smaller* minds compared to the medium which is a *bigger* mind. The sender is called *ādibhautika,* the receiver is called *ādiatmika,* and the medium is called *ādidaivika.* Since the medium is capable of redacting and deleting messages, just as it is capable of transmitting and receiving messages transparently, hence, the medium becomes the "controller" of the sender-receiver communication.

When the material medium is treated as an inert substance, a false notion of "objective science" is constructed under which if a message was sent, it must be received without redaction or deletion. Under this "objective science", everyone must see the world in the same way, and because humans cannot see the world in the same way, therefore, the world must be measured by instruments. Scientists don't understand that measurement is a transmit-receive process of information exchange—akin to sending emails or letters—which cannot be objective if the mail server or post office can redact or delete the emails or letters, making even the instrument measurement a subjective process.

The material medium of communication is *ādidaivika* controller of communication in which letters pass through a hierarchy of post office officers—called demigods—who can redact, delete, enhance, or alter the messages. Thus, someone can see what others cannot see and someone cannot see what others can see. What one sees is not just a function of what they are capable of seeing, or of the properties the thing they are seeing, but also of the post office system of controlling the message exchange between a sender and a receiver. If the post office burns the letters, then we cannot communicate with other minds. We might insist that what we are not perceiving must not exist, when factually the post office is burning the letters intended for us.

The medium of communication we call "matter" is not impersonal. It is rather a "bigger mind" which controls the "smaller minds" just like we control thoughts in our mind. Due to this control, each individualistic sender and receiver is to varying degrees under material control. What they can perceive and do, how much happiness or distress they can or cannot get, and what goals they can accomplish or not, are all finely controlled simply by intercepting all messages and redacting, deleting, enhancing, or modifying them while in transit.

Matter is like the German Stasi or the Russian KGB which snooped on all communications and had the power to modify messages in transit. Frontline soldiers would get redacted letters from their families during wartime if the secret police deemed them inappropriate. If they found that the letters were emotional, they would just burn the letter or delay its transmission to its intended recipients. The secret police hid the minds from each other. The material energy controls individualistic minds in the same way.

However, unlike the secret police, the material medium is not evil. She controls everything to improve the senders and receivers—to make them give up their individualism and selfishness and transform them into selfless personalistic minds that have no hidden agendas, no desire for mental privacy, and no desire to cheat and exploit others. They are like clean mirrors which transparently reflect, understand, and accept all other mirrors. They don't think that they are separate from others, although they are still distinct individuals.

Only a mirror that has cleaned itself can perfectly reflect another—clean or unclean—mirror. The clean mirror sees everything perfectly, including the unclean mirrors. The unclean mirror sees nothing clearly, including the fact that it is an unclean mirror that can be cleaned to see everything perfectly. The unclean mirror thinks that every other mirror must be unclean, feels guilty about its uncleanliness, hides its uncleanliness from others in the name of mental privacy, makes no effort to clean itself, and calls others unclean.

The Creation of Smaller Minds

The only remaining question now is how the bigger mind creates a smaller mind as its thoughts. This requires us to understand that imagination comprises three aspects—thinker, thinking, thought. The thinker may not think, and the thought would not exist. When the thinker thinks, the thought is only an expression of what was previously in the thinker. Once a thought is created, by the thinker's power of thinking, then the thought can also become a thinker—capable of expanding into more thoughts—*if* the thinker's idea of the thought is that the thought is also a thinker with its own power of thinking.

I often have mental debates with imagined opponents who have different personalities and views than me. Once an alternative persona is created in my mind, that persona challenges me, questions me, and doubts me in various ways. I respond to these challenges, questions, and doubts, but every response is met with more challenges, questions, and doubts. I wrote several books arguing with these imagined personas in which I and the imagined persona go back and forth discussing various objections. I could easily shut down these imagined personas because they are my mental creations. But I let them be the kind of person that I have created them to be in my mind and allow them to challenge, question, and doubt me because I *enjoy* this debate and dialogue.

In simple words, if a person thinks about other persons, who have their own personas, then those self-created personas start interacting with the person who created those personas as his thoughts in the first place. If the creator persona doesn't want to tamper with the created persona, then these personas can argue, debate, challenge, question, and doubt each other, merely for enjoyment. They can also support, love, nourish, encourage, nurture, and fulfill each other, merely for enjoyment. Thus, one person becomes many persons.

This is the essence of the Vedic theory of creation in which God—the original mind—thought of various personas, and let them be the kind of person that He had created them to be in His mind. He could shut everyone down, and force them to comply with His will—after all, they are all thoughts in His mind—but He lets them be, merely for enjoyment. Some of these created personas challenge, question, and doubt God, while others nurture, fulfill, and love God. They are all part of God because they were created as mental personas. And yet, as created personas, they are different from the creator persona. We can say that everything is an illusion because it is all God's creation within His mind. And yet, for God, everything is real because He is enjoying the experience.

We have to remember that there is no difference between mind and body if the mind is pure because then, whatever is in the mind is also outside the mind, and whatever is outside the mind is also inside. The mind-body difference exists due to mental impurity in which what is inside the mind is not outside, and what is outside the mind is not inside. That impurity doesn't exist in God, and hence the mind-body distinction also doesn't exist for Him. There is also no mental privacy in the spiritual world—we cannot hide our thoughts, feelings, intentions, and judgments from others. Everyone can see the mind as clearly as they see the face right now. Hence, a dirty mind cannot enter the spiritual world because others can see the dirty mind and they will be repulsed by it. Unless the mind has been completely purified of this dirt, and all notions of mental privacy have been completely destroyed, there is no entry to the spiritual world.

The mind-body distinction is a result of (a) thinking contrary to reality, (b) thinking contrary to other persons, and (c) hiding one's thoughts from others. Since this is aided and abetted by matter, therefore, it becomes a fact for *us*, although it is not true. In Sañkhyā, we speak about three kinds of bodies—sthūla śarīra, linga śarīra, and sūkshma śarīra—or gross body, gendered body, and subtle body. In each body, everything is three things—knower, known, and knowing. Knowing is a power, knower is a sense, and the known is a type of meaning. The linga śarīra is mind, intellect, ego, and morality, and each of these is a sense with a power of knowing, along with the known meanings called thoughts, judgments, intentions, and values. If these senses are working, and matter is not redacting or deleting messages, then we construct a *composite* picture of reality that includes both mind and body, in which the mind is the deeper and broader reality that explains the shallower and narrower reality of the body. For instance, if you hear a person speaking—a narrower and shallower reality—then you can perceive their mind, as the *explanation* of why they are saying what they are saying. If the mind is perceived along with the speech, then we get behavior and its explanation, without mind-body duality.

I often meet toxic people while trying to teach. They give innocuous explanations of their actions because they assume that we can only see their words and not their minds—after all, the words, in their estimation, are the public realities and the minds are private realities. They don't know that the mind is also public for one who can see. Mind is yet another body, which can be seen just like the body most people can see. There is no mental privacy. That privacy is an illusion of egotism and individualism aided by material energy.

Since antiquity, Western philosophy has assumed that there is a reality behind the phenomena—which is true. But they have also incorrectly assumed that we can never see the reality behind the phenomena. This is the essence of the Socratic "dancing men in the cave" problem where you see shadows on the wall (phenomena) but you can never see what is causing those shadows (reality). The conclusion is: To know the "hidden" reality, we must *speculate*. No speculation can ever be proven because nobody can see. Hence, all knowledge is guesswork that may sometimes work, but it can always be falsified. This is the genesis of all problems in Western thinking—go on speculating, or accept some reality on blind faith, or forcibly assert your ideas on others, or become nihilistic due to the impossibility of knowledge. Not a single philosopher, theologian, scientist, or thinker has ever talked about the possibility of developing our perception.

All the struggles that people have between solipsism and realism are merely the result of the mind-body divide when factually there is no divide. God can see our mind. It is not hidden from Him. So, for God, there is no mind-body divide because there is no mental privacy. The mind is also a public reality for Him. Hence, the mind is not a private reality *per se*. It is not equally private for everyone because some people with mental acuity can read other minds. It is a private reality because it is obscured by material covering. It is obscured because of individualism and egotism. Otherwise, it is also a public reality.

Egotism narrows the mind into selfishness. When this ego is dissolved, then the mind becomes broad and selfless. It is just like unshackling an animal by cutting all the ropes that are binding it and letting it roam freely. An unshackled mind can see everything, including other minds. Therefore, anyone can develop their mind to perceive all the hidden realities by giving up selfishness. If we become unalloyed devotees of the Lord, then we become most selfless. Then we can also see all hidden realities. The mind connects to other minds when it gives up individualism. Otherwise, there is the illusion of mental privacy.

The infinite world we see is a movie within God's mind. God is also within that same movie as His self-image. Since the world is within God's mind, therefore, the world is a part of God. Since His self-persona is part of the created world, therefore, God is a part of the world. There is no contradiction in saying that God is a part of the world and the world is a part of God, just as there is no contradiction in saying that yellow is within color and color is within yellow. These contradictions result from thinking about object separations, the inability to reconcile the mind-body duality, and rejecting the mind to model everything as objects. When many falsehoods are accepted as truths, then we think that there is a contradiction between God in the world and the world in God. If we peel away these falsehoods one-by-one, then there is no contradiction.

Person vs. Personality Distinctions

Spiritual and Material Personas

The distinction between material and spiritual realities now arises due to two kinds of personas—selfish and selfless. God has egotism in Him, so when He creates personas, they have the *capacity* for egotism. But they have the capacity for selflessness too, just like God. All these capacities are simply potentials in a persona, and they can be prioritized and combined by choice. When selfishness is prioritized over selflessness, then a person makes a show of selflessness to fulfill his selfishness—akin to a capitalist who makes a show of philanthropy and charity with ulterior motives to enhance his power and profit. When selflessness is prioritized over selfishness, then a person makes a show of selfishness to fulfill his selflessness—akin to a mother who pretends to not hear the crying and wailing of a child who has been behaving badly.

Selfishness and selflessness never disappear, but they can be combined and prioritized in different orders. Choice is about combination and prioritization. By creating different priorities—akin to the sequencing of elements in a set—infinite different experiences can be created from the same potentiality. All these experiences are choices of sequences. Hence, there is no fundamental distinction between a spiritual and material persona, because a persona is a set of potentialities that are prioritized differently by a person's choices.

This is important to answer the question: Did God make some souls evil, only to condemn them to suffer in the material world, while He made other souls good to have them enjoy in the spiritual world? The question assumes a dualism between good and evil—if one of them exists then the other must not. The question is asked because we don't understand how good and evil are created from the same personal traits by prioritizing them through choice. A mother who pretends to be selfish and a capitalist who pretends to be selfless are not necessarily different personas. They can be the same persona—i.e., a set of personal traits—being prioritized in different orders by choice.

Therefore, what we mean by a "persona" is a set of traits, and a "personality" is a combination and prioritization of these traits by choice. God creates personas with different sets of personal traits, but not their personality. Each person can shape their personality using a finite set of personal traits by combination and prioritization. Personal traits are not good or evil, but the personality created from these traits by choice is good or evil. Thus, a person enters a spiritual or material realm based on choice, not because God made them good or evil.

The Impersonalist Confusion

Since a personality is constructed by choice operating on personal traits, therefore, both choice and personal traits are eternal. The fundamental contention of an impersonalist or voidist—that these traits are byproducts of a material covering—is false. Both the capacity for choice and the capacity to exhibit personal traits are eternal. However, since choice can be self-negating (you can choose to deny the possibility of choice), therefore, a person can enter states of thoughtless waking or thoughtless sleeping. In the former, one is aware of the ability of choice. In the latter, one is unaware of the ability of choice.

The impersonalist and voidist confusions are subtle—equating a personality to a persona, perceiving choice as a problem, and rejecting choice, personality, and persona to become thoughtless. Personalism doesn't reject the possibility of such rejection. But it also doesn't consider it the ultimate conclusion. Moreover, it describes a spiritual person as one who makes good choices, not merely one who rejects choice. The contrast is not between evil choice and no choice, although the no choice alternative also exists. The real contrast is between evil choice and good choice. That doesn't make a person eternally, fundamentally, or essentially good or evil—as we find in some present religions.

Nobody is fundamentally, eternally, or essentially good or evil. Each person is capable of many personal traits, and they have the power of choice to combine and prioritize traits. All these traits are just like instruments or tools. A knife or a hammer is not fundamentally, eternally, or essentially good or evil. Choice makes a tool good or evil. Hence, any philosophy that relies on killing the patient to cure the disease is fundamentally problematic.

Multiple Incarnations of God

Impersonalists see deities in the temple, and ask: How can God be the source of the infinite universe, and yet, be a part of the universe? They read about His pastimes of childhood and ask: How can God be the Almighty and yet become a child in a mother's lap? They read about the incarnations of God and ask: How can God be one, and yet, appear in different forms? These questions pertain to the confusion between a *person* and a *personality.* God takes on many forms just like an actor plays many characters. The impersonalists cannot digest this simple answer and conclude that all characters are illusions.

While impersonalists suffer from indigestion, monotheists—or mind-body dualists—lack the appetite for God's personhood; they attack many forms of God as polytheism. They imagine the freedom to exhibit many alternative personalities, but they do not want to afford the same freedom to God. In their minds, eternal truth must be a *fixed truth.* An eternal world must be a fixed world. Eternity is therefore never about choice. Eternity is about the elimination of choice, to arrive at one final and fixed truth.

There is no reincarnation in monotheism, which means that one soul cannot take on different bodily forms. Monotheists don't understand how the soul changes bodies in this life from childhood to youth to old age while retaining his individuality. If they knew how the soul takes on many bodily forms in this life, then they would understand how the soul takes on many other forms in other lives. Then it would be much easier to understand how God can also take on many forms—just like the many bodies of the soul. The rejection of incarnations of the soul becomes the rejection of the incarnations of God.

Monotheists don't know that the body is shaped after the mind. If the mind changes form, then it gets a new body, without changing the person. This principle is involved in deciding the next body of the soul at the time of death. If the mind is fixed on one idea, then the body is also fixed. By fixing their mind, the yogis stop aging in present life because going from childhood to youth to old age is the change of soul's body, but if the mind is fixed then the body is also fixed. If anyone understands reincarnation, then they understand how God takes many forms. Those who do not understand reincarnation also do not understand God's many forms, because both are based on the same principle.

Multiple incarnations of God are different from the multiple incarnations of the soul only in the sense that multiple incarnations of the soul are *mutually exclusive* while the multiple incarnations of God are not. This is related to the capacity in God to make multiple choices at once, while a soul is capable of making only one choice at a time. A sequence of choices constructs a personal time. God is simultaneously in many personal times, while the soul is generally in one personal time. Thus, the sequencing of bodies in the case of the soul is not the sequencing of bodies for God. All those bodies are simultaneously possible and present, due to the capacity for multiple choices at once.

We have all heard about multitasking. Some people can do more multitasking than others. As a soul progresses in spiritual life, he is able to multitask more. Some advanced souls have talked about the ability to do up to eight things simultaneously. Musicians playing string instruments learn how to coordinate both hand movements. Drummers learn how to coordinate both hand and leg movements at once. Some drummers who also sing, learn to coordinate hands, legs, and speech at once. God has an infinite capacity for multitasking. He can be multiple personalities doing multiple things at once. God appears in many forms based on His varied ideas about Himself. He thinks "I am a lion" and He becomes Narasimha. He thinks "I am a fish" and He becomes Matsya. He thinks "I am a dwarf" and He becomes Vamana. He thinks "I am a seductive woman", and He becomes Mohini. He thinks "I am a tortoise" and He becomes Kūrma. He thinks "I am a dutiful husband and king" and He becomes Rāma.

God has a vivid imagination and the power of multitasking. Shouldn't these be considered a part of what we mean by God? But people without a vivid imagination and the ability for multitasking want to limit God's imagination and multitasking. Their critique of "polytheism" is equating their weakness to God's. According to monotheists, God must always think "I am God". According to impersonalists, God must stop thinking. When we contrast this against the infinite thoughts that God has about Himself, then we realize how far monotheism and impersonalism are from personalism—because whether God has zero thoughts or one thought, both are infinitely fewer thoughts than all the thoughts that God has about Himself under personalism. Monotheism is also infinitely farther from personalism and infinitely closer to impersonalism because there is little difference between one thought and zero thoughts.

Incorrect Use of Logic in Religion

The Aristotelian dictum "A is A" ensures that God must always think "I am God". God can never think that "I am a dwarf" or "I am a fish" or "I am a tortoise" or "I am a seductive woman", let alone become a dwarf, fish, tortoise, or a seductive woman, because the moment God thinks any thought other than "I am God", He is in violation of logic's most fundamental principle called the *Principle of Identity*. We don't want God to be illogical, do we? To preserve logic, we must limit God's imagination. God cannot but think of Himself to be God. He must always follow the rules of logic while thinking about Himself.

We don't realize this, but logic is contrary to multitasking. "I am running" and "I am talking" are not permitted in logic at once, because by the equivalence of two things that are equal to a third thing, we must conclude that they are equal to each other. Or that running must be synonymous with talking.

Logic makes everything a thing-in-itself. Reality can no longer be a mirror that reflects everything in itself, because a mirror is everything reflected in it, and yet, it is none of those reflected things. How can a thing be itself and not itself simultaneously? Only a mirror covered by dirt is a thing-in-itself because it reflects nothing so it is nothing other than itself. Hence, using logic is covering all mirrors with dirt and it works only for thing-in-itself mirrors.

The impersonalist realizes the problem with a mirror (i.e., that a mirror that reflects everything is simultaneously itself and not itself, breaking the principle of logical identity), and concludes: The mirror must not reflect anything. Thus, we arrive at two kinds of impersonalism—(a) the mirror is covered by dirt and has no reflection, and (b) the mirror is clean but still has no reflection. Cleaning the mirror is just as useless as leaving it dirty because in neither case can the mirror have any reflection. This is due to logic because one thing can only be one thing, and it must be a thing-in-itself, not a thing that is both itself and not itself. This is why the thing-in-itself logic becomes non-semantic and incapable of describing the mind because while knowing the world, the mind is itself and yet not itself—the picture of the world is mine, at the point of knowing the world the mind has become the picture, the picture is precisely the world, and hence the mind is precisely the world, creating an equivalence between two distinct things, which by definition is forbidden by logic. To solve this logical paradox, the impersonalist insists: To just be me, I must shut off the world, because then "I am I" would be true whereas "I am the world" would be false.

Principles of Identity and Identification

This problem is solved in Vedic texts by talking about three aspects of the soul—relation, cognition, and emotion. At the point of observing the world, the consciousness "moves out" like a tortoise stretching its limbs out of its shell, and attaching itself to the world. In some animated movies, we see the eyeballs of a character pop out of the eye sockets when they see something attractive. That is just like the tortoise putting its limbs out. The cognitive aspect of the soul then takes the form of the world to know it. Then, the emotive aspect of the soul becomes attracted to this world if the world is a source of its happiness. Finally, a person starts identifying with the world. This is also how the soul stretches outward, attaches to the body, knows the body, enjoys the body, and then identifies with the body to say that "I am the body". Logic cannot handle this problem because something that is not the self is equated to the self because of stretching, attaching, knowing, enjoying, and identifying.

The attachment to the world and the body is destroyed only when life becomes *painful*. When the world or body is a source of intolerable pain and suffering, then the process of stretching, attaching, knowing, enjoying, and identifying is reversed—the consciousness *withdraws* from the world and the body to realize that it is not the world and not the body. Pain and suffering are methods for this withdrawal, and they are sometimes necessary to break the attachment to the world and the body. No pain no gain. Austerity is hence a prescribed method to realize that I am not the body, although I am currently attached to the body.

However, if the world and body were not painful, then we would never stop identifying with the body. That is the situation with God—He creates a form, and then stretches, attaches, knows, enjoys, and identifies with that form in the same way that we identify with our body. The difference is simply that our body gives pain and suffering, and forces a withdrawal of consciousness but God's forms do not. We conclude that "I am not the body" only when we suffer. If we never suffer, then "I am the body" is taken to be true, although it is not true in the way that logic equates an identity to the essence of a thing.

"I am not the body" only in the sense that this body is not my essential nature. But I can identify with it. That identification establishes an equivalence between two things that are factually not identical to each other. It is true and yet it is not true. It can be temporary due to suffering. It can be eternal due to enjoyment. And despite this temporary or eternal truth, it is not true as a logical identity.

The simple thing we call "I am", which is also called *aham* and *om* in Sanskrit (in different contexts), is a very complicated problem involving six aspects of creating, stretching, attaching, knowing, enjoying, and identifying. Descartes oversimplified this problem by saying "I think therefore I exist", where he equated the self to thought, when the fact is that the thought is created, and over the next five steps—including the enjoyment of the thought—we identify with that thought to *become* thought. If that thought is painful, then we quickly withdraw from that thought and to become not that thought. Hence, "I think therefore I exist" is not always true. It is true only for pleasurable thoughts.

Thus, "I am X" is a choice. It is not a necessity. When Aristotle equated choice to a necessity—as entailed by the logical necessity of "A is A", which must always be upheld by everything—he killed the essence of personalism and replaced it with materialism devoid of choice. When we apply choice to religious topics involving the soul and God, then we are treating them as material objects.

Impersonalism is the application of logic to consciousness to say that *aham brahmāsmi* or "I am soul" and therefore "I am not body". It is true in the sense that the material body is painful so we cannot always identify with it. But then to extend it to say that there is no pleasurable body is idiocy. I can be many things, some of which are painful while others are pleasurable. When I become that which is pleasurable to me, then I have no problem saying "I am that". "I am that" is not a logical necessity which Aristotle called "A is A". It is merely identification with something that I find pleasurable. If I find something so pleasurable that I never want to give it up, then "I am that" is also eternally true.

Personalism is Rooted in Choice

The Depersonalization of God

Monotheism is just one step from impersonalism under which God becomes omniscient to know everything without a choice (a) to know some things and not know other things, (b) to know some things more than other things, (c) to know the same thing in different ways, and (d) to know oneself differently. Omniscience is the destruction of choice because, under its dictates, God must watch—like a sadist—traumatic occurrences, worldly catastrophes, diseases, and death. He has been deprived of choice due to His omniscience.

The fact is that there is no omniscient God because God has a choice. He has the capacity to know everything, but He doesn't *want* to know everything. When He wants to know something, He uses His capacity to know and He knows that which He has chosen to know. Generally, He wants to know all that is pleasing. He is not interested in knowing that all that is displeasing. Hence, He is not omniscient. Similarly, God can do everything, but He doesn't *want* to do everything. He can be kind to everyone, but He doesn't *want* to be kind to everyone. When monotheism calls God omniscient, omnipotent, and omnibenevolent, it deprives God of His choice. He has to know, He has to do, and He has to love. This is the mechanization and depersonalization of God.

The hallmark of personalism is *choice*. That means God has the choice to be what He wants to be. He is not eternally condemned to play God. He can be an irresponsible child, a seductive woman, a bird, or a fish, if He so wants. Impersonalism and monotheism take away choice from God—impersonalism by removing self-thought and monotheism by fixing the self-thought for eternity. God deprived of self-thought or fixated on one thought is infinitely *not* the person who has innumerable different thoughts about Himself. The choice of being whatever He wants to be, rather than being eternally fixated on just one thing, is the difference between personalism and monotheism.

Whatever monotheism calls polytheism is a mark of its depersonalization of God. The Vedic system is not polytheistic. But monotheism has depersonalized God by robbing Him of choice to an extent that His choices to define Himself in the way He wants have become a problem for monotheism. God exists to serve people in monotheism—tell them what to do, answer their prayers, solve their problems, forgive their sins, and accept someone who has accepted Him.

Does a woman automatically marry a man who wants her? Does an employer automatically employ a person who wants to be his employee? Does a country automatically give citizenship to one who wants to become a citizen? And yet, God in monotheism accepts everyone who accepts Him. Effectively, God has *less* choice than a man or woman, employer or employee, country or citizen.

Monotheism is the attempt to bind God using laws, contracts, covenants, and logic while giving every human a choice about whom they want to employ, whom they want to marry, whom they want to make friends with, whom they want to be close to, define themselves in their chosen way, decide if want to accept God or not, and whom they want to give citizenship to their country or kingdom. A God who is bound by laws, contracts, covenants, and logic is not God. Hence, a monotheistic God doesn't exist. It is a sheer mental concoction.

The Host Has the Most Choices

Impersonalist and monotheist theologies are trivial because they focus on God being nothing or just one thing. Personalist theology is immensely complicated because it focuses on why God wants to be infinite different things, although He wants to be some of those more eagerly and urgently than others. The things that God wants to be occasionally are His rare incarnations. Those that He wants more are His frequently seen forms. That which He wants always over everything else is His original form. Every person is defined by their capacity for choice, so God must also have a choice. In fact, God must have infinite choices to be what He wants to be, compared to other persons whose choices can be constrained. This is then the meaning of the Supreme Person—He wants to be more things than anyone else, and His ability to be everything that He wants to be, makes Him infinitely more *types* of persons than everyone else.

This idea of supremacy based on choice is different from the supremacy based on power, control, and authority over others. God is of course supreme because He can control everything. But His desire for supremacy is overridden by His desire to be all other things where He is not supreme. When compared to all the ways in which He wants to be non-supreme, His desire to be supreme is infinitesimal. In effect, if we were to draw a space of all desires that God has, His desire to be supreme would be just one point. The rest of the space would constitute infinite other desires where God wants to be non-supreme.

Hence, when we talk about the *Supreme Lord*, we are not talking about His supremacy based on power, control, and authority over others. We are talking about His infinite other desires that far exceed anyone else's desires to be other things, and which involve Him being non-supreme. We are small compared to God, not because of power, but because our choices or ideas about ourselves are small compared to God's uncountable ideas about Himself. Most people in this world, for instance, just want one thing—to be supreme. They don't have the power to be supreme, but they get that power when they ascend to the spiritual world. And yet, that idea of supremacy is just one of the infinite ideas about the self. God has been supreme for so long that He has no charm for supremacy. Supremacy is a boring idea for Him and His desires for non-supremacy are infinitely greater. So many people worship God as supreme and ask Him for something. Thereby, His desires for non-supremacy remain unfulfilled.

The Personalist Idea of Supremacy

That ocean of desires in which the desire for supremacy is just one drop, while the rest of the ocean constitutes the infinite other desires to be non-supreme, is Kṛṣṇa. His lust for supremacy is a drop in the ocean. The rest of the ocean is wanting to be non-supreme. Everyone goes to Kṛṣṇa considering Him to be the giver of benedictions, and they treat Him as supreme. He is not satisfied by that because He wants to be non-supreme. Every other form of God that displays supremacy, is a part of that one drop of desire for supremacy in Kṛṣṇa.

The monotheistic idea of God is that He is the most powerful and He is inclined to use that power. The impersonalist idea of God is that He has no idea of who He is. But the personalist idea of God is that He has infinite desires other than the desire to remain ignorant about who He is and to know Himself as supreme. Whatever people call God or infinite Brahman are just two drops in an ocean of desires in Kṛṣṇa. If we equate personalism to monotheism, then we are equating an ocean to a drop. If someone says that they can merge into the ocean called Brahman, and that would be identity with God, then they are equating the state in which Kṛṣṇa has no clue what He is, to the infinite other states where He has a different idea of Himself. Not knowing oneself or knowing oneself to be supreme are just two drops in an ocean of desires.

An impersonalist or monotheist theology is so small compared to the theology of Kṛṣṇa that we can dismiss it as almost totally irrelevant. Kṛṣṇa theology is so vast that we can never fully fathom Kṛṣṇa even in infinite lifetimes. That is because He has so many desires. To know a person is to know what they desire. Those who know a person from a distance know a fraction of their desires. Knowing God as a powerful ruler is knowing Him from a great distance. It is true that God is the supreme ruler, but only as a drop in the ocean of desires. Brahman is also knowing God from a great distance where we think that God wants nothing. It is true in the sense that God has everything so He wants nothing. But that is also true only as one of the drops in the ocean of desires. However, as we go closer and closer to God, we realize that although He controls everything, and He wants nothing, there is still so much that He wants.

Three Measures of Greatness

Impersonalists ask how the infinite world could spring from a finite person because they don't know that infinite universes are created simply from the desire for supremacy, which is just one drop in the ocean of desires of Kṛṣṇa. The universe is an ocean, but the desire it fulfills in Kṛṣṇa is just a drop in the ocean of desires in Him. Brahman is created from the desire to not have any desire. Brahman is also an ocean, but the desire it fulfills in Kṛṣṇa is just a drop in the ocean. Vaikuṇṭha is created from the desire to be free, independent, and autonomous. Vaikuṇṭha is also an ocean, with free, independent, and autonomous individuals who treat God as their equal. But the desire that Vaikuṇṭha fulfills in Kṛṣṇa is a drop in the ocean. Collectively, the desires to be the master, to be self-satisfied, and to be equal to others, are drops in the ocean of desire in Kṛṣṇa. If we keep aside these trivial drops, then the rest of the ocean is about the desire to be non-master, non-self-satisfied, and non-equal.

Kṛṣṇa's greatest desire is to be possessed, owned, and controlled by His devotees. Those devotees who don't see Kṛṣṇa as a superior master, a self-satisfied individual, or autonomously independent, but consider Him to be helpless, hungry for their love, and totally dependent on their care, are the dearest to Kṛṣṇa. The idea that God is powerful, autonomous, or self-fulfilled is therefore very insignificant in the ultimate analysis. The idea that God is vulnerable, needy, dependent, and helpless is the most significant idea.

There are many ways to measure greatness. There is a measure of greatness based on the power one holds over others. There is a measure of greatness based on one's knowledge and skills. And there is a measure of greatness based on bliss. Impersonalism and monotheism measure greatness by power—the impersonalist wants to be beyond anyone's control while the monotheist imagines that God controls everything. This is the most primitive method of measuring greatness. A better measure of greatness is variegated knowledge and skill. The more types of things you know, and the more types of things you can do, make you greater than others. The knowledge and skill to control others or become free from their control is a primitive form of knowledge. Much better knowledge and skill are art, poetry, music, literature, dance, and science. The best measure of greatness is happiness. The happiness derived from controlling others or becoming free of their control is primitive. A much better type of happiness is involved in producing art, poetry, music, literature, dance, and science. The best happiness is found in intimate relationships devoid of the considerations of mastery, self-satisfaction, and autonomous equality.

Since the impersonalist measure of greatness is based on the lowest idea of greatness, and he has no idea about superior measures of greatness, he thinks that becoming free of all entanglements is the greatest achievement. It is factually greater than the state when a person is bound by the material energy. Under the inferior idea of greatness, he thinks that becoming free from entanglement is itself becoming God and he imagines that any form of God tied by relationships must be an entanglement. All these are false concoctions.

Impersonalists mount the argument about how the infinite came out of the finite because they are thinking of the body as matter and the material universe as a lot more matter than found in the body. If they could just think of the body as knowledge and skill, then there would be a much smaller problem because immense knowledge and skill can reside in a person even with a small body. Finally, if they knew that real power was willpower, and everything else works under the control of that willpower, then there would be no problem in understanding how willpower in a person controls the universe.

All these types of issues are rooted in materialism where to move a big body one needs a lot of force, so if the universe is moving, then the agency that moves it must be a bigger body and a bigger force. There is no understanding that the world is thoughts being moved by willpower. You can create infinite thoughts by willpower. You can control all these thoughts by willpower. If one has developed willpower in their life, then they will know how it is used to control the mind and channel it appropriately. Finally, if one has willpower, then he will know how it is used to acquire happiness. The thoughts can be infinitely variegated, but willpower is one. Even as willpower is one, happiness is infinitely variegated. So, one willpower can produce infinite thoughts and happiness. Many kinds of worlds that deliver different kinds of happiness can simply be created by a mind with strong willpower. The world is created by willpower. But willpower is used because it delivers happiness. The choice made by willpower that delivers the greatest happiness is the greatest measure of a person. The best person is not one who controls a universe, who is most talented and knowledgeable, or who is self-satisfied, but one who is the happiest. Calling self-satisfaction happiness is the lack of imagination about happiness.

The Meaning of Kṛṣṇa's Greatness

If one dreams of escaping material suffering, he thinks of God as one who controls the world. If one dreams of being free of entanglement, he thinks of God as one who has no responsibility. If one dreams of leading a self-satisfied life, he thinks of God as one who is capable of knowing and creating anything. If one dreams of a happy life, he thinks of God as one who loves selflessly. The journey from the worst to the best situation in life is the journey from thinking of God as power to thinking of God as love. We cannot arbitrarily mix these ideas. We cannot claim that because God is most loving and powerful, hence, He must use His power and love for me to help me ensure my enjoyment and forgive all my misdeeds. When the idea of power applies, then the idea of love does not. Hence, if we want to see God as power, then we must obey His laws. But if we want to see God as love, then we must be fully devoted to Him.

Monotheists mix and conflate all these ideas to create many problems because they cannot recognize that God has many natures, that these natures are mutually exclusive, and the tenets of one nature cannot be applied to another nature. This is just like a person may be both a boss and a father, but he is not a father to his subordinates just as he is not a boss to his children. Similarly, the fact that God is both a boss and a father doesn't mean we can mix both just as we please. If we want God to be a boss, then we have to be subordinate. If we want Him to be a father, then we have to be a child. Those who mix these into hodge-podge theology, probably don't know the first thing about relationships.

The idea of God as one who has power over others is the lowest idea of God. The idea of God as one who is free of all responsibilities and entanglements is a better idea of God. The idea of God as one who can know and create everything and fulfills himself through his work is an even better idea of God. The idea of God who is loved by everyone and is constantly enjoying that relationship is the best idea of God. While greatness is measured in different ways in these four progressive conceptions of Godliness, the final measure of greatness is also the greatest. Under it, we don't say that God is great because He has so much power, authority, knowledge, skill, or autonomy. Rather, we say that God is the greatest because He is the happiest. He is happiest because He has given up all the previous ideas of greatness rooted in power, authority, knowledge, skill, and autonomy, and become non-supreme. Before arriving at this greatest measure of greatness, we have to reject every other inferior measure of greatness that is considered great by materialists, impersonalists, voidists, or monotheists.

To understand God's greatness, we have to conceptualize four tiers of greatness, successively reject them to progress to a better idea of greatness, to then arrive at the best measure of greatness, which would most likely seem not great to those who haven't yet ascended this ladder. Those whose idea of greatness is control over others will naturally think that a person who is controlled is not great. Those who are obsessed with self-satisfaction will always think that those who have succumbed to amor must not be great. Those absorbed in acquiring knowledge and skill will think that those who are not pursuing knowledge and skill must not be great. And yet they will be wrong. The problem is their yardstick of greatness. They are using an inferior yardstick. But since it is better than a previous yardstick, hence, we can say that they are better than others. God's greatness is known not by measuring against our chosen yardstick, but by progressing through a ladder of yardsticks in which the yardstick of greatness itself changes into something that seems not great to others.

People measuring God according to an inferior yardstick may say that Kṛṣṇa seems ordinary because (a) He is so small that He could not have created a gigantic universe, (b) He is so humble in front of His devotees that He could not be the all-powerful ruler of the universe, (c) that He is always hankering after love so He must not be the most self-satisfied, and (d) that He is conquered by His friends and girlfriends that He must not be knowledgeable and skilled.

Everybody measures according to their yardstick. They think that their yardstick is the best, but we can learn about the ladder of yardsticks. Kṛṣṇa can excel in all these yardsticks. But He finds excelling in the lower yardsticks boring. This is Kṛṣṇa's greatness. He is not trying to be great according to so many other yardsticks because He finds those yardsticks boring. After rejecting all boring yardsticks, He has chosen to define Himself against the most interesting yardstick.

Those unaware of the ladder of yardsticks think that Kṛṣṇa is not great, and that He cannot be God according to their yardstick. This is their foolishness because they don't know that there are many superior yardsticks. Kṛṣṇa has rejected their yardstick, so it is not hard for Him to reject the measurement result based on that yardstick. The devotees of Kṛṣṇa also use Kṛṣṇa's yardstick to measure themselves. They are not interested in becoming a king of the universe, free of the control of the imaginary self-deluding kings, self-satisfied, or knowledgeable, skilled, and independent. They are just happy talking about Him. They also want to hear others talking about Him. But if nobody is talking about Him, then they just talk about Him, listen to that sound, and forget about everything else because nothing else is comparable.

Is God Omniscient?

Two Notions of Omniscience

There are two versions of omniscience, one in Abrahamic religions and the other in Vedic philosophy. The Abrahamic version of omniscience is that God knows everything, and the Vedic version of omniscience is that knowing is a *power* of God, which God can use as per His will. If that power is used, then God knows, otherwise, He does not. In Vedic philosophy, God doesn't *want* to know everything. And yet, He has the *power* to know everything. That power operates under the control of God's will.

Divine Masculine-Feminine Distinction

The power to know everything is called *Chit-Śakti*. God has many kinds of Śakti, which are sometimes divided into three, and sometimes into five. If we talk about all the divisions, it will take a very long time, therefore, I will restrict the discussion to just the power of knowing, also known as *Chit-Śakti*.

The existence of Śakti in Vedic philosophy, distinct (but not separate) from God, is articulated as the distinction between masculine and feminine forms of the Supreme Truth. That masculine-feminine distinction does not exist in Abrahamic religions. Hence, omniscience is a power of knowing in Vedic philosophy, which operates under the control of will, but that omniscience becomes a necessity in Abrahamic religions because the masculine-feminine distinction between God and Śakti is absent.

Numerous Expansions of the Feminine

Even the Śakti is further divided and expanded into many subordinate Śakti, which are all considered the parts of the complete

Śakti. Each complete or partial form of Śakti is also a person. The Śakti sometimes becomes immanent in a person, so they are also said to be an incarnation of Śakti.

Long story short, knowing is a power of God, that power is a person, and if God wants to know, He asks His Śakti, who may then ask subordinate Śakti, and through this consultative process, God knows. This is just like a CEO can know everything going on in his organization, but he may not know everything. If he wants to know, he can ask the next-level leader, who may then consult the next-level leader, and the question-and-answer process moves down and up the hierarchy, and thus the CEO can know everything if he wants to know.

The Śakti is also an expansion of God, and that which is expanded doesn't cease to be a part of God, but it remains *inactive*. Thus, we don't say that God doesn't *have* the power. We rather say that His Śakti is expanded from God, serves God, and yet She remains inactive within God. The inactive form of Śakti is therefore a part of God, and the active form of Śakti is expanded from God. There are lots of details within this, which will make us digress from the main topic, so I will not get into them.

Problems Arising From Omniscience

All these distinctions are important for several reasons:

First, if God necessarily knows everything, then He must be watching every individual suffer, which will then make him a sadist. This problem appears in Abrahamic religions as the counter to His omnibenevolence: God is watching people suffer, so He cannot be loving in nature. In Vedic philosophy, God is not watching everyone suffer. He is not omniscient as a necessity. If He wants to know, He can know. But He doesn't want to know the soul who has no desire to know God. But if the soul is deeply interested in God, then God is also deeply interested in the soul. He is watching us in that case.

Second, God's omniscience leads to the problem in Abrahamic religions that God must know that the soul would commit evil deeds, and He has the power to stop him from those deeds. But if God doesn't stop the soul from committing those deeds, then either God doesn't know, or He is incapable of stopping it. The answer in Vedic philosophy is that there is no element of surprise if we know everything that is going to happen in the future. Without that surprise, there is no novelty, and without that novelty, there is no enjoyment. God wants to enjoy. For that, He doesn't want to know the future.

Third, the actions in the material world are recorded in an unconscious memory, which is continuously erased as new actions are created. Thus, there is no record of what happened in the distant past. As a soul is liberated from the material condition, there is no recollection of what the soul has done in the material world. Not even God remembers all that has been done in the past. This is essential to reestablish the loving relationship between God and the soul. If we remember all the bad things someone has done in the past, then we cannot have a relationship with them. Forgetfulness of a bad past is essential for that.

Knowing Only When It is Better

There are possibly other reasons and nuances for which omniscience is a problem, and the absence of omniscience is not a problem. There are similarly many reasons why the absence of omniscience is a problem, and presence is not a problem. When we take into account all these nuanced positions of presence and absence, we will find that Vedic philosophy answers all these questions in a way that omniscience is rejected when it is better to not know, and it is accepted when it is better to know.

Therefore, we don't attribute omniscience to God as a necessity. Our question is: It is better to know? Or is it better to not know? This is the ultimate meaning of omniscience being a power operating under the control of a will. The will chooses when it is better to know and does not choose when it is worse to know. This is the *rationality of the will*. It operates under the principle of better and worse, not a necessity of knowing or not knowing. The situation will always be worse if we make omniscience a necessity as we can see from the above examples. Hence, will and power are separately active, and they are one when they are inactive. This oneness and distinction is not a contradiction due to active-inactive.

Diverse Descriptions of Śakti

There are numerous descriptions of Śakti found in various Vedic texts. Each reference describes a different aspect of Śakti. All of these references are true. By understanding all these statements, we develop progressively better understanding of the Śakti.

na tasya kāryaṁ karaṇaṁ ca vidyate
na tat-samaś cābhyadhikaś ca dṛśyate
parāsya śaktir vividhaiva śrūyate
svābhāvikī jñāna-bala-kriyā ca

"In that, neither effect nor instruments are known. Nor is anything seen to be greater than that whole. The powers of the Supreme are said to be varied. Also, they are His personal or natural (powers of) knowing, willing, and acting". [Śvetāśvatara Upaniṣad 6.8]

sṛjāmi tan-niyukto 'haṁ
haro harati tad-vaśaḥ
viśvaṁ puruṣa-rūpeṇa
paripāti tri-śakti-dhṛk

Brahma says: "I create in that arrangement. Har (Shiva) destroys under His control. The universe is maintained by the owner of three energies, in the form of Puruṣa." [Bhāgavata Purāṇa 2.6.32]

viṣṇu-śaktiḥ parā proktā
kṣetrajñākhyā tathā parā
avidyā-karma-saṁjñānyā
tṛtīyā śaktir iṣyate

"The powers of Viṣṇu are said to be transcendental. In the same way, He is famous as being transcendent to those known as knowers of the field. He is the master of the third power, which is known as the combination of ignorance and fruitive activity." [Viṣṇu Purāṇa 6.7.61]

Three-Fold and Five-Fold Śakti

The Śakti is also divided sometimes into three and sometimes into five. The three-fold division corresponds to sat-chit-ānanda while the five-fold division corresponds to the powers of intention, emotion, cognition, conation, and relation. Both are distinct from the will.

The world is maintained by some Śakti constantly observing the world. For instance, if we concentrate our minds on something exclusively, it will stop changing. It will start changing only when the mind is withdrawn. So, something is fixed in one state when the awareness is fixed. Something is changing when the awareness is moving. So, the awareness of the world is the cause of its existence, maintenance, or sustenance. When that awareness is withdrawn from the world, the world ceases to exist. This awareness is the power of relation. The capacity to move the awareness from one thing to another is the power of conation. When the awareness moves to or from something, there is a power of cognition to know its nature.

Finally, the awareness moves from one thing to another due to the power of emotion and intention. The power of emotion is the capacity to enjoy. If this power weakens, then the awareness is withdrawn. The intention pertains to the motive to enjoy different kinds of emotions. When that intention is fulfilled by the movement of awareness, there is pleasure as a result of the cognition, conation, relation, and the fulfilment of the intention.

The Nature of the Puruṣa

The three- and five-fold Śakti moves under the control of will, which is called Puruṣa or God. Sometimes, even the soul is called Puruṣa because it also has three- and five-fold Śakti. Because of its presence, even the soul has intention, emotion, cognition, conation, and relation. If these powers are withdrawn, then the soul loses motivation, becomes unhappy, falls into ignorance, its power of action is destroyed, and its relation to the world is broken.

The acquisition of Śakti is thus sometimes called the pursuit of material wellness. But since the acquisition of Śakti creates the desire to acquire more and more Śakti, therefore, it is called bondage to the world, and the relinquishment of Śakti is called release from material entanglement. The Śakti is worshipped both for acquisition and relinquishment.

The fact that the soul is also called Puruṣa doesn't make it God. Factually, the soul can never acquire all possible Śakti. That acquisition is limited to God. Ultimately, the pursuit of Śakti therefore becomes a frustrating experience, and the soul seeks salvation from Śakti. That salvation is never sought by God because every possible Śakti is at His disposal.

The Polytheistic Origins of Monotheism

Introduction and Overview

There are widespread misconceptions about monotheism at present—(a) that it is about a transcendent God, (b) that it has had no connections to polytheism, and (c) that it has always been monotheistic. These are far from the truth. The truth is that monotheism emerged out of polytheism, that its "God" was originally a low-level demigod but later transformed into an all-powerful God by abrogating other gods, and the reason for this transformation was political and worldly rather than transcendent.

In this article, I will discuss the origins of monotheism in polytheism, and the syncretic construction of monotheism by applying numerous traits of polytheistic gods to a monotheistic God. We will then try to understand the problems arising out of this syncretism, namely, that there is no God who possesses the traits of a syncretic God.

The Less Known Story of Yahweh

In her recent book "God—An Anatomy", Francesca Stravrakopoulou writes many revealing passages about how Yahweh came to be the God of monotheism. I will cite some of them here. Those interested in this subject may want to read the whole book. It may prove an eye-opener. If we go through these passages, what monotheism is, and how it emerged historically, will become quite apparent.

1. "As one of the many deities in the Late Bronze and Early Iron Age Levant, Yahweh was originally a god rooted within a polytheistic world—and remained comfortably so for much of his early career. This was a world in which the gods were imagined as a sprawling heavenly household, broadly reflecting the family bonds and social structures of their human worshippers. In most Levantine societies, this pantheon was headed by an aged progenitor of the cosmos, the god El or (in some dialects) Il—a name functioning both as a proper noun and the generic Semitic term for 'deity'. Beneath him were ranked a younger generation of gods each charged with a particular portfolio in the management of the universe–from storms, seas, sunlight, and starlight, to fertility, birth, warfare, and death. As frontline deities, they were the most prominent gods of ancient Levantine societies, and those most closely tied to the territorial identities of their worshippers."

2. "Thanks particularly to a wealth of literature dated to the fourteenth and thirteenth century BCE, recovered from the ancient city-state called Ugarit, on the Syrian coast, El's multitiered household has come into sharper focus. He was understood to be the gentle father of the gods, enjoying a comfortable semi-retirement from the day-to-day running of the cosmos, accompanied by his consort, the mother goddess Athirat. Between them, they had 'seventy sons'—a collective term for the frontline deities. These included Ugarit's special patron, the powerful storm-god Baal, and his sister, a fearsome warrior, as well as a boisterous sea-god Yam, and the underworld king of death, Mot, each of whom dwelt in his own domain located at the very edge of the divine realm. Ranked between them were the relatively minor deities of practical skill and cultural arts, including architecture and design, healing, music, and magic, while below them was a collection of divine attendants and messengers, who variously served the gods and commuted between the heavens and the earthly realms. Despite their differences in rank, the gods met together as

a divine council or assembly chaired by El in his role as the highest god to decide on matters both divine and mortal."

3. "Ugarit's pantheon was typical of Levantine religions in the second and early first millennium BCE when early forms of Yahweh worship emerged. The pantheon's shape and composition was determined by the very human idea that to be a god isolated from any other was to be bereft of the benefits of collaboration, status, and kinship. In short, it was to be socially impotent—and frankly useless, therefore, to mortals. Against this cultural backdrop, certain theological claims asserting that Yahweh had only ever been a solitary deity look more than a little implausible."

4. "Yahweh appears as one among El's many divine children. Ancient pieces of poetry in the Hebrew Bible tell something about Yahweh's early career. Far from portraying Yahweh as the supreme king and creator of the cosmos, they present him instead as a minor but ferocious storm deity, at the margins of the inhabited world in an ancient place variously known as Seir, Paran, and Teman—cast in the Bible as a dangerous, mountainous wilderness, seemingly located south of the Negev desert, beyond the Dead Sea, in what used to be called Edom and is now southern Jordan."

5. "Scholars have long suspected that El, not Yahweh, was the original god of the people known in the Bible as 'Israel'. Yahweh would gradually come to usurp his father El by supplanting him as the head of the pantheon. But quite how this happened remains frustratingly unclear. As a storm god, Yahweh was naturally a god of warfare, equipped with weapons of thunder, lightning, and rain clouds, and it was Yahweh's personal patronage that the kings of Israel and Judah claimed."

6. "Yahweh was acclaimed as the 'national' or state deity, and the divine patron of each kingdom's royal household. A

number of other deities, who likely played their part in the polytheistic governance of the cosmos, were worshipped alongside him, with the most prominent among them being Yahweh's wife Asherah. The biblical writers cannot help but reveal that she was worshipped alongside Yahweh in his temples in Jerusalem and Samaria, while inscriptions dating to the eighth century BCE attest to seeking blessings from 'Yahweh and his Asherah'."

7. "Historically, the goddess's fall broadly reflects the decline of traditional, state-sponsored polytheism—a decline triggered by the Assyrian annihilation of the kingdom of Israel in about 722 BCE, and the Babylonian destruction of Judah in 587 BCE. As patron deity and divine warrior of his peoples, Yahweh had seemingly failed to protect them. It would prompt a profound theological and cultural shift among certain priestly and scribal groups, some of them in exile, whose work would shape the central traditions reflected in the Hebrew Bible, and eventually craft a new image of their god—the deity who would become the God of the Bible. Despite the destruction of his kingdoms, Yahweh himself had not been defeated, they insisted. Rather, he had engineered the collapse of the states of Israel and Judah in punishment for his worshipper's religious deviancy: the worship of other gods. Yahweh would come to be presented as a god intolerant of other deities, and Yahweh worship would become increasingly monolatrous."

Understanding the Story of Yahweh

Years ago, I wrote a book entitled "Cosmic Theogony" tracing the diversity of world religions emerging from a very large pantheon of demigods in the Vedic tradition. These diverse religions cannot be reconciled without understanding the Vedic tradition. However, if one knows that tradition, then it is far easier to reconcile them. I will try to explain the story of Yahweh as seen through the lens of Vedic descriptions. We can see what others cannot see if we use that lens.

- The first stage
  - Originally, there is a very big multi-tiered polytheistic family of gods
  - There is a parent god called El, with seventy sons, whom we call Brahma
  - There is a child god of rain and thunder, called Yahweh, whom we call Indra
  - Both of them have their feminine consorts—Athirat and Asherah
  - They are respectively called Saraswati and Shachi in the Vedic texts
- The second stage
  - At some point in history, El is substituted or replaced by Yahweh
  - The historical reasons for this substitution are obscure to scholars
  - Even after the substitution, a polytheistic system under Yahweh continues
  - Yahweh and Asherah are now primary deities, along with many other gods
  - Rulers of Israel primarily worship a smaller pantheon of gods under Yahweh
- The third stage
  - There are major defeats in wars, and Yahweh's patronage is questioned
  - These defeats are blamed on Israel worshiping gods other than Yahweh
  - To prevent future defeats in wars, Asherah and other gods are dropped
  - After dropping all other gods, Yahweh remains the only god
- The fourth stage
  - At this time, the theological concept of "one god" or monotheism appears
  - Monotheism now pertains to Yahweh, an originally lower god, Indra
  - Priests and scribes rework the Hebrew Bible to remove

all other gods

- Still, there are uncleansed remnants of the past referring to other gods

Most people today think that monotheistic religions were monotheistic from the start. They also think that monotheistic religions were opposed to polytheistic religions. All these notions are false. The truth is that the original state of monotheism was polytheism, which included a large pantheon of gods. Over time, this pantheon gradually shrunk, and eventually, it was stripped of all but one deity. Different sects within these traditions continued with a fewer or greater number of deities, making the same tradition totally polytheistic, a mixture of polytheism and monotheism, and totally monotheistic. The militant opposition to polytheism came much later in the historical evolution.

The polytheistic system of worship that involved dozens of gods (which we call devatas in the Vedic system) closely resembles the Vedic pantheon of demigods. It was headed by a creator god El (whom we call Brahma in the Vedic tradition). These gods had their feminine consorts. But as time passed, most of these gods—including the top creator god, and their feminine consorts—were dropped, and a lower god called Yahweh (whom we call Indra in the Vedic tradition) was appointed as the supreme being. This is then the origin of monotheism—stripping away deities from a bigger hierarchical pantheon of demigods, appointing a lower demigod as the top deity, and rejecting all feminine consorts of these deities.

The Story of Adam and Eve

The story gets more interesting as we go along this journey. For example, God gives a place for Adam and Eve to live, but asks them never to eat the fruit of the tree of knowledge or wisdom. We can interpret this story in more than one way, and I will try to note two such interpretations here.

- We could call it karma-yoga—God gives Adam and Eve a place to live, there is a tree of knowledge (which we call the

Vedas) and which has a karma-kānda portion (signified by the four Vedas) by which one can obtain many material benefits; however, God forbids Adam and Eve to eat these "fruits" of the tree, and accept the *other* parts of the tree. Eschewing karma-kānda, while doing one's duties with renunciation, is called karma-yoga in the Vedic tradition, and the Adam and Eve story can be seen as accepting karma-yoga and rejecting karma-kānda.

- We could also say that God gave Adam and Eve a place to live, with a tree of wisdom, while forbidding them from eating the *real* fruits of wisdom, namely, devotion to a transcendent personality. The Śrīmad Bhagavatam, for instance, is called nigama-kalpa-taror galitaṁ phalaṁ or the "ripened fruit of the desire tree of knowledge". Hence, there is a tree of knowledge, called the nigama-kalpa-taru, in which there are numerous subdivisions of knowledge found on the different branches of the tree, and the fruit of this tree is perfect devotion to the Supreme Being, but whichever God gave Adam and Eve a place to live, forbade them from eating the ripened fruit, which means to remain entangled in the world of material enjoyment.

If God is Yahweh or Indra, then there is ample information in the Vedic texts to understand why he would not want his followers to attain transcendence—Indra is known to seduce attractive wives of other men, disturb the austerities of sages, pollute the yajñá of kings, and always remain in conflict with demons. From the Śrīmad Bhagavatam, we know how he is infuriated when Kṛṣṇa stops his worship and causes a flood. He fits the bill of a "jealous god" perfectly—he is always demanding exclusivity, trying to destroy any potential threats, and punishing those who disobey or disregard his commands.

But if God is not Yahweh or Indra, then there is literally no scenario in which people who don't practice karma-yoga but take to karma-kānda, would be condemned from a heavenly place as sinful persons. The fact is that living entities ascend to heaven due to the performance of sacrifices or yajñá. Doing these things is the norm rather than the exception. To condemn someone for doing the normal thing would be an exception. Hence, if God gave Adam and Eve a place to live, and asked them to not eat the fruit of the tree of knowledge, the best inference is that God is Indra.

Syncretic Enhancement of Monotheism

In a polytheistic pantheon of demigods, each demigod performs a unique function and role. Thereby, no demigod is "complete" because they have their respective departments—wind, water, fire, earth, sky, planet, stars, punishment, arts, architecture, healing, music, etc. If we reduce a polytheistic system to one God, by elevating one of the demigods to the status of God, then the monotheistic deity elevated thus would also be incomplete. Then we cannot call the monotheistic God the most powerful God because he lacks the capacities of other demigods. Thus, after abrogating numerous demigods, monotheism had to attribute their powers and stories of all the polytheistic gods to the monotheistic god.

For example, in the Bible, God creates the world, which means that Yahweh created the world when it was originally created by El. The creation of the world originally attributed to El must now be attributed to Yahweh. This is the equivalent of attributing the work of Brahma to Indra, after removing Brahma.

The removal of Brahma's worship is not "frustratingly unclear" in the Vedic tradition. We can find hundreds of temples of various demigods in India, but never a temple of Brahma. This is because Brahma was cursed by Lord Shiva to never be worshipped after Brahma lusted for his daughter—Shatarupa. Brahma is excluded even in Vedic yajñá, although he is recognized as the father of all the demigods and the topmost demigod in the pantheon. Thereby, there is a double standard regarding Brahma even in the Vedic tradition—(a) he is excluded from the standpoint of worship, and (b) he is recognized as the creator of the universe. It is likely that El or Il was never worshipped, although he was recognized as the creator of the universe. The usurping of El by Yahweh is therefore a natural consequence of the fact that Brahma is not worshipped and Indra is identified as the leader of the lower-level demigods after that.

Likewise, when God causes a catastrophic flood, the work of the water and wind would be attributed to Yahweh. In the Vedic system, Indra is the god of rain and thunder. But floods require cooperation from other demigods like Varuṇa and Vāyu (the demigods of water and wind). Ideally, all three demigods—Indra, Varuṇa, and Vāyu—must be noted while attributing the occurrence of a flood, although under one supervising deity. This is understood in the Vedic system as the subordinate role played by Varuṇa and Vāyu under Indra. But if other demigods are removed, then everything would be attributed to Indra.

I wonder which God would ask people to cut off their foreskins as a mark of a covenant with him and why such a covenant ritual would exclude women from participating in the covenant. The fact is that this ritual predates monotheism for thousands of years and was widely practiced in Africa. Egypt is cited by historians as the most prominent case of ritualistic circumcision. But the chief god of Egypt wasn't Indra or Brahma. It was the sun god, called Ra. Again, by continuing the practice of circumcision and attributing it to the monotheistic god—Yahweh or Indra—the practices related to the sun god were misattributed.

The practices of animal sacrifices, followed by the consumption of meat as a ritual, used to be highly varied. Each demigod was offered a different kind of animal, sometimes a different gender animal, only at specific times for specific reasons. The offerings for male and female deities were also different. But when the diversity of demigods is removed, then the stipulations of time, place, animal, and gender were abrogated and animal killing and consumption were normalized even outside of rituals. There are numerous such examples of acts found in monotheistic texts which should be attributed to other demigods, but they are just attributed to God. The syncretic construction of a monotheistic God does more harm than good—it makes God a very confusing personality, often engaged in acts that we would not attribute to a truly divine and transcendent personality, but only to the powerful demigods.

Concepts of the Kingdom of God

The fact that monotheism emerged purely out of earthly preoccupations—namely, a religious reform movement initiated after the defeat of Jews at the hands of Assyrians and Babylonians—is clearly evidenced in the numerous references to the "Kingdom of God" abundantly found in monotheistic texts. There is a famous Christian prayer: "O God, our Father in heaven, thy kingdom come". Clearly, this cannot refer to a heavenly kingdom where God's rule already prevails so it cannot "come" because it never went away. This has to be speaking about the desire to revive an earthly kingdom. Such prayers indicate that there was once an earthly kingdom, which was then lost, the loss was interpreted as a punishment from Yahweh, which then led to a monotheistic reform, and having done that reform, the reformers pray for the revival of their lost kingdom.

The Old Testament speaks to this too. King David had been promised by God that his descendants will forever rule over Israel. That was true for about 400 years, after which the descendants of David were overthrown by invasions. The reforms of monotheism that followed thus began speaking of the new "King of the Jews", who was expected to arrive, free the Jews from foreign rule, return the Jews living in exile to their homeland, and reestablish a Jewish kingdom on earth. The references to king and kingdom are about an earthly king and an earthly kingdom, assumed to return after a monotheistic reform.

Addition of Salvation Doctrines

Traditional polytheistic religions were not about salvation from the world or going to a transcendent realm after death. They were about worshipping demigods to get a good life on earth. We have to remember that in polytheism, going to the heavenly kingdom of gods requires a person to *become god*, or something equivalent to him. But how can man become a god? In the Vedic system, we talk about how men can become demigods due to their pious deeds, that they will die and will be reborn, that the soul will be transferred from earth to heaven through a process of soul transmigration, and after some time, the demigods will lose their position, only to be replaced by a new generation of demigods.

But all this is too complicated. The simple version is—gods will be gods and men will be men, men need the favor of the gods, but they cannot become gods. This version of god works only so long as people can see the favor of their gods upon them. If that favor has been replaced by misery, then people will naturally start questioning if God even exists. This is not a new phenomenon, by the way. Many modern atheists became atheists after seeing the misery in their life—their argument is that if God is so kind, then why would He make everyone suffer, for no apparent fault of theirs? The answer to that question involves past lives, deeds in past lives, and reincarnation. But if these ideas do not exist in a religion, then how do you assure and placate people to keep their faith in religion while enduring bad times?

The answer is that you can solve the problem of diminishing faith by adding a doctrine of salvation where you could say that God tests people, that He gives heaven to people who pass that test, etc. Now, monotheism drives in two directions—(a) even if people are not seeing God's favor right now—since they haven't regained the kingdom—religion is still important for going to heaven, and (b) due to persistent faith in God, the Kingdom of God will arrive soon to give people a good life. The former is a monotheistic doctrine of salvation and the latter is a monotheistic doctrine of a good life on earth. Good life on earth is the original motivation and salvation is added as compensation to keep the faith.

We see this addition through the transformation of the concept of *redemption* in Judaism. Right after the Assyrian attacks around 700 BCE, redemption meant the return of Jewish people from various exiles to their homeland as a result of accepting a monotheistic god. Almost 500 years passed before this idea of redemption was enhanced to speak about a *final redemption* when a Jewish Messiah would come, the world would end, the dead would be revived, and people would then enter an afterlife in heaven. Jewish belief in an afterlife in heaven did not exist before 200 BCE. It was added because 500 years had passed, the "King of the Jews" had not arrived, and religious faith in the people was declining.

The late addition of the doctrine of salvation to the religion indicates that salvation was not the motive for religion previously. It wasn't even a motive after monotheism was created. The goal of monotheism was only to get back the lost kingdom. When that did not happen, and people began losing faith in religion and the possibility of ever returning to their motherland, then salvation was added. Until that time, gods lived in heaven, and men lived on earth, and men needed the favor of gods for a good life on earth. The concept of going to heaven and becoming God or something like Him came later.

The Causes of the Crucifixion of Jesus

The earthly preoccupation of early monotheism played a central role in the crucifixion of Jesus because when Jesus began teaching the Jews, he was quickly hailed as the "King of the Jews" who would bring back the Jewish kingdom. This is because the preponderant idea in the mind of the Jews wasn't a messiah savior who would come to tell them about what is wrong with their beliefs and practices. Their preponderant idea was that Yahweh will send a new warrior king who will then fight with the Romans to bring back their kingdom. Hence, when they saw Jesus speaking, they thought the new king had come.

The news of Jesus possibly reviving a separate Jewish kingdom reached Roman governor Pontius Pilate, who obviously had no intentions of returning Israel back to the Jews, and he ordered the crucifixion of Jesus. Jesus was crucified by Romans because he posed a political threat. If Jesus had been portrayed merely as a preacher, savior, or messiah, who was bringing the message of God, which posed no political threats to Romans, then he would not have been crucified. Jesus says in the Bible: "Render unto Caesar the things which are Caesar's and unto God the things that are God's." Jesus was factually not a threat to the Roman empire. But the Jews were not interested in his teachings. He was crucified because Jews were expecting a warrior king to revive their kingdom and hailed his arrival as the future king who would soon fight and defeat the Romans in a battle. That possibility posed a serious threat to Romans.

The Separatist Birth of Christianity

The dreams of a Jewish kingdom either ended or faced a serious setback when Jesus was crucified. But for most Jews, the crucifixion just meant that Jesus was not the savior that had been prophesized. Jesus was not a warrior and he would have never revived the Jewish kingdom. For most Jews, the crucifixion of Jesus was an aberration caused by their misunderstanding that the Messiah had arrived.

But for a smaller sect of followers of Jesus—later to be called Christians—Jesus was indeed the Messiah. The Christians gave a radical interpretation of the crucifixion in which Jesus had been sent by God to be sacrificed for the sins of Jews (committed when they were polytheists), and through this sacrifice, Jews were finally free of their sins. In this interpretation, the Jewish kingdom could not be established until the Jews had been completely purged of their sins of polytheism. But God had now purged the sins of the Jews, to prepare them for a new king and kingdom. Therefore, the crucifixion of Jesus was the mark that the kingdom of God was soon to arrive. Thereby, calling Jesus the "King of the Jews" was a mistake, but his arrival and crucifixion weren't to be treated merely as accidents of history because, through his sacrifice, he had paved the way for a "Kingdom of God", which would soon arrive.

Since most Jews did not accept this interpretation of crucifixion, the Christians broke off from Judaism to start a new religion called Christianity which focused on the doctrines of how the sacrifice of Jesus was essential for the revival of God's kingdom on earth, and how those who accepted this sacrifice were the rightful inheritors of God's earthly kingdom, destined to rule over those who did not accept this sacrifice. Thereby, the "Kingdom of God" was itself given a new interpretation—it was not a kingdom for the Jews who did not believe in the importance of crucifixion. It was rather a kingdom for Christians who accepted the crucifixion as a divine plan to revive God's kingdom on earth. Thus, Christians converted the previous idea of God's kingdom for the Jews in Israel to a worldwide kingdom for the Christians.

The Christian Doctrine of Salvation

Christians borrowed the Jewish doctrines of salvation—under which those who accept the monotheistic God not just enjoy an earthly kingdom but also go to heaven in an afterlife—almost completely, except that the coming of the Jewish Messiah just before the end times became the second coming of Jesus. This subject pertaining to the end times is called Eschatology and the end time is called the Apocalypse.

The Christian doctrines, however, further simplified the problem of salvation by saying that anyone who has accepted Jesus in this life would receive salvation, thereby progressively reducing the importance of moral human deeds in deciding one's salvation. If at all a deed is important, it is only to accelerate the second coming of Jesus. Thus, Christians proselytize all over the world to pave the way for Jesus' arrival. They believe that Jesus hasn't come so far because many parts of the world have still not accepted Jesus. Thereby, Jesus is waiting for most people to accept him before he arrives to end the world.

This doctrine serves two important purposes. First, it ameliorates the objection of why people are still suffering in this world if Jesus has already suffered for their sins—the answer is that the Kingdom of God hasn't yet arrived, and it will not arrive until the second coming of Jesus. Second, it creates incentives for the conversion of people to Christianity in their self-interest—namely, that if most people in the world converted to Christianity, then Jesus would arrive sooner, and that will put an end to all suffering.

Popular Incarnations of Salvation

After the collapse of the Soviet Union, there was a widespread belief that the hurdles to the spread of Christianity due to the prevalence and power of communism had been removed. The fact that a conservative Christian President in the US—Ronald Reagan—was instrumental in bringing an end to the Soviet Union and the power of communism, just added to the conviction in most people that this would now lead to a rapid spread of Christianity. Many territories that were previously parts of the Soviet Union were rapidly inducted into the NATO alliance to bring them under the influence of the US, ostensibly to spread or revive Christianity in them after the atheistic onslaught of communism.

Thus, in 1992 Francis Fukuyama published "The End of History and the Last Man" in which he noted that humanity has reached "the end-point of mankind's ideological evolution and the universalization of Western liberal democracy as the final form of human government". Such was the euphoria at the end of the Soviet Union that people started calling this end the final state of humanity.

But many parts of Asia were still non-Christian. China was the biggest communist nation at that time. The plan to convert them to Christianity involved bringing capitalism and democracy to them. The West strongly believed that if people accept the Western culture, then they will also accept Christianity. The Western formula for bringing Christianity to them was to give them capitalism under the hope that this will transform China into a democratic society, which will then accelerate their conversion to Christianity. Thus, if liberal democracy and capitalism take over the world, then Christianity cannot be far behind. This process of Christianizing the world was called "globalization".

Thus, a little over a decade after the collapse of the Soviet Union, Thomas Friedman wrote a book in 2005 entitled "The World is Flat: A Brief History of the Twenty-first Century" in which he talked about how free trade and globalization have finally dissolved the boundaries between nations, and this would be the story of the world for the remainder of the 21st century. This was another euphoric moment in which the spread of capitalism meant the inevitability of democracy and the arrival of Christianity.

The fact is that after the Ukraine war, globalization is reversing, Western liberal democracy is teetering, there are talks about World War III, and an economic crash is predicted to occur soon. This has been the fate of the second coming of Jesus or that of a Jewish Messiah for 2000 years. Every few years there is talk about the arrival of a messiah who will then end the world. If that messiah doesn't come, then there are plans to accelerate his arrival. Colonialism was the preferred method earlier. It went bust at the end of the two world wars. It was democracy and capitalism after the two world wars. It is going bust now. This is a serious personal issue for many Christians because their ascent to heaven is tied to the second coming of Jesus, and he is not coming until most people have accepted Christianity.

Every now and then, thinly disguised Judeo-Christian puffferies—e.g., the books by Francis Fukuyama and Thomas

Friedman—celebrate the arrival of mankind to their final destination in history signaled by a comprehensive victory of Judeo-Christian ideals. We cannot help but yelp in joy at the end of reading such propaganda pieces: "And the Judeo-Christian messiah is just about to arrive".

A Brief History of Monotheism

These are then the simple conclusions we can draw from the history of monotheism:

- The original religion of Israel had a multilayered pantheon of demigods
- At some point, all layers in this pantheon above Yahweh were removed
- After this, Jews were defeated in wars by the Assyrians and the Babylonians
- Jewish priests blamed their defeat on the presence of gods besides Yahweh
- Monotheism was thus crafted by stripping away all the remaining demigods
- The acts and qualities of some demigods were retroactively imputed upon Yahweh
- Redemption in Judaism originally meant the return of Jews to their homeland
- When that did not happen, a doctrine of an afterlife was added to preserve Judaism
- Jesus was crucified due to the Jewish idea of a king who revives a Jewish kingdom
- Crucifixion was reinterpreted by Christians as God's plan to absolve their sins
- Jews rejected this interpretation of crucifixion due to its factual incorrectness
- Christians then broke away from Judaism to create a separate religion
- But they carried forward the Judaic eschatology and apocalyptic theories
- Predictions of this eschatology have not come true for two

millennia
- Tricks and tactics used to realize eschatology are periodically reversed

The fact is that if Jews had accepted Jesus as a messiah or savior, Judaism would have been reformed, there would be no crucifixion, there would be no need to reinterpret crucifixion as God's plan to absolve the Jews of their sins, and Christianity would not exist as a religion. All these things would occur if Jews had earlier not interpreted their defeat at the hands of Assyrians and Babylonians as indicative of a need for religious reform and hoping that the reform would automatically bring back their kingdom.

I'm not trying to conjure an alternative course in history. I'm just trying to point out the historical chain of events in which monotheism is created from polytheism for political objectives—i.e., the return of the Jewish kingdom. Then a doctrine of the afterlife and redemption is added to extend and preserve Judaism. Then the arrival of a messiah is interpreted as the arrival of a king. Then the crucifixion of that supposed messiah-king is interpreted as God's plan to absolve sins. Since that plan is rejected by most Jews, a breakaway religion—Christianity—is created, primarily to extend and reify the theories of crucifixion.

Why is Monotheism So Successful?

There are several theories about why Christian monotheism became so popular.

- Most Powerful God: The earliest converts to Christianity were most impressed by the concepts of virgin birth and resurrection as these indicated the miraculous powers of Jesus. Christianity gained enormous popularity by talking about the miracles of Jesus. Constantine won a major battle after accepting Jesus although he knew pity little about Christianity. One of the earliest persecutors of Christians—Paul—underwent a transformation to become its greatest advocate writing the most gospels included in the New Testament. The transformation of a persecutor into an advocate signified the power of the Christian faith. While pagan gods had powers only in one domain, the Christian God—due to the aggregation of powers from many domains ruled by many demigods into one god—had greater powers than any individual pagan god.

- Most Merciful God: The God of the Old Testament is depicted as demanding, punishing, and harsh. But Jesus is known as a merciful healer. The God of the Old Testament punished Jews by forcing their exile. But Jesus had appeared to forgive the previous sins of people, and suffer for them if needed. The God of the Old Testament was giving commandments to people. But Jesus was teaching love and brotherhood. For all these things to be beneficial for Christianity, Christians had to establish that Jesus was God. He wasn't merely a Jewish messiah but was God himself.
- Most Accessible God: The God of the Old Testament lived in the sky and did not speak to everyone, but Jesus as God appeared among the ordinary people. God of the Old Testament was talking to prophets, patronizing kings, and accessed by priests, and a complicated set of rules were necessary for obedience to Him. But Jesus was accessible to everyone. Religion was no longer a greater privilege for priests, prophets, or kings. Religion was for the common man. The rejection of Jewish laws and the adoption of simple ideas like love and brotherhood appealed to everyone. God had walked among common men, become one of them, and He was no longer distant.

The attraction of Christian monotheism can be summarized through three simple principles—Our God is the most powerful, most merciful, and most accessible. Everyone can approach our God, everyone can receive his mercy easily, and he can do anything for you. Our God is loving and kind, rather than harsh and fearsome. Having the most powerful person on your side, ready to ignore your faults, accept you as you are, and always be available to solve your problems, is undeniably an unbeatable combination.

The Contradictions of Monotheism

This popularity required a radical transformation from the harsh, judging, and demanding image of God in the Old Testament to a kind, giving, and forgiving image of God in the New Testament. The God of the Old Testament is Yahweh, but the God of the New Testament is Jesus. Everything rests on Jesus being God, and yet, not being the kind of God that Yahweh is. Does that mean there are two Gods—one who is kind and the other who is harsh? That would not be monotheism. Or, does it mean that Yahweh is not God and only Jesus is God? That would mean that God had died on the cross and was then resurrected. The question would also be: If God had died then who resurrected Him? You need two ideas of God, which are in total contradiction to each other, but you cannot have a religion with just one of those.

These contradictions in Christianity make it a malleable religion because you can go to the extremes of kindness and harshness whenever and whichever seems convenient. You can talk about the mercifulness of Jesus on those who follow Jesus and then talk about the unkindness of Yahweh on those who don't follow Yahweh. You can forgive the sins of Christians because Jesus is merciful and punish the sins of non-Christians because they haven't accepted Yahweh. You can send the followers of Jesus to heaven because Jesus is merciful and send everyone else to hell because they have rejected Yahweh.

Most people are attracted to Jesus and most people are repelled by Yahweh but Christianity cannot reject either of those. They cannot call them two separate Gods, because it would not be monotheism. These two personalities cannot be reconciled, because they are fundamentally opposed. This duality within monotheism has been seen over the ages in the cruelty that Christians have shown to people of other religions while talking about the kindness, love, and brotherhood within Christianity. This duality has allowed people to interpret Christianity in thousands of different ways with different people taking different parts of the Bible literally and metaphorically and everything in between those extremes. Thus, apart from the problems of how monotheism emerged from polytheism and how the interpretation of crucifixion is contrary to the facts, there is the issue of two radically opposed depictions of God.

Trajectory Away from Monotheism

Followers of the Vedic tradition have no problem accepting the many *aspects* of God, which appear as lower deities, along with a complete form of God. Vedic darshan is specifically about studying everything in terms of six aspects. God has both cruel and kind faces, which He shows to different people, based on their natures. Those different aspects of God are always possible, but they become real to a specific person, at a specific, time, place, and situation. These aspects of God are His many forms. The followers of the Vedic tradition accept that everyone has a unique relationship with God, through which he can see a different form of God. God is one, and yet, He exists in many forms.

Therefore, contrary to monotheism, there is no exclusivism of multiple forms of God in the Vedic system. The fact that one form exists doesn't mean only one form exists. There are infinite forms. And yet, those forms are not experienced by everyone. This is demystified through the problem of the five blind men trying to understand the elephant—they touch different parts of the elephant and they are not wrong in saying that the elephant is the part that they are currently touching. However, they become wrong when they say that the other part of the elephant doesn't exist.

Therefore, apart from all the historical, conceptual, philosophical, and logical problems in monotheism, the fundamental problem—as far as other religions are concerned—is their *exclusivism.* In the five blind men problem, this exclusivism comes from the blindness of the men trying to understand the elephant. The man touching the leg of the elephant says that the elephant cannot be the ear or the tail. Exclusivists attack other religions because they don't have the philosophical framework in which they could think of reality as multiple aspects of one thing, seen differently by different people.

This is why we have to contrast monotheism with personalism. Monotheism says that God can either be like the tail or the leg. Personalism says that God is actually an elephant of which tail and leg are aspects. God is one as an elephant and God is many as the elephant's tail and leg perceived by the blind men. Therefore, the Vedic tradition is neither monotheistic, nor polytheistic, but something that is neither and both (as detailed in the earlier article The Conception of God in . Vaiṣṇavism). Every aspect of God is not equally important; some aspects are more important than others, quite like the head of the elephant is most important, the stomach is next, the legs are next, the ears are next, and the tail is last. We can grade the parts of an elephant in a hierarchy, and talk about the more important aspects of God. This is how the Vedic system rejects both the blind equality of all religions and the blind rejection of other religions.

Personalism requires a non-binary system of reasoning in which there are many aspects that are neither the whole, nor separate from the whole. The problem of exclusivism is easy to state. But it is so deep and broad that to solve it, we need to discard ordinary principles of logic, objectivity, and universality. We have to revise even the notion of truth. When such radical differences are understood in their full resplendence, then the semblance between personalism and monotheism is like the superficial whiteness of chalk and cheese without any deep similarity.

Lakśmi—The Personification of Wealth

The separation of religion and economics, like so many other separations in modern thinking, is the gift of the Western reductionist methodology of drawing arbitrary boundaries within reality and treating them as isolated systems. These separations never occurred in Vedic thinking. Wealth, for instance, is one of the qualities of Lord Viṣṇu, personified as Lakśmi. Thus, when Viṣṇu is worshipped, Lakśmi automatically arrives in that place. Economics is therefore the science of how Lakśmi goes from one place to another. In this post, I will talk about why Lakśmi is called restless, why She goes from one place to another, and how She becomes fixed only where Viṣṇu is fixed.

Divine Religion-Economics Connection

Religion cannot be separated from economics because where there is Viṣṇu, there is Lakśmi. The devotees of Viṣṇu don't pursue Lakśmi but Lakśmi comes automatically to them. Trying to separate religion from economics is trying to divorce Viṣṇu from Lakśmi. That attempt is futile. Wealth is one of the aspects of God. The devotees of Viṣṇu ask everyone to focus on Viṣṇu, and not merely on the aspect of wealth. But they do not reject Lakśmi, because She is an aspect of Viṣṇu. The focus on Viṣṇu and the acceptance of Lakśmi are for the same reason.

The fact is also that any attempted separation of religion from economics in the minds of some people will not separate them in most minds because religion has been connected to prosperity in other religions: God rewards a religious person with power, beauty, and prosperity.

Our disagreement with this connection is simply that it holds in one direction but not another. Where there is God there is prosperity, but where there is prosperity there may not be any God. The truth is wealthy, but wealth is not the truth. The truth is powerful, but power is not truth. The truth is beautiful, but beauty is not truth. Wealth, beauty, and power can exist *temporarily* even where God is absent. But where God is present, wealth, beauty, and power are *eternal*. Therefore, the equivalence of religion and prosperity is accepted in the sense that truth is wealthy but rejected in the sense that wealth is not truth. If wealth, power, and beauty are obtained through theft, then the acquisition is short-lived. If dharma results in the acquisition of wealth, power, and beauty, then those acquisitions are also long-lived.

The philosophical principle is that beauty, wealth, fame, power, and renunciation are *adjectives* of the truth but they can also be treated as *nouns*. If they are treated as nouns—i.e., things independent of the truth—then they are temporary. But if they are treated as adjectives of the truth, then they are eternal. This principle is called Puruṣa and Prakṛti–Puruṣa is the noun and Prakṛti is the adjective. Where there is Puruṣa, the Prakṛti is always present. But, Prakṛti can also *seem* to be a noun temporarily, separated from the Puruṣa. That seeming objectivity of wealth is an *illusion*. Thus, if we think that there is Prakṛti to be taken because She doesn't already belong to the Puruṣa, then that is an illusion.

Puruṣa may be obscured by Prakṛti because we want to see the Prakṛti and not the Puruṣa. For example, a man may lust after a woman's body without any interest in the person itself. The body doesn't exist without the person. But due to lust, one disregards the person and lusts for the body. Similarly, Prakṛti has no independent existence from the Puruṣa. But due to lust, we disregard the Puruṣa and focus on the Prakṛti. This is why devotees of Viṣṇu say: Focus on the person, and when you do that, then the body is included. This is just like a man may genuinely love a woman, and not simply lust for her body. Then, love doesn't exclude the body, and yet, the body is not the exclusive focus. Likewise, wealth doesn't exist independently of a person. Only a person is wealthy. And yet, we can lust for wealth to create the illusion that there is wealth to be taken because it is not already owned by the Puruṣa. This independent existence of wealth is an illusion.

The Personalist Idea of Economics

Wealth is one of the adjectives of Viṣṇu, personified as Lakśmi, and called Chanchala or "restless". She walks around in the material garden playfully twirling the lotus in Her hand, and people want to grab Her. Since She seems to appear in this world without Viṣṇu, therefore, an illusion of wealth as a noun is created. Everyone wants to possess Lakśmi and make Her their adjective—i.e., become *wealthy*. But Lakśmi is neither an independent noun nor is She everyone's adjective. She is always the adjective of Viṣṇu. Thereby, She doesn't stay with anyone except Her husband Viṣṇu. Her appearance in this world where She seems like a noun to everyone is just an illusion.

This illusion is created by Lakśmi playfully to attract the fools to Viṣṇu through the allurement of wealth—i.e., if you become devoted to Viṣṇu, then I will also bless you. Since there is truth in this allurement, therefore, the connection between religion and economics cannot be severed. And yet, because allurement is just playfulness without devotion to Viṣṇu, therefore, without Viṣṇu, all the wealth is eventually lost.

Poverty and prosperity are equally the results of Lakśmi playfully twirling Her lotus and giving sidelong glances to Her suitors, and when these suitors are attracted by Her sidelong glances, Lakśmi goes to another suitor, if they just want Her without Her husband. Lakśmi is always playing with prospective suitors so that they may follow Her and eventually come to Viṣṇu due to their allurement for wealth. She goes to some people to check if they will become devoted to Viṣṇu due to prosperity. She goes away from people to check if they will become devoted to Viṣṇu due to poverty. Some people become gracious and humble when they obtain riches. Others become gracious and humble when they lose their riches. Since different medicines work for different people, therefore, these are just playful methods of attraction.

Economics for the Vedic tradition is the sidelong glances of Lakśmi playfully twirling Her lotus to attract everyone to Viṣṇu.

That same economics in the Western world is mathematical equations, cycles of boom and bust, graphs and charts, with arrows pointing upward and downward. The Vedic tradition replaces those upward and downward arrows with the sidelong glances of Lakśmi looking here and there for the most suitable candidate to be blessed by Her either through prosperity or through poverty. Those who forget Viṣṇu lose their wealth as a reminder to remember Viṣṇu as Lakśmi moves to the previously poor people hoping that they will turn to Viṣṇu after becoming wealthy. If they don't reform even after getting wealth, then Lakśmi goes to those remembering Viṣṇu just to gain wealth.

Lakśmi can come because—(a) She wants to check if a person will be devoted to Viṣṇu after he gets wealth, (b) She comes to a person who is devoted to Viṣṇu for wealth or despite poverty. Lakśmi can leave because—(a) the person has forgotten Viṣṇu and She wants to make Him remember Viṣṇu again, and (b) She considers wealth a hindrance in the devotion to Viṣṇu, and She leaves the person to make him even more devoted to Viṣṇu. In every case, Her goal is to make a person remember Viṣṇu.

Wealth can come to us because we are religious, or because we can become religious out of gratitude for having received wealth, or because we are expecting wealth as the recognition of our religiosity. Wealth can go away because we are not religious, or because we have no gratitude for having received wealth, or because we think that religiosity is not a precondition for wealth, or to strengthen our religiosity, or to remind us that good things happen to those who are involved in doing good to others.

Those who measure themselves by wealth rather than character will eventually lose their wealth. But those who have character can again accept Viṣṇu and Lakśmi, and if they do so, then they will regain wealth because Lakśmi likes to stay with the decent person who treats Her respectfully and not with the person who tries to grab Her by force and abuse Her grace for immoral activities. When Lakśmi goes to the decent person, then those allured by wealth will naturally start following the decent person.

Therefore, wealth is not the long-term decider of truth. But the truth is the long-term decider of wealth. Those strutting around arrogantly due to their wealth have to be impoverished to bring them to the truth. The poverty of those who worship wealth can be solved by worshipping the worshippers of truth.

Economic Failures of Impersonalism

Impersonalists say that Viṣṇu and Lakśmi are human concoctions, which is why we invite them to produce economic theories that explain the rise and fall of societies without reference to Viṣṇu and Lakśmi. Western academics have already tried that, and their economics is now known as a "dismal science". Impersonalists can also try. We can accept their views on morality and spirituality if they can produce better economics. Otherwise, their claims are empty rhetoric.

The fact is that they cannot produce a better economic theory. The fact is that they cannot create economic prosperity. The fact is that their ideologies have led to the economic decline of the most prosperous nation. Hence, their morality and spirituality have already been proven to be bankrupt.

Anyone trying to make an equation that predicts the upward or downward trend in economics will be frustrated by the indeterminism in economics because Lakśmi comes and goes due to many different reasons. Whichever equation is universalized, it will be undone by another reason why Lakśmi comes and goes. We can never solve the problem of economics without personalizing wealth. Personalization is the rejection of mathematical equations, cycles of boom and bust, graphs and charts, with arrows pointing upward and downward. One who can understand how economies rise and fall due to the playfully moving glances of Lakśmi will find mathematical equations disgusting. They will be able to see Her in this world and reject the ignorance found in Impersonalism masquerading as truth.

When God Spreads Delusion

The Fear of Missing Out on Religion

There is a new internet slang called FOMO. It means fear of missing out. It arises because of jealousy. We see someone else doing something and we fear that they will get something good that we will not. That jealousy makes us want the other thing too. But we cannot do it as well as the person who is dedicated to it. Our priorities are different than theirs. Hence, we put on a charade of doing something while not being committed to it. By that charade, we put our FOMO to rest. Of course, it achieves nothing. We do actually miss out. But we pretend that we will not be missing out because we are doing something minimal. Therefore, FOMO engages us in ridiculous and fruitless activities.

Religion is also subject to FOMO. True religion involves complete devotion and dedication to God. Most people don't want that. But they are jealous that the truly dedicated people will get something that they will not. They want the greatest result in religion without exclusive and complete devotion to God. Such people create new religions where the results are supposed to come without total devotion to God.

The Ladder of Religious Practices

In the Bhagavad-Gita, Lord Kṛṣṇa offers Arjuna a ladder of six types of practices in which the topmost rung is complete and exclusive devotion to Him. But if Arjuna cannot do that, then there is something lower. If he cannot even do that, then there is something even lower. The lowest rung in this ladder is the cultivation of knowledge by studying the Vedic texts. In doing this, one doesn't have to sacrifice most of their materialistic aspirations but they can still be on the lowest rung of the ladder.

Thus, Lord Kṛṣṇa offers Arjuna five different alternatives to the best path. All the paths are not equal. There is a clear hierarchy between these paths. The lower steps are for those who cannot do the higher step, but get FOMO. They realize that whatever I am doing is not going to get me the best result, especially the result attained by those devoted to God. To deal with it, they can follow the lower path. Lord Kṛṣṇa doesn't give any path lower than the cultivation of knowledge.

The Creation of Multiple Religions

But in this age of lies, hypocrisy, and deceit, people have created dozens of religions. In some religions, you just have to believe that because you accepted some savior, you will be going to eternal heaven, without any change in personal character. The bar of religion has been lowered so low that everyone can jump over it.

People are jumping over low bars due to FOMO. They want to spend their life earning money, enjoying sex, building their careers, buying a house and car, going to all the possible social events, celebrating all the routines, and feeling good as a result of all these things. But sometimes they look at others who are fully devoted to God and not focusing on any of the above materialistic pursuits. They get FOMO. They don't want to miss out on what the devoted people will get as a result of their dedication. They want to do the bare minimum to feel that they will also receive what others are going to receive. Multiple religions are created due to FOMO.

Each religion exists for people with different commitments to their own upliftment but they take to a religion to overcome their FOMO. They don't want to be left out of the possibility of eternal heaven if such a thing indeed exists. But since they are not convinced that such a thing indeed exists, they don't want to invest their whole life in its pursuit. They want all the other things, just in case eternal heaven doesn't exist.

FOMO Religions Reduce Requirements

Each alternative religion reduces what one has to do to attain perfection but hides it from its followers because the purpose of the religion is to alleviate FOMO. Indeed, it promises to give the same result without the same level of dedication and devotion. The lowest level of required dedication is seen in religions that say that if you just have faith in God and His savior then you will go to heaven. Once in a while, you should just donate some money to those who are doing more than you, namely, trying to spread the message that nothing is required except faith in the savior and some money. This is hugely attractive to billions of people. The bar is so low that anyone can jump over it. They jump over it to evade their FOMO. They think that they will receive the most valuable thing without doing anything.

Then there are religions that demand more commitment. You have to practice non-violence, control your mind and senses, and lead a clean and cultured life, whose immediate benefits are mental peace and fewer diseases arising from endless anxieties about failure in materialistic pursuits. Materialism is still very important to such people. It is, in fact, the key measure of success in life. But to keep materialism going for a long time without suffering, one has to add some practices. Such people choose a religion that helps them lead a good life for a long time by following a practice that gives a healthy body and mind for continuous materialistic pursuit. The religion also says that this is the be-all and end-all of life. There is nothing more to religion than a peaceful mind and a healthy body which is then used for getting material success.

Then there are religions that demand even more commitment. They say that the world is a delusion, that you must practice simplicity and renunciation for personal salvation, through the cultivation of knowledge and the practice of some meditation. Generally, all this comes along with the renunciation of other duties, so this type of religion substitutes one thing with another. However, the standards of knowledge and meditation are very low. Some meditators say that we must just "observe" our thoughts and by that, we will become "observers" of reality, as if you can just keep observing those coming to kill you. Their standard for knowledge is even lower. Just study the seven centers of concentration in the body where you can focus your awareness for observation as if anyone can actually see anything in these places.

Basic Traits of FOMO Religions

When real dedication, devotion, and commitment are missing, then hundreds if not thousands of religions are created due to FOMO. Everyone is scared of missing out but unwilling to dedicate their life to the greatest thing either because they are not convinced or they don't want to invest the energy and time necessary to get convinced. They rubber stamp themselves with a religious title, practice, and allegiance to some sectarian group to overcome their FOMO. They also claim or like to believe there is nothing more to religion than what they are doing.

The basic trait of a FOMO-driven religion is that it attacks all other religions closer to complete devotion to God. The mere presence of a religion that teaches the highest result only in return for the highest sacrifice is greatly troubling for the FOMO-driven religion because it entails that the FOMO-driven religion is not going to attain the highest result.

Many people who want the highest result may start questioning the tenets of the FOMO-driven religion and ultimately abandon it. The reduced size of the band of followers will then prompt other followers to ask the same questions and possibly abandon the religion. Through this process, the FOMO in the FOMO-driven religion increases greatly. To put an end to the FOMO, the FOMO-driven religion attacks all other religions to keep its band of followers intact. All FOMO-driven religions seek the safety of numbers. Abandonment greatly increases their FOMO.

Misleading Incarnations of God

When religion is practiced due to FOMO, then God appears to separate the wheat from the husk. He pied-pipers people suffering from FOMO to a separate intellectual, ideological, or sectarian land where they will find safety in numbers with similarly FOMO-driven people and stop attacking and confusing the people who are prepared to make the greatest sacrifice to obtain the greatest result. The FOMO-driven people then gather together and form a new religion that promises to give a lot for a lot less.

The Vedic texts recognize two incarnations of God—Buddha and Shankaracharya—in this age to pied-piper away the people who are in a religion driven by FOMO and constantly challenge and question the people who have dedicated their full life to the greatest pursuit. The pied-piper produces enchanting music. At least, it is music to the ears of those who are in the religion due to FOMO and are a continuous distraction, disturbance, and nuisance for those who have dedicated their life to the greatest pursuit. The pied-piper takes away these nuisance makers to their own separate place where they can dance to the pied-piper's tunes and leave the rest of the people dedicated to the highest purpose alone.

These pied-piper incarnations are glorified by the greatest devotees of the Lord because they know that taking the people disinterested in the highest truth away from the highest truth is a glorious activity. Instead of bothering others, the disinterested people can just dance to the tunes of the pied-piper, truly believe that the pied-piper is taking them toward deliverance and salvation, and leave the rest alone. But the same devotees also say that these incarnations are pied-pipers and their music is delusional. These two are not contradictory things. The glorification and criticism pertain to the same situation. It is true that the Lord has incarnated to protect the true dharma. It is also true that the Lord has incarnated to enchant the mischief makers away from those who can devote themselves to the highest purpose.

How God Plays Multiple Roles

Thus, in this age called Kali-Yuga, hundreds of religions are created because (a) people are not interested in religion, (b) they have FOMO, (c) they attack those who devote themselves to the highest goal of life, and (d) they have to be separated from those who are devoted to the highest goal of life. The cook cleans the raw uncooked food before cooking it. Cleaning is also a cook's job. But since cleaning requires separating the grain from the chaff, hence, it looks different from cooking. Cleaning and cooking are two sides of the same coin, although cooking is the desired goal, and cleaning is a necessary evil.

There are two kinds of contaminations in every conditioned soul. They are called guna and karma. By guna, each person is accustomed to bad habits, ideas, and practices. By karma, each person is born in a society addicted to bad habits, ideas, and practices. Guna is nature and karma is nurture. Nurture increases nature and nature increases nurture. Therefore, when we start changing nature, then we have to stop nurturing the previous nature. Medicine may not always work without a change in diet. That change in diet is the change of nurture. Stop eating bad things while you are trying to get cured. If those bad things are people poisoning a person trying to heal, then they have to be removed from the association of those cultivating devotion to the Lord. That removal happens through the creation of a new religion.

We can clearly see that the other religion is different. That it has separate books, practices, and places of worship. We can clearly see that the people of such religions assemble in different places to do different things. They dance to different tunes because some pied-piper has enchanted them away to (a) fulfill their desire for practicing a FOMO-driven religion, and (b) relieve others from their disturbing influence.

Interactions with FOMO Religions

The thumb rule for those dedicated to the highest purpose is to never criticize the FOMO-driven religion because any attack will simply increase the fear in the FOMO-driven religion and cause a bigger attack in retaliation. The purpose of separating the FOMO-driven people from those dedicated to the highest purpose would be defeated. Therefore, the general principle for those dedicated to the highest purpose is to not question, criticize, or attack other religious sects. Let them dance to the tune that the Lord has created for them—precisely so that they will leave the seekers of the highest truth alone. The exception to this thumb rule is that we must counterattack in response to attacks from FOMO-driven people.

Of course, we cannot dig a well after the house is already on fire. We cannot start recruiting an army after the country is already under attack. We have to anticipate, prepare, and train for such an attack in advance. These attacks from FOMO-driven people are inevitable and anticipated. The well is dug in advance to put out the fire. The army is recruited, trained, and prepared for repelling an attack. But the army is called the Ministry of Defense rather than the Ministry of Attack. The army serves to defend and occasionally counterattack. It doesn't exist to attack proactively. The proactive step is to recruit, prepare, and train the army. For that, we need to understand the attackers and how to defend and counterattack them. But if there is no attack, then the army is not utilized to attack the others proactively. Defense and counterattacks are not proactive aggression. They are meant to hold and defend a position. A country should not stop preparing for an attack and a country should not attack other countries proactively.

This nuance must be upheld in case of aggression from FOMO-driven religions too. When they attack, we have to respond aggressively. Before that, we have to prepare proactively without attacking them. But if they do not attack, then we have to let them dance to the tune of the pied pipers who have taken them away from those dedicated to the highest purpose and allowed different people to live peacefully.

Understanding God's Many Natures

Even as God spreads the truth, He also spreads delusion. The truth is spread to those who want the truth. The delusion is spread to those who want the delusion. God is the supplier of both truth and delusion. That doesn't mean He equates both truth and delusion. His preference for the truth is always higher. But that preference is not the absence of the delusion. Since everything is coming from God, therefore, both truth and delusion are coming from God. The delusional act of God is also an act of mercy on those interested in the truth, just as it is very pleasing to those who are not interested in the truth. God is the marketplace to get everything.

The better things are priced higher than the worse things. The pricing is honest. The intelligent look at the price tag and ask the shopkeeper: Why is this priced so high when the other things are priced so low? Then, the shopkeeper explains the features of the highly- and lowly-priced products. The intelligent customer also realizes that the cheaper product is also the worse product. If he wants to get the better product then he also has to shell out the higher price.

However, the shopkeeper doesn't proactively criticize the cheaper products in his shop. He will sell whatever the buyer wants to purchase. He will of course display everything very clearly, and display the better products more prominently. The shopkeeper wants to sell the best and the most expensive products the most. But he knows that most people cannot afford the better products. He looks at each buyer, assesses their capacity to purchase, and directs them toward the correct aisle or display to let them evaluate. The buyers who want to get expensive products are treated with greater respect, courtesy, and regard. The buyers who want to get the cheaper product are not so treated.

Knowing the Nature of Truth and Delusion

Those buyers who are already buying the most expensive products should not attack the other buyers. Of course, they can feel happy that they are getting better products and tell their trusted friends, relatives, and associates about the better product. If they find a friend in the same shop buying the worse product, they can just go up to them and inquire what they are buying. They can also tell them that they prefer to buy the better product, see if their trusted friend, relative, or associate is interested, and then act accordingly.

Unless the person buying the cheaper product attacks the person buying the better product, there is no need for retaliation. But the person buying the expensive product must also know the features of the more expensive thing he is buying. Nobody pays more money out of blind faith.

All these nuances are not difficult to understand. They are just not widely known because of binary good-bad thinking created by FOMO-driven religions that cannot justify their beliefs and actions based on the features of what they are buying or selling. Those interested in the highest truth must understand the features of both the expensive and cheaper products and then buy the best quality product.

Arguments for the Existence of God

The Difference Between Existence and Truth

Many people try to construct proofs of God's existence. These proofs generally operate under equivalence between truth and existence, which is false because untruths can also exist. For instance, I can think that the sky is purple. This thought exists but it is not true. Similarly, someone can make a fictional movie, write a fictitious novel, or create a fictional work of art. All these things exist, but they are not true. Hence, existence doesn't equal to truth.

There is also a subtle but important difference between *true* and *truth*. Facts are true, but they might be true only for some time, not eternally. For example, I can think that the sky is blue. It may be true right now, but false later on when the sky becomes black or yellow. Hence, the existence of a blue sky can be true, not truth. Something is truth only if it exists eternally. Hence, we have to distinguish between eternal existence, temporary existence, and false existence. Existence itself can never be truth.

The non-equivalence of existence and truth is recognized in Vedic texts by the category called māyā, which exists, but it is not eternal truth. It may be a temporary existence or a false existence. Since nearly the whole material world (barring exceptions such as Vedic texts, the deities, and eternal spiritual activities enacted in the material world) falls in the category of temporary or false existence, the material world is called māyā. It is an overgeneralization because eternal truths also exist in the material world. But the mere characterization of the world as māyā means that existence is not truth.

The Creator of the Universe is Not Necessarily God

If by God we mean a creator, trying to prove that such a person exists is also not enough because that existence may be temporary. For example, suppose that our idea of God is one who creates heaven and earth and the life in them. This person is called Brahma in the Vedic texts. Suppose we prove Brahma's existence and think that we have proved the existence of God. In many religions, this proof would be considered the eternal truth. But in the Vedic system, it is just a temporary fact, that lasts for 311 trillion years. Since the person who presents this proof wouldn't be alive for 311 trillion years, hence, everyone who accepts that proof until then would have held a false belief for trillions of years. Hypothetically, we could also have a person meet Brahma and have him see the process of creation of heaven and earth. Even then, the empirical evidence of Brahma creating the world would not be proof of God's existence because this creation is temporary. Then if we don't see other Brahmas in other universes, and think that just seeing one Brahma is the proof of a creator, then too our empirical proof of the creator as God would be a false belief.

Thus, the proofs for the existence of God are useless until we can prove that this existence is eternal. Moreover, we must also know all that exists before we can talk about the creator of everything. If we don't know all that exists, and we don't know for how long it exists, then giving proof of a creator who has created something relatively small for a relatively short duration doesn't constitute proof of God's existence. In other words, we must know the greatness of God before we can give proof of God.

Most people don't know how great God is. They have talked about proofs of God as the creator of heaven and earth and the life in them. Only if they knew that there are trillions of material heavens and earths created by trillions of Brahmas and trillions of spiritual planets created by many partial although eternal forms of God, would they begin to comprehend the scope of the proof of God's existence.

The Supreme Person is the Original Self-Born

If this problem is still unclear, then we can rephrase it. When we try to prove God's existence as a creator, people often ask: If God created the world, then who created God? The answer most people would give is that God is self-born. But that is not true for Brahma who is born from the navel of Garbhodakśāyi Viṣṇu. Even Garbhodakśāyi Viṣṇu is born from Kāraṇodakaśāyī Viṣṇu. This process continues over several stages until we come to Kṛṣṇa. Only Kṛṣṇa is self-born. Everyone else is born either directly or indirectly from Kṛṣṇa. Hence, who created the creator of the world is not an invalid or irrelevant question because Brahma is born from Garbhodakśāyi Viṣṇu who is born from Kāraṇodakaśāyī Viṣṇu, and so on, until Kṛṣṇa. And yet, there is something about Kṛṣṇa that makes Him self-born.

What is the trait of Kṛṣṇa that makes Him self-born? Why are Brahma, Garbhodakśāyi, Kāraṇodakaśāyī, and many other forms not self-born although many of them may be eternal truths? The problem of the proof of God's existence is now further complicated because all eternal truths are not *self-born*. Even creators of eternal planets are not self-born. Rather, there is an original, complete, and supreme person from whom many subsequent, partial, and subordinate persons (including creators) are born.

The issue is that if we don't know the meaning of original, complete, and supreme, then we can prove the existence of subsequent, partial, and subordinate persons and think that we have proved the existence of God because he or she satisfies the limited criteria we have set for God. Hence, before we try to prove the existence of God, as someone who is self-born, we should try to understand the meaning of original, supreme, and complete. We should also try to understand the meaning of a person.

Direct Experience is the Basis of Logical Inference

In the Vedic texts, each person is defined as sat-chit-ānanda. A scripture is not necessary to prove this although a scripture is provided to describe the self so that we can obtain a theoretical understanding of the self and then pursue experiential self-knowledge.

We need self-experiential self-knowledge to know the meaning of sat-chit-ānanda. This is called Brahman realization and liberation.

Once we attain experiential self-knowledge, then we also know that we are *incomplete* sat-chit-ānanda. That is because we exist although we are not all that exists; we know but we don't know everything; we are happy but that is not all the happiness. Through such realization, we develop the quest for a more complete sat-chit-ānanda and a complete sat-chit-ānanda. This quest is meaningful only if there are more complete sat-chit-ānanda and a complete sat-chit-ānanda. The self-knowledge of sat-chit-ānanda is pratyakṣa while the inference of more complete versions of sat-chit-ānanda is anumāna. If we don't have the pratyakṣa that we are sat-chit-ānanda, then the anumāna that there must be a complete sat-chit-ānanda is baseless speculation. To be a valid inference, anumāna must always be based on pratyakṣa.

Self-Knowledge Necessary Before God-Knowledge

Thus, the Vedic system progresses from self-knowledge toward God-knowledge. Initially, we experience who we are. Then we can infer what God should be and then we get a direct perception of God. Trying to prove the existence of God without knowing that a person is sat-chit-ānanda, that most persons are partial sat-chit-ānanda, that there are more complete sat-chit-ānanda than us, and all these partial and incomplete sat-chit-ānanda are born from a self-born complete sat-chit-ānanda is baseless speculation.

Therefore, the proof of God's existence has to begin with establishing that I am a person defined as sat-chit-ānanda. Then we have to prove that everything that we can see in this world right now is also a sat-chit-ānanda. Then we have to show that there are more and less complete sat-chit-ānanda. For example, rivers, mountains, seas, and planets are more complete sat-chit-ānanda and the living entities living under their control are less complete sat-chit-ānanda. This establishes a hierarchy of sat-chit-ānanda. Then we can talk about demigods who are even more complete sat-chit-ānanda than the ones that we can perceive right now culminating in Brahma who is the ancestral sat-chit-ānanda of all the species into which we could be born. Then we can talk about progressively more complete sat-chit-ānanda divinities such as Shiva, and forms of Viṣṇu, until we come to the complete sat-chit-ānanda, Kṛṣṇa.

Progressive Incompleteness Drives God-Knowledge

If we focus on the creation, we can never know the Supreme Person unless we know all the creations. Factually, we will never know all the creations. Then how can we know the Supreme Person? The answer is simple: We must know ourselves and realize our incompleteness. The materially incomplete person tries to complete himself. But one who has obtained self-realization tries to complete others. His completeness rests upon making others complete. As one progresses in completing others and thereby completing oneself, he begins to understand the nature of God as the person who tries to complete others and feels more complete by that. Nobody can complete everyone like God. Hence, everyone is inferior to God. And yet, they become more complete by completing others.

This process of completing oneself by completing others is in stark contrast to material desires where we try to complete ourselves by denying others completion. Under material desires, we acquire things to fill the inner hollow and compete with others to deny them fulfillment of their hollows. Therefore, material desire is a zero-sum game in which my satisfaction entails someone else's dissatisfaction. Conversely, spiritual desire means experiencing an inner hollow and giving away what we have to fill that hollow. Happiness grows when it is distributed. Therefore, spiritual desire is an infinite-sum game in which each person feels happier by giving others happiness. However, an unhappy person cannot understand this. Only a person who has attained self-satisfaction at the bare minimum can understand it. God is that person who fills His inner hollow by distributing His happiness. He becomes happier by making others happy.

In the self-realization journey, we must first become self-satisfied. Then we can try to make others satisfied. The self-satisfied state is not the end of self-realization, as the impersonalists claim. It is just the beginning of the self-realization journey. Once the material desires end, we stop seeking things to fill the inner void. Instead, we start distributing the happiness within to others to make them happy. The spiritual desire is the inversion of material desire and it follows the termination of material desire. The spiritual desire never ends because one always feels incomplete as he hasn't completed everyone else. We progress in the hierarchy of more complete persons by progressively completing others. We know the Complete Person when we realize how He completes everyone and feels completed by that.

Thus, God-realization follows self-realization. If someone thinks that they are the complete sat-chit-ānanda, then they have no God-realization. If they consider themselves the byproducts of matter, they don't even have self-realization. Hence, the ladder of realizations involves self-realization, understanding how this self is still hollow, and distributing what one has to overcome that hollow. This is the process by which one understands the true nature of God as a spontaneous being. The spontaneity is that happiness is overflowing and there is still a desire to distribute and grow it.

The Necessity of Defining Personhood Hierarchically

The study of the world around us, which most people call science, is the study of things as sat-chit-ānanda. Even atoms are persons and not objects. Persons are defined in relation to each other whereas objects are defined as independent of each other. This relationality is why atoms are entangled in quantum physics. Science is modeling atoms as objects when they are actually persons. We cannot define an incomplete person in isolation. All incomplete persons must be defined in relation to other more complete persons. However, a Complete Person can be defined in relation to itself, becoming the only *thing-in-itself.*

Factually, God or the Supreme Person is the only thing-in-itself, which means that He is defined in relation to Himself. Everything else is a thing-in-relation-to-other-things. These relations are hierarchical such that the lower thing is defined in relation to the higher thing (which is higher because it is more complete) and this goes on until we come to the highest point of definition in which there is something that is defined in relation to itself. He is God. He is supreme because He is defined in relation to Himself.

If things were not defined in a hierarchy, then we would end up with circular definitions, such as A is defined in relation to B, which is defined in relation to A, so nothing can ever be completely defined. If we have circular definitions, then factually nothing can be defined. Conversely, a hierarchy is loop-free. Therefore, unless things are defined in a hierarchy, they must be defined circularly, and hence not defined at all.

When the only ontology in reality is persons, and the persons we can see are defined in relation to some other person, then the proof of the existence of God is very simple. It says: A is defined in relation to a higher B, which is defined in relation to a higher C, and so on, therefore, ultimately these things must be defined in relation to something self-defined. If this self-defined thing doesn't exist, then nothing else exists. The mere existence of one thing that is defined in relation to other things through a hierarchy, which terminates in something that is self-defined, establishes God's existence as the one and only self-defined thing.

This is a rational and empirical proof because it relies on the entanglement of ordinary things for their definition and explains that entanglement to present an explanation of their existence. We cannot explain entanglement with objects, since they are things-in-themselves and self-defined. We can only explain entanglement when the ontology is persons, as they are by definition things-in-relation-to-other-things. This cascading definition of things-in-relation-to-other-things mandates a hierarchy of definitions that terminates if and only if something is self-defined. If that self-defined thing doesn't exist, then nothing else can exist. Since something exists, therefore, the self-defined thing exists. The mere existence of the world establishes God's existence if the ontology of this world is persons.

Aristotelian Objectification of Personal Reality

The problem of God's existence arises because since Greek times the ontology of this world is objects rather than persons. Objects are things-in-themselves. Each object is defined in relation to itself. Aristotle phrased this idea as the Law of Identity, or A is A. The first A is the thing being defined. The second A is the thing in terms of which it is defined. The first and the second things are identical. Hence, everything is defined in relation to itself. Thereafter, every logical thing became a thing-in-itself. Now, God is unnecessary for any thing-in-itself to exist because it is already a thing-in-itself so it is self-defined and whatever is self-defined doesn't need anything else to define whatever it is defined as.

The genesis of all problems of modern science, religion, and philosophy is in Aristotelian logic and its conception of identity as something that is self-defined. We can call this conception *objects*. Factually, this logic and ontology is false. There are no objects. There are only persons. These persons are defined in relation to more complete persons, creating a hierarchy of definitions. This hierarchy terminates in a self-defined person. Since He is self-defined, hence, He is self-born. Everything else is born from this self-born person where birth simply means defining a part-thing in relation to a whole-thing. Since there are many levels of wholes, therefore, there is a hierarchy, which terminates in the complete whole.

The problem of atheism and the subsequent necessity of trying to prove God through an argument is the result of using Aristotelian logic and its object (i.e., thing-in-itself) ontology. If we reject this ontology and logic, then we don't have the problem of atheism or the need to prove God's existence because the mere existence of the world establishes the existence of God. We must reject this ontology to explain why ordinary objects are entangled (because they are not things-in-itself). The object ontology has collapsed even in what people call *physical science* because there is nothing physical. Everything is persons, not objects, hence it cannot be self-defined. Ultimately, everything is defined through a cascading hierarchy in relation to the Supreme Person. Hence, atheism is false.

A Scientific Program for Religious Conviction

Thus, we can outline a simple scientific program for religion, to establish—(a) that all object models of reality are false, (b) that the problems of object models can only be solved by person models, (c) that incomplete persons are defined in relation to more complete persons, and (d) therefore, for anything to be defined and to exist at all, the Supreme self-defined and self-born person is necessary.

This bypasses the need to define supremacy but necessitates the definition of personhood. Supremacy is defined through a cascading hierarchy that terminates in a self-defined, self-born person. However, we don't need to know how big this hierarchy is. We just need to know that this hierarchy must terminate for anything to be defined and to exist. Since something exists, therefore, the hierarchy terminates.

Thereby, we can also say that the Supreme Person created everything without restricting it to a universe or a heaven and earth within that universe. Factually, we don't know all that exists. We can also accept that we may never know. But we can accept a hierarchy of more and less complete persons as the solution to the problem of circular definitions. This is then the logical evidence for many temporary demigods and eternal but partial forms of God. This process also establishes the necessity of the feminine form of divinity as the method of dividing the whole into parts and establishing a relation between the whole and the part. Logically speaking, the whole is the father, the part is the child, and the connection between the whole and the part is the child's mother.

Finally, since each person can be defined in many ways—both temporary and eternal—it establishes the possibility of continuous redefinition of the self in different ways as parts of different wholes until one arrives at the unchanging eternal definition, which is the process of reincarnation of the person.

Objective vs. Personal Ideas of Whole and Part

It is important at this juncture to define the meaning of whole and part. We can begin with the whole-part idea in the case of objects and then demarcate it from the whole-part idea in the case of persons. If one object is inside another object, then it cannot be outside that object. However, if a person is inside another person, he is at once outside the person. We can take the example of one person observing another person. The observed person is inside the consciousness of the observer and yet the observed person is outside the observer. The outside connotation of a person arises because each person is free. The inside connotation of a person arises if they agree to be bound by the will of another person. When two persons willingly look at each other, they have willingly agreed to be inside each other. But because they can will a change, hence, they are potentially free and therefore outside each other. Inside simply means being controlled by another person. Outside simply means independent of other persons.

Thus, we define a hierarchy based on persons rather than objects. In this hierarchy, the higher-level person controls lower-level persons, and hence, the lower level is inside the higher level. However, the lower-level person can choose to be free and therefore he is outside the higher-level person.

We can never describe this whole-part theory in object logic because two things can never be both inside and outside in object logic. We can never subsume this whole-part theory in binary logic because one thing can never be both inside and outside another thing in binary logic. Thereby, we can never describe persons in object and binary logic. Since persons are the only ontology in reality, we can never describe anything in binary and object logic. This is the fundamental problem of modern science in which every scientific theory created to date has been (a) incomplete and (b) inconsistent with other incomplete theories. Each theory is incomplete because it tries to model a person as a different kind of object. Each theory is inconsistent with other theories because each theory employs a different object concept incompatible with other object concepts. This problem can never be solved until we shift modeling from objects to persons. There are many kinds of persons, compatible with some other persons. This compatibility between persons is the hierarchy of persons. A new logic—which we can call non-binary logic—must be constructed to describe persons instead of objects. It will allow each person to be simultaneously inside and outside other persons.

Non-binary conditions are essential for all knowledge. For example, if I observe an apple, then the apple is inside my consciousness, otherwise, I don't know the apple. Conversely, the apple must also be outside my consciousness, otherwise, my experience would be just a hallucination. Then, my consciousness must be inside the apple for me to know the apple. And yet, because I can focus my consciousness on something else, therefore, it must be outside the apple. The proposition that "I choose to see an apple" requires four conditions—(a) the apple is inside me, (b) the apple is outside me, (c) I am inside the apple, and (d) I am outside the apple. Any less, and we don't have the choice of knowing.

Problems With Current Proofs of God's Existence

The scientific problems of logic and entanglement are not separate from the philosophical problems of knowledge and consciousness. These philosophical problems are in turn not separate from the religious problems of the existence of God and the relation between soul and God. The separation between science, philosophy, and religion is the gift of object thinking rooted in binary logic. If we change that to person-based thinking rooted in non-binary logic, then all problems disappear at once.

Most people crafting arguments for the existence of God at present operate under the separation of science, philosophy, and religion. They believe that they can construct an argument for God's existence without thinking about logic, entanglement, knowledge, consciousness, whole, and part. This is because arguments for the existence of God have an Abrahamic history, which in turn adopted Aristotelian logic as the foundation of its rationality and thereby the conception of thing-in-itself individuals.

Most people trying to prove God's existence assume thing-in-itself individuals bypassing person hierarchy. They don't establish the meaning of personhood. They don't establish the existence of more and less complete persons. They don't delve into the hierarchy of persons. They leap into discussing the Supreme Person without prior defining supremacy or personhood. When the individual terms in "Supreme Person" are undefined then the composite term is also meaningless.

For instance, the Ontological Argument for God's existence says that a perfection that exists is more perfect than one that does not. However, no definition of perfection is given. Depending on one's personal conception of perfection, the purported "God" could be Indra, Manu, Brahma, Shiva, Viṣṇu, and so on, because perfection is undefined. This is how some people have earlier come to the conception of the Supreme Person as the creator of heaven and earth although there are trillions of such creators. Similarly, there is no justification for why perfection has to be a person. Can perfection not be a computer computing mathematical formulas? So-called proofs of God's existence have many holes because neither perfection nor personhood are defined. Their necessity is also not established. This is because the proof for the existence of God doesn't begin in self-realization.

Why Vedic Society Never Gave Proofs of God

Arguments for the existence of God were never advanced in the Vedic system because the argument for the Vedic society was trivial—there is a whole person of which we are part persons. As long as we show that the part persons are not mutually separable, we have proved the existence of the whole person and hence God.

Vedic society was constructed as a single body. The parts of the body were inseparable. Even as there were higher and lower parts of the body, there was no oppression just like the head cares for the legs and the legs care for the head. The head and leg perform different roles without oppression. Within this society, great emphasis was placed on duties toward the members of the family and society. The family was also another body within the larger social body. The head of the family did not oppress the children nor did the children want to replace the head of the family. Without any philosophy, people growing up in a family or society understood the concept of the inseparability of persons. It was not individualism and it was not oneness. It was a family, a body, an organism. Thereby, practically nobody needed an argument for the existence of God because they thought of God as the head of the cosmic family. If we are not at war within the family, community, society, planet, and the universe, then there is a cosmic family, and it must have a head that unifies everything into a family. An argument for the existence of God is required when family and society have been fragmented by thing-in-itself individualism.

Those advancing arguments for the existence of God might want to study the Vedic system, specifically why such arguments were never advanced in the Vedic system, and why they became necessary in Christianity. The reason is that material things were described in the Vedic system using concepts of inseparability (such as the three modes of prakṛti that are co-defined hierarchically) whereas they were described as separate objects in the West since Greek times. When there are many separate things-in-themselves, then no such thing-in-itself needs God. Then you have to supply an argument for God's existence as yet another thing-in-itself but that argument is always tenuous because (a) nobody can see that thing-in-itself right now, and (b) a thing-in-itself needs no other thing-in-itself. Thereby, all religious dogmas have to be forced on people through institutional power. The moment people get freedom from such institutions, the first thing they would do is get rid of God. Atheism is the natural and logical conclusion that no thing-in-itself should require another thing-in-itself.

This is why when people turn against religion and God, they adopt one of two things. One, they rely on their powers of reason and observation to find the truth. Two, they turn toward a spiritual system that focuses on the self rather than God. This is because the self has been defined as a thing-in-itself. So, why should it need anything else?

Hegel's Failed Attempt to Revive Spirituality

Hegel is by far the only Western philosopher who tried to break away from Aristotelian orthodoxy. He postulated that God was a spirit that needed to see His own reflection. The world was supposed to be His reflection and by seeing it, God would cognize Himself. The world had to become a perfect reflection of God to fulfill His will. When that happened, it would mean the end of history. The problem with Hegel was that he never defined what God looked like and hence what His reflection must look like. Tyrants who followed Hegel elevated themselves to the level of God to shape society as their own self-reflection, using people to fulfill their personal imagery of grandiosity, producing totalitarian dictatorships.

The only contribution Hegel made to the history of philosophy is that God changed from thing-in-itself to a thing-for-itself. The inert God was replaced by a selfish God. Thus, Hegel failed to revive spirituality. This failure is the direct result of a person trying to produce philosophies without any self-realization. A person needs to realize the nature of the self as sat-chit-ānanda before he tries to speculate on the nature of God. If one cannot become good then he cannot know God. The bare minimum goodness is self-satisfaction. This is the meaning of ānanda. It is not complete ānanda, but it is enough that one doesn't need the ānanda from the world. The incompleteness in the ānanda experienced at this juncture drives a person toward distributing his current happiness. When happiness is distributed, it grows. The answer to the incompleteness of happiness is not seeking happiness. It is distributing happiness.

This is the juncture at which a person understands that God is distributing happiness rather than seeking happiness. His creation is meant to reflect His infinitely happy self in the world. He doesn't need the reflection to know Himself. He already knows Himself. But He is so happy with Himself that He wants to distribute this happiness to everyone. If one doesn't have this understanding and he talks about God seeking self-reflection in the world, he just encourages and motivates narcissistic psychopaths who try to elevate themselves to the status of God hoping to shape the world in their self-image because they need the world to give them happiness by becoming the extended arms of their selfish wills.

False Reliance on Ideas that Led to Atheism

Barring the disastrous failure of Hegel's philosophy, there have been no attempts to break away from the Aristotelian hegemony of thing-in-itself thinking. This is the foundation of modern physics, biology, economics, sociology, and politics. Every man for himself. Trust your mind and senses alone. Greed is religion.

Abrahamic faiths too have been crafted around the idea of a jealous God who doesn't tolerate other gods. God's jealousy has become the exclusivism and supremacism of Abrahamic faiths as they wage endless, lawless, and needless wars against each other and everyone else. Those who crafted these religions did not have the minimum goodness of self-satisfaction. They were fearful, envious, and hateful of others. Such people talking about God is just like Hegel talking about spirit. They have no self-realization.

So, how can they give insights into the nature of God? They simply project their jealousy onto God.

There were many good religions until a few thousand years ago. We call their followers pagans today. They encouraged family traditions, organized society as an organism, worshipped nature, and treated animals as members of their extended community. All these have been progressively destroyed initially by Greek thinking, then by Abrahamic faiths, then by modern science, and finally by Hegelian thinking and its Marxist and Communist offshoots. The result of this history of bad ideologies is atheism.

We cannot counter atheism by relying on ideas that have led to atheism. Trying to construct arguments for the existence of God using the same logic and theories that have previously led to atheism will change nothing even if they give us a feeling of intellectual accomplishment. We should try not to poison the nectar, just because everyone is used to drinking poison. We should reject the poison and focus on the nectar. The Vedic system is the sole surviving system distributing the nectar of self- and God-realization. That nectar can be enjoyed, for those who are eager for it, through science, philosophy, and religion.

Pagan religions were destroyed because they did not have science and philosophy, although they had good religious practices. The Vedic system was not destroyed because it has science and philosophy apart from good religious practices. The Vedic system is so morally, intellectually, and spiritually strong that it cannot be defeated. However, it can be forgotten, ignored, and marginalized by foolish people at the risk of their own unhappiness. And yet, people who want to go to heaven don't want to die to get there. Similarly, those who want to know God intellectually don't want to discard the false ideologies that have earlier led to atheism.

The Equivalence of Supreme Truth and Person

If we still want to prove God's existence, then we have to define God not as the Supreme Person, but as the Complete Truth, the Perfect Truth, and the Supreme Truth. The complete truth means that there is nothing outside of this truth. The perfect truth means that we don't need anything outside this truth. The supreme truth means that we can explain everything based on this truth. God's existence now becomes the question: Does truth exist? The proof of God's existence now involves showing the presence of complete, perfect, and supreme truth. The proof is just like saying that we are partial persons, not inseparable from each other, and hence, there is a complete person.

Now, "God exists" means "the perfect, complete, and supreme truth exists eternally". Since existence is equated to true (and not always truth, unless it is eternal existence), we can also rephrase this as "truth is eternally true". This truth is not a static idea, formula, equation, ideology, or theory because all these do not generate or control anything. Ideas never exist outside a person. Therefore, the truth is a person. The burden of proof that the truth is an idea, formula, equation, ideology, or theory lies on the person who believes in such claims. He cannot prove his suppositions. Therefore, we don't need to subject ourselves to unprovable standards of separating truth and personhood.

The Truth is Known Only by the Selfless Person

The proof of the existence of God rests on rejecting the long history of thing-in-itself and thing-for-itself thinking. The proof rests on each person realizing that they are things-for-something-else. Unless we can make this transformation, the proof may be logically correct but it will still be rejected by self-centered people. As we noted above, proofs are not contradictory to choice. It is only when people have become frustrated with their self-centered ideologies, will they seek an alternative. Then we can say that the best thing to become a thing for is the Supreme Person. We are not defined by ourselves. We are defined in relation to the Supreme Person. When we accept our definition to become a part serving the whole, through the hierarchy of better persons, then we become self-satisfied.

That is because the essence of the Supreme Person is distributing His happiness. Just by associating with Him, we become happy, quite like proximity to a happy person makes us happy. Don't ask God for anything other than His association, which can be had just by calling Him. He goes wherever He is called. We just have to learn how to call Him earnestly and lovingly. When we have His association, then we will not desire anything else. We will be filled with happiness. This is the juncture at which we can begin distributing our happiness, making others self-satisfied, and then distributors of happiness.

The invitation to the Vedic system is the offer to live this selfless life. The selfish life is a life of the struggle for survival. A selfless life is that of distributing happiness to increase that happiness, unceasingly and unendingly. Those who can understand the meaning and purpose of life, have self-realization, and then God-realization, can give arguments for the existence of God because they are talking about the existence of something they understand. Everyone else should try to understand God before arguing for His existence. There are no counters for the arguments that are accurately rooted in the true understanding of God. There is no value in arguments without such an understanding.

Who Are Āditya, Rudra, and Vasu?

The Big Picture of Vedic Cosmology

The universe in Vedic cosmology is divided into three parts—upper, middle, and lower, as follows: (1) Four upper realms, called Mahar, Jana, Tapa, and Satya, (2) Three middle realms, called Bhu, Bhuvar, and Svarga, and (3) Seven lower realms, called Tala, Atala, Vitala, Talātal, Mahātala, Rasātala, and Pātāla.

Three groups of deities—Āditya, Rudra, and Vasu—who are collectively called *deva*, or demigods, are controllers of the middle realm. They live in Svarga and Bhuvar, and control Bhu. The control of the upper and lower realms is not discussed in the Vedic texts at any great length because the readers of these texts are the inhabitants of Bhu, the lowest of the three in the middle part of the universe.

In Vedic cosmology, we always talk about living *in* a place, not living *on* a place. For example, we don't live *on* Earth. We live *in* Earth. A place of living is not strictly a planet (we live on a planet rather than in a planet). It is just a place (we live in a place and not on a place). This is just like our body. We live in the body and not on the body. When we live *on* something, then we are controllers, dominators, rulers of that thing. When we live *in* something, then we are controlled, dominated, and ruled by that thing. We are not free. The body or place is a prison. It has trapped us and limited our freedom. It is bondage. The moment we talk about living *in* a place or body, the immediate next question is: How to get out of this bondage? The discussion of cosmology, therefore, naturally initiates the discussion of liberation. If this curiosity is not immediately sparked, then there is something wrong with our understanding.

The soul can move from one place to another, one body to another, in the material world. Through such change, it sometimes becomes the controller and at other times the controlled. The lower part of the universe is controlled by demons and the middle part by demigods. The control of demigods is meant to make and keep a person moral. The control of demons is meant to make and keep a person their slave. Demigods reward morality and punish immorality. Demons reward when their self-interest is served and punish when their self-interest is violated. Demons enforce self-serving laws upon others whereas demigods enforce moral laws upon others. As one comes under the control of demons, he works for their pleasure. As one comes under the control of demigods, he works morally. The laws of the demons are flexible—they keep changing to whatever is convenient for them. The laws of the demigods are rigid—they always concord with the contextual and individual application of universal moral principles.

Morality is the basis of spirituality. As one becomes obedient to the demigods, he becomes moral and progresses to spirituality. He eventually gets liberated from the control of both demigods and demons. He develops self-control instead of being controlled by demigods. He serves the Supreme Lord instead of the demons. It is almost impossible to get liberated under obedience to the demons because they keep a person immoral. It is also very hard for demigods to themselves get liberated because they keep enjoying controlling others, although to keep them moral. So, the best place for liberation is where one is neither controlled by the demons nor a controller like the demigods. That place is the middle of the universe, called Bhu. It is the best place in the universe for those interested in pursuing liberation from the world.

Varied Systems of Civilizational Gods

In the Vedic texts, there are many *classes* of higher beings—Apsarā, Gandharva, Chāraṇa, Deva, Siddha, Asura, Devarṣi, Manu, Prajāpati—that total 330 million. They are higher and lower controllers within the middle realm of the universe. We can call them the members of a cosmic government. The order in the nature we experience is the result of this government rather than the so-called laws of nature.

There aren't many laws of nature in the Vedic texts. There is just one law—choice and responsibility. As you sow, so shall you reap. Those in the government are reaping the results of good deeds they have sown. They have been given power over others because they are moral, pious, and dutiful, for the most part. They make mistakes occasionally, for which they suffer immensely, including being evicted from Bhuvar and Svarga and being forced to take birth in Bhu. Their position is not eternal. It can be taken away if they become immoral. It is definitely taken away when the results of their good deeds are finished. Hence, there is no tolerance for misconduct. You cannot get more than your due. The order in nature is maintained by the demigods due to their extraordinary diligence and dutifulness.

The Vedic system of demigods existed formerly in all parts of the world and became their system of gods. This includes Greek gods, Roman gods, Nordic gods, Celtic gods, Egyptian gods, Sumerian gods, Assyrian gods, Canaanite gods, Ugarit gods, Babylonian gods, Aztec gods, Mayan gods, and possibly many more. If we try to correlate the deities of demigod religions, we see cross-cultural similarities because these are based on a cosmic government. For example, there are deities of natural elements such as ether, air, fire, water, and earth. There are deities of truth, beauty, and justice. There are deities of different directions that represent qualities and activities. There are significant commonalities between these deities.

But we also see differences arising out of local events and geographic conditions in which these religions were practiced. Since natural events were attributed to gods, as unique events occurred in varied places, the gods acquired additional traits and characteristics. For example, in places where sea routes were also commercial routes, the god of seas was also called the god of commerce. In places where storms caused great destruction, the destruction god was called the child of the storm god. In places where prosperity led to war and war led to prosperity, the goddess of war and prosperity became one and the same. In places where tornados were common, the wind god was depicted with circular wings. In places where red-colored birds flew in the east, the god of the east was depicted in ruddy clothes and decorations.

A cross-cultural comparative analysis of traditional deities reveals the presence of both common and unique traits. The latter makes the cross-cultural analysis harder but not impossible. We have to look for both common and unique traits. We have to understand how the unique traits arose due to local events and geographical circumstances. It is difficult but important for reasons that we will now turn to.

Failures of Mathematical Modeling

This desire to see the will of the gods in the world was overturned by Abrahamic religions. They claimed that the world works according to mathematical laws rather than the will of God. However, all mathematical laws are indeterministic, probabilistic, and incomplete. They cannot explain everything in the domain they are applied to. Many conflicting laws are required to explain observations in different domains. Each law is incomplete and together they are inconsistent. The universe governed by mathematical laws is also irrational. If God made these laws, then He wasn't a rational thinker. If the universe sprung out due to mathematics, then it is devoid of meaning, purpose, and morals and not fully intelligible.

The attempt to replace gods with mathematics has failed. Mathematical laws cannot solve the problem that scientists had set for them—explain natural occurrences based on mathematics rather than the will of the gods. In fact, attempts at such substitution ended up replacing a dozen gods with hundreds of laws. Concordance and dissonance between these laws is no better than the love and hate relations between the gods which mathematical laws were supposed to end. Many centuries have been spent trying to change the model of natural causation from the will of gods to mathematical laws. The failure of this experiment has put us back to where we were—i.e., without a model of natural explanation.

The order in nature controlled by gods was moral. Things that happened in a society were correlated to the actions of the people in them. The model stated that if people were moral then societies would prosper. Immoral societies would decline. This is true. A society's longevity, prosperity, and strength depend on morality. Therefore, even if people were wrong about which god caused which event, the long-term broader societal trends were correct. Mistakes in natural explanation did not cause a social collapse. A society guided by such explanations could still be long-lived, prosperous, and strong.

This is not an endorsement of people trying to create speculative connections between natural events and the will of gods. It is rather an articulation of the fact that attempts to replace the will of gods with mathematical equations are worse. Through such attempts, science removed meaning, purpose, and morality from nature and life. Even if technology improved, life became immoral, meaningless, and purposeless. The programs of science produced improved machines and primitive humans.

The theoretical problem with mathematical laws is that all laws are inconsistent and incomplete. They cannot be called rationality. They cannot be true. The practical problem for those relying on these laws to guide and run society is that they will run their society into the ground after destroying it morally. Hence, understanding the cosmic governance system of gods is both a rational and moral necessity. We can call these the depersonalized and personalized models of natural explanation, respectively.

Vedic Description of Material Bodies

The depersonalized system of causation rests on an object, property, and force model of reality. Objects have properties, which exert forces on other properties, which cause the objects to move or change. Modern science has created many such object, property, and force models of causation. In contrast, the personalized system of causation rests on a six-fold understanding of persons. The will of the person is the object, the intention, emotion, cognition, conation, and relation are the person's properties, and a life force—called prāṇa—acting under the control of the person and his properties is the force.

A willing person is the same in material and spiritual realms. But the person's properties (i.e., intention, emotion, cognition, conation, and relation) along with the life force (i.e., prāṇa) become material. In the spiritual realm, the person defined by his will regains his own properties and the life force. Thus, the same person (i.e., the embodiment of will) goes between material and spiritual realms. A person's body is produced from the five properties when the prāṇa acts on these properties. Thereby, a person gains or loses different bodies in the material realm and regains an eternal body in the spiritual realm.

The use of the term body in the singular is misleading. Vedic texts discuss multiple bodies, layered on top of each other, like the layers of an onion, the outer layers being produced from the inner layers. While there are many systems of classifying these bodies, I prefer the four-fold system (because it is the most comprehensive) called kāraṇa-śārīra, sūkṣma-śārīra, liṅga-śārīra, and sthūla-śārīra. These are translated as causal body, subtle body, gendered body, and gross body. The causal body is the unconscious realm, the subtle body is the preconscious realm, the gendered body is the subconscious realm, and the gross body is the conscious realm. Matter is layered from the unconscious to the conscious. Those interested in a detailed discussion of these different bodies can refer to the classical text called Sāñkhya Sūtra.

Each of these bodies is progressively manifest from the soul by the effect of prāṇa. The previous body is the cause and the later body is the effect. The soul is the object and the bodies are its properties. The properties are produced by aggregating material elements under the soul's presence. The same soul can get many bodies just like one object can have many properties. The cause of these bodies (i.e., the soul) and the effects of the cause (i.e., the bodies) are embedded within each other in Sāñkhya. Hence, each of the bodies is distinct from the other bodies and yet inseparable from them. The soul is also inside each of these bodies and yet outside all of them. The mutual embedding of the cause and the effect is the root cause of material entanglement. The soul is entrapped by the body. Hence, by controlling the body, the soul can be controlled because the soul is inside the body. Becoming free of this entanglement requires us to realize that the soul is *also* outside the bodies, and can therefore control them.

Thus, there is a distinction between a bounded soul and a liberated soul. The liberated soul can control his body because he sees himself outside these bodies. The bounded soul is controlled by his body because he sees himself embedded in the body. Even though everyone is originally a free person, they are not currently free, unless they can see themselves as distinct from the body. Typically, nobody is born free. However, they can earn back their freedom through the processes of extricating themselves from the four bodies. This extrication is the primary goal of human life called the quest for liberation.

The Hierarchy of Natural Controls

The bodies we consider our own are just like puppets in the hands of puppeteers—the demigods. The bodies of the demigods are also puppets in the hands of higher-level puppeteers. As we have discussed, there are several levels of control in the universe. They are the levels of puppets and puppeteers.

The whole universe is described as an animal dragged by a rope—a different analogy to describe the puppet and puppeteer scenario. The universe is called Paśu (animal), the master of the animal is called Paśupati, and the rope binding the Paśu to the Paśupati is called the Pāśa of material nature. The Paśupati is Cosmic Time. The rope that binds the animal is Pāśa of material nature. The living entity bound by these ropes is the Paśu or the animal. The situation is pretty grim. We are animals dragged by the rope of nature under the control of time. Even the demigods are not free. They are animals dragging other animals under the control of nature and time. The goal of life is to become free of the desire to attain higher- or lower-level animal status.

In the middle of the universe, the controlling system is divided into three categories called Āditya, Vasu, and Rudra, as we have noted earlier. Together they are the 33 primary demigods from the perspective of Bhu (i.e., our plane of existence). They are also puppets in the hands of higher-level puppeteers. But their rule establishes morality rather than selfishness, which slowly takes a person to spirituality.

The Evolution of Natural Explanation

Classical cultures in different parts of the world took one part of this complex system—Āditya, Vasu, or Rudra—and considered it to be the only system of cosmic control. Over time, they removed higher levels of control and the demigods became independent gods. Under Abrahamic religions, this moral government was replaced by the rulership of a Monotheistic God. The bigger problem was that monotheistic religions rationalized, justified, and normalized violence against nature, animals, and humans. Immorality became common. Science gave greater power to violent tendencies and even greater violence was unleashed on nature, animals, and humans.

Without this big picture, we cannot understand the global trajectory of religion, philosophy, and science. Conversely, understanding this big picture reveals the lessons of history. First, the hierarchy of control cannot be flattened to claim that demigods are independent controllers; if we do so, we will get many independent controllers destroying the unity of the cosmic government and the understanding of natural order. Second, only one part of the system—Āditya, Vasu, or Rudra—cannot be selected while rejecting others; doing so will result in inadequacies to compensate for which, more traits will have to be added, creating even more confusion. Third, all these gods cannot be replaced by a Monotheistic God because each personality controls different aspects of reality; if we merge all controllers into one, then the single controller will become unintelligible. Fourth, the Monotheistic God cannot be worshiped without morality; no genuine system of spirituality can exist without morality; if morality is discarded, then people will degrade themselves instead of progressing spiritually. Fifth, nature is governed by persons and not equations; if we replace persons with equations, all laws will be collectively inconsistent and individually incomplete.

No present education system teaches us this comprehensive picture of religion, philosophy, and science. Modern science begins with mathematical laws. Abrahamic religions with a Monotheistic God. Diverse traditional cultures across the world are incommunicado due to ignorance of their commonalities and shared origins.

They have forgotten their traditional system of religion as these were belittled during colonial times and their followers were forcibly converted. They are ignorant about the rational and moral problems of the mathematical modeling of nature. The Vedic system is fragmented into numerous competing schools as a result of its internal problems.

And yet, there is no reason for despair if we understand the big picture of religion, philosophy, and science. That helps us comprehend history. It helps us to bring seemingly unrelated pieces together. The task is still not trivial. But it becomes conceivable and feasible with the picture. If the big picture exists, then different pieces of the puzzle can potentially fall into the right places over time and with effort.

Vedic Deities and Abrahamic Religions

Some years ago, I wrote Cosmic Theogony, describing how pagan religions preceded Abrahamic religions. They worshipped one part of the system of demigods before they shifted to monotheism. The ancestors of Jews worshipped Vasu personified as seven stars. The ancestors of Christians worshipped Āditya personified as the Sun in Mithraism and the Twelve Olympians of Greeks and Romans. The ancestors of Muslims worshipped Rudra personified as Allah with three consorts Allat, Mannat, and Al-Uzza.

The monotheistic religions did not have common ancestry during pagan times. They did not identify with each other culturally or ethnically. Their interconnections were conjured with the desire to create an alternate lineage, ancestry, and history of monotheism separate from pagans. The monotheists wanted to wash their hands off the pagans from whom they had evolved. They claimed to be the original people of God. They claimed that God gave them monotheism, which the pagans subsequently corrupted.

The facts were just the opposite—the pagan religions worshipped multiple deities with one supreme deity. There was no pagan religion without multiple deities and a supreme deity. The monotheists made the pagan supreme deity their monotheistic deity and abrogated all others. Thereafter, they claimed that they were the original civilization created by their monotheistic deity, and the pagans who came after them had corrupted their true religion by adding many deities. Since this fictional history was factually the opposite of what had truly happened, monotheists either violently converted or killed the pagans.

False Claims of Abrahamic History

Abrahamic supremacist attitudes rest on one claim—they were the *original* people of God and pagans corrupted their religion. Facts of history disprove this over and over—(a) pagan religions existed all over the world thousands of years before the Abrahamic religions arrived, (b) all of these worshipped many deities along with a supreme deity, (c) pagan religions shared many commonalities showing a common ancestral origin, (d) all Abrahamic religions elevated the local pagan deity to the supreme deity so they took from the pagans rather than pagans taking from them, (e) the result of elevating the local pagan deity to the supreme deity created differences between the different monotheistic religions when such differences should not exist if there was just one monotheistic deity, and (f) Abrahamic history is a false tale of independent origination and the truth is evolution of monotheism out of pagan religions.

The Abrahamic religions have been propagating a false history for so long that it has become the default folklore. They believe that civilized humans did not exist before 6000 years ago, the farthest point in their history. They try to minimize everyone else's history to make them fit theirs. Colonialists invented the Aryan Invasion Theory to reduce Vedic history to under 6000 years. They belittle older civilizations to prove their superiority and claim that no advanced civilization existed on earth before their arrival.

Secular historians and archeologists have now conclusively established an alternative history. They show the presence of other civilizations from which Abrahamic religions took their ideas. The Jewish Yahweh is the Greek Zeus. The Ten Commandments are taken from the Egyptian Book of the Dead. The stories of people dying and resurrecting existed before Jesus. Christmas was the harvest festival in Europe 1600 years ago. The Sun god was worshipped as he went into Capricorn, a festival still celebrated in India as Makar Saṅkrānti. Allah had three wives, and one of them called Allat was symbolized by the moon, the crescent, and worshipped through cubic stone deities. The worship involved offering barley items and circumambulating the cubic deities. The concept of covenants was taken from Babylonia. The idea of Messiah and Apocalypse came from Zoroastrianism. Herodotus had created the trend of using fake triumphalist stories as factual histories for nationalistic propaganda.

The central ideas in all Abrahamic religions are plagiarized. They are either not divine revelations or God had already revealed them to others before the messiahs and/or religions arrived. The messiahs and/or religions took preexisting material and called it *their* divine revelation. The destruction of older societies, the trend of writing false belittling histories of other civilizations to expound one's superiority, and the insularity toward other cultures and civilizations, greatly elongated the ignorance of history. Most people did not know the extent of theft and appropriation and did not suspect any wrongdoing. They thought that their scriptures were revelations by God to His messiahs. These claims do not work anymore because historical information is now readily accessible. Historians and archeologists are now discovering the facts and the picture is completely different. A need to rewrite the history of the world has arisen with the discovery of grand historical deceptions.

The Actual History of the World

The historical truth is that India is the source of all prominent world religions. Different societies took different parts of the Vedic system of deities, then added, modified, and evolved their systems to adapt them to their local context. The divergences grew over time, but not enough to completely wipe out the common source. To see the commonalities, we have to compare the world religions to the Vedic system of deities. To unite them into a common understanding, we have to understand the unity in the Vedic system. By understanding the unity, and who took which part of that unity, we can harmonize them.

This is not hard because a single idea binds Vedic texts—that reality is personal. The order in the universe is not due to impersonal mathematical laws. That order exists because the universe is run by a government. The members of this government may be in powerful positions, but they are persons and they control persons. All persons are defined in the same way as the triad of *sat-chit-ānanda*. These three are the causes of three material *guna* called *sattva, rajas,* and *tamas,* which are personified in Viṣṇu, Brahma, and Shiva. These three are in turn the controllers of Āditya, Vasu, and Rudra, who are in turn the primary members of the cosmic government controlling the persons living in Bhu.

The question is: How does a government control? The answer is: It creates laws, rewards those who follow the laws and punishes those who don't. If the laws are very complex—as indeed morality is—then we replace the law with knowledge. If the laws controlling people are based on the contextual and individual application of universal moral principles, then knowledge pertains to the order in nature. Nature rewards and punishes. Most people consider reward order and punishment chaos. But they are simply two aspects of order for those who obey or disobey laws. Law is not whimsical if we know how nature works—i.e., the knowledge of morality and how it leads to reward and punishment.

The Tripartite System of Demigods

The Vasu personify the laws of nature. They are the sons and disciples of Brahma, also called the "mental sons" of Brahma. They personify Vedic knowledge, and so they are also known as Brahmarṣi, or Brahma's sages. In the cosmos, they are the seven stars, circumambulating the pole star. These are their places of residence. Collectively, they are called the eight Vasu. Typically, in each Manavantara (a period of 71 x 4,320,000 solar years) the Vasu change. However, the 8th Vasu called Dhruva (residing in the polestar) is blessed by Lord Viṣṇu to rule for a very long time. Hence, the Vedic texts talk about the seven sages named Gautam, Vasiṣṭha, Atri, Kaśyapa, Bhārdwaja, Viśvāmitra, and Jamdagni. Brahma divided the Veda into seven portions and distributed it among these seven sages for dissemination, after receiving it from Viṣṇu. Subsequently, these sages became the primary teachers from whom knowledge was disseminated all over the universe.

Viṣṇu, Brahma, and the eight Vasu are the teachers of morality or natural law.

The Āditya personify rewards. They are twelve in number. One human year (calculated as 360 instead of 365 days) constitutes one day of their life. They live for 100 years based on this calculation, which means 36,000 years. Āditya are sons of Aditi, who is the wife of Kaśyapa, one of the above seven sages. Being the children of one of the Vasu, they are thus lower situated than the Vasus and hence subordinate to Brahma and Viṣṇu, the guru of the Vasu. The Āditya are worshipped in rituals and reward society based on their good deeds. Good deeds are just like money in the bank, which can be spent in many ways. One earns good deeds by their actions and then chooses to spend those deeds in different ways through ritual worship. Rituals stop working if people don't have good deeds because their situation is just like a person without money in the bank trying to choose how to spend it. Thus, an immoral society doing rituals is a waste of time. They have to earn before they can spend. The twelve Āditya control the delivery of twelve areas of material rewards. These are the twelve signs of the zodiac, with each sign denoting a different kind of material reward.

The Rudra personify punishments. They are subordinate to Shiva who is the cosmic deity of destruction. Of course, destruction is not always bad; the destruction of evil is good. Therefore, Rudra are not evil, although they are depicted in horrific forms. The prescribed forms of Rudra worship in the Vedic texts pertain to the destruction of evil. It could mean the destruction of demons or the destruction of one's evil tendencies. Through the worship of the deities of destruction, persons and societies are purified of evil. The Rudra number eleven. Together with Shiva, they are counted as twelve. They denote twelve areas of destruction, counterparts of the twelve areas of rewards. Rudra assist the Āditya in wars with demons. The sinful deeds are punished by the Rudra through destruction. Then if we get the knowledge of Vasu, and want the boons of Āditya to reestablish the natural law, we can worship the Āditya again.

The Vedic texts describe two Ashvin, also called Ashvini-Kumāra, who personify the knowledge of how to keep a healthy mind and body. And yet, they are not included among the Vasu.

The knowledge of health and healing has been separated from the study of dharma and liberation in the Vedic tradition. This knowledge is called Ayurveda and excluded from the Samhita, Upaniśad, Purana, Itihāsa, Tantra, and Darśan. Surya and Chandra—two of the twelve Āditya—deliver the results of good deeds as bodily and mental health respectively. Thus, by exclusion from the group of Vasu and Āditya, Ashvin are spoken of as a separate category of deities. But this knowledge has always prevailed in the traditional Vedic society in the form of foods, cooking, spices, medicines, clothing, housing, routines, conduct, and recreation that we call Vedic culture. Culture is the science of mind-body health. It is distinct from duty and liberation and yet knowledge. Some people like to take the knowledge of duty and liberation without the Vedic culture. Hence, we can include the Ashvin among the category of knowledge or law without calling them the Vasu. Along with Viṣṇu, Brahma, and eight Vasu, the Ashvin constitute the twelve divisions of knowledge.

This is then the basic structure of the Vedic government. The twelve Āditya, the eleven Rudra, the eight Vasu, and the two Ashvin constitute 33 demigods. When Viṣṇu, Brahma, and Shiva are added, they are counted as 36. Each of these has a feminine consort. If we add them, then they are counted as 72. By their combination, many other demigods are produced. However, they are all subordinate to these 72 deities. We could call them the staff, secretaries, and assistants in the government departments.

Confusions Regarding the Demigods

Too much or too little of any material thing is bad. Thereby, even as Āditya give rewards, they can also give punishments by increasing or decreasing what we call a reward. For example, sunlight is a reward. But too much or too little of it is a punishment. Rain is a boon. But floods and droughts are a curse. Similarly, pestilence and plague are never a boon. But if they destroy a bad society, they are not evil. Earthquakes are never a boon. However, if they destroy an evil empire, they are truly good. This is a source of great confusion about demigods and the key reason why they are not understood.

To understand the workings of demigods, we have to understand duty. It involves (a) doing the right thing, (b) not overdoing it, and (c) not underdoing it. While doing a duty, one must try to uphold the principles of truth, kindness, austerity, and cleanliness. If all principles cannot be upheld, then the least bit of sacrifice to the least number of principles must be accepted in the interest of upholding all four principles for greater times, places, situations, and persons. Duties and principles are violated due to convenience: (a) it is convenient to not do the duty, (b) it is convenient to only do the duty partially, (c) it is convenient to do more than the duty, and (d) it is convenient to do something other than the duty. When duties are not done properly, due to considerations of convenience, then (a) bad things happen while trying to do good things, and (b) good things happen while trying to do bad things.

When good and bad outcomes are mixed as the result of overdoing or underdoing duties, disregarding the collective importance of moral principles, and focusing on convenience, then demigods of reward also deliver punishment and the demigods of punishment also deliver rewards. The society that loses the understanding of the complexities of duties, and simply focuses on demigods, over time gets confused about the nature of these demigods. It starts adding and removing demigod attributes while trying to explain natural outcomes based on demigod attributes, overlooking its role in demigod actions.

The situation can be compared to an ordinary thing like a pen. Ideally, it is a pen. But non-ideally, it is also a toy, weapon, paperweight, and doorstop. It is not incorrect to say that a pen is infinite other things, although not all conceivable things. But it is ideal to say that a pen is ideally just a pen. The ideal or non-ideal behavior of a pen depends on how we want to use it. In the same way, both God and demigods are ideally one thing, but non-ideally infinite other things. That ideal or non-ideal behaviors are the result of our ideality or non-ideality. The non-ideal outcomes tell us that we have been non-ideal, rather than God or demigods being non-ideal. The ideal outcomes tell us that we have been ideal and so God or demigods are just reciprocating our ideality. If the understanding of our ideality declines, then the ideal understanding of demigods and God declines and many non-ideal attributes are added to them while removing many ideal attributes. The non-ideal person misrepresents the ideal person.

The understanding of demigods cannot be divorced from that of duty. If the latter is perfect, then the former is perfect. Unfortunately, when people start worshipping God or demigods, they overlook their duties and think that God or demigods have the *power* to overcome their shortcomings. Their focus shifts from their duties to the power of God or demigods. As God and demigods reward and punish based on our ideality or non-ideality, our non-ideal conduct results in non-ideal outcomes which are then attributed back to God or demigods. Many societies deviated from the perfect understanding of God and demigods due to a decline in their understanding of duty. Depravity resulted in deprivation. Abrahamic religions attributed this deprivation not to their depravity but to God's power. Instead of making themselves more moral, these religions made God violent, selfish, and narrow-minded.

Personal vs. Impersonal Law Systems

The solution to all such problems lies in the understanding of morality and duty. This is the real law of nature. It is a natural law and a moral law. A single law covers natural, social, and moral spheres. At present, modern science describes natural order in terms of impersonal mathematical laws. These are also called *descriptive* as opposed to *normative* laws. European Enlightenment posited that natural laws were only descriptive while human laws (both social laws and moral laws) were normative. However, classical societies did not separate natural law from social and divine law. They did not think that descriptive laws were different from normative laws. All laws were normative. Nature was reward and punishment. It was a reward if we followed the law. It was punishment if we disobeyed the laws. It was understood that if society does not punish criminals, then nature will do so. The earthly government had to abide by the cosmic government. If it created its whimsical laws, it became a criminal for the cosmic government.

Abrahamic cultures borrowed the Greek system of depersonalizing nature. Greeks retained the natural elements called Earth, Water, Fire, and Air, but removed their demigods. They tried to model their behavior mathematically. Aristotle said that morality could not be known rationally. Only geometrical shapes were rational knowledge. It meant that there was no natural, rational, and definite system of morality. Different societies could choose their laws. Democracy was necessary to determine the social laws. Thereby, the truth was split into natural sciences and social sciences. The laws of natural sciences were universal. The laws of social sciences were local. This separation of natural and social laws, based on the depersonalization of nature using mathematics, was instrumental in the intellectual, cultural, and social destruction of pagan religions that were trying to live according to the cosmic government.

Abrahamic religions replaced *morality* with *ethics*. Morality is a contextual and individual application of universal principles. Ethics is laws created by a group of people to govern themselves. A small select group of people have always been involved in lawmaking. And yet, these laws are then forced upon the rest the society, including those who had no say in selecting the lawmakers. Nature, flora, and fauna are automatically excluded from the process of lawmaking. A select few people make all the laws.

This is why Abrahamic societies give so much emphasis to their elites, who are lawmakers. They make self-serving laws to accumulate power and oppress others. They don't worry about punishment since they made the laws to ensure they are not punished. When criminals make the laws, then we cannot expect society to become moral. This problem is as old as the Greeks. They dissolved the cosmic government. Now they are free to do as they please.

God is standing in front of everyone as nature's reward and punishment. They are not accidents of nature. Nor are they caused by mathematical equations. They are the result of demigods operating under God's will. All those who dissolve the cosmic government are atheists. They replace God's will with their own whimsical system of laws, including the false idea that God forgives their sins. Their whimsical system of laws makes everyone progressively nihilistic. After all, what goodness, truth, and morality will come out of mathematical laws? How will people trust their leaders if they are criminals? Why will they hope for happiness completely surrounded by suffering?

The discussion on Āditya, Rudra, and Vasu helps us understand how the natural system of duty and morality works. This understanding also makes us dutiful and moral. It is the first step toward true religion. It is also the first step toward happiness. Attempts to replace true religion with various cheating religions result in catastrophic failures. Those who fail catastrophically, use false propaganda to hide their failures. But that only delays the inevitable. It may make it harder to find the truth. But the truth is still accessible to those who seek it.

THE MEANING OF DEMIGODS

Recently a controversy has arisen regarding the use of the term *demigod*. In the Vedic texts, we find many kinds of powerful personalities, such as Apsarā, Gandharva, Chāraṇa, Deva, Siddha, Asura, Devarṣi, Manu, Prajāpati, etc.—that total 330 million. There are three forms called Viṣṇu, Brahma, and Rudra, who respectively embody the three *guna* called *sattva, rajas,* and *tamas,* respectively. In different places in the Vedic texts, some of them are sometimes called Bhagavān. At other times they are called Deva. Shiva is called Mahādeva. The Devas are often divided into 33 (Vasu, Aditya, Rudra, and Asvin).

European languages don't have this variety. The English word God comes from the German word *guđan,* whose origin is not certain. It probably means "the person to whom sacrifices are made". The word was picked up in the 6th century into English. Before that, the Latin *deus* was used. It meant divine or deity. Even before that, there was a Greek word *theós*. Similarly, Greeks used the word *hemitheoi* to mean half-gods. There is a Latin equivalent of this word too—*semideus*. These terms evolved into the English word demigod. They refer to the lower pagan deities, namely those born of gods and humans combining.

Before we come to the problem of mapping words in one language to those in others, let's discuss the meaning of Bhagavān. Viṣṇu Purāṇa 6.5.47 gives the below definition.

aiśvaryasya samagrasya
vīryasya yaśasaḥ śriyaḥ
jñāna-vairāgyayoś caiva
ṣaṇṇāṁ bhagam itīṅganā

The complete origin of (samagrasya) wealth (aiśvarya), power (vīrya), fame (yaśa), beauty (śriyaḥ), knowledge (jñāna), and renunciation (vairāgya), is respectfully or devotionally called (ṣaṇṇāṁ) Bhaga (bhagam) counted in this way (itīṅganā).

Bhagavān is also called satyam-param (Supreme Truth) and jñā-nam-advayam (Non-Dual Knowledge). The combination of these two kinds of descriptions is that knowledge is the primary trait while beauty, renunciation, power, wealth, and fame are secondary. We can also say that beauty, renunciation, power, wealth, and fame are traits of knowledge. The layering of traits results in multiple non-binary conditions, such as—the truth is beautiful but the beautiful is not the truth, the truth is powerful but the powerful is not the truth, the truth is famous but the famous is not the truth, the truth is renounced by the renounced is not the truth, and the truth is wealthy but the wealthy is not the truth.

The word *truth* (or knowledge) is not so simple. There is a metaphysics of truth, which means the description of what constitutes truth. In this metaphysics, truth is defined as that which is eternal. That which is not eternal can be *true* but not *truth*. For example, facts are true, but not truth. That is because facts are temporary and truth is eternal. The distinction between true and truth is not enough because there are infinite truths. Each ātmā is eternal, so it is a truth. But the ātmā is not param-satya or Supreme Truth.

How do we know the difference between truth and Supreme Truth? This is where the metaphysics of truth becomes important. The Supreme Truth is that which is also most beautiful, renounced, famous, powerful, and wealthy. Every truth is not on par with the Supreme Truth. Even as there are infinite truths, they are laddered from bottom to top based on the metaphysics of truth—i.e., a more beautiful truth, a more powerful truth, a more independent truth, a more complex truth, and a more pervasive truth is a higher truth. Infinite truths are stack-ranked all the way to the Supreme Truth—Bhagavān.

It is worth mentioning that the Vedic system doesn't accept the binary true-false condition. Rather, it accepts a stack ranking of truths from the Supreme Truth all the way to *apara-vidya* or inferior truths. Nothing is completely false. There is some truth even in the inferior truth. To understand this, we have to know that Bhagavān is called *samagrasya* of the six qualities above. He is the whole, the foremost, the original, and the complete. Everything else is a *part* of that *samagrasya*. A part is neither the whole nor zero. Hence, there is some truth, beauty, power, wealth, fame, and renunciation in everything. They cannot be called Supreme Truth. And they cannot be equated to the binary false condition. Binary logic has to be rejected to understand the ladder of truths. We will now turn to examples of this.

Brahma, Indra, Surya, Chandra, and many others are *occasionally* called Bhagavān. By and large, they are called Deva, Shiva is called Mahādeva, and Viṣṇu is called Bhagavān. This is based on the ladder of truths. The Supreme Truth is Bhagavān. A slightly lower truth is Mahādeva. An even lower truth is Deva. And yet, the term Bhagavān is sometimes used even for Mahādeva, Deva, and others even lower in the ladder, because the word Bhagavān denotes anyone with the six qualities. Even great sages are sometimes addressed as Bhagavān. Typically, however, the term is reserved for Lord Viṣṇu or Kṛṣṇa. Non-binary conditions are also seen when Viṣṇu or Kṛṣṇa are called *param-deva, param-iśvara, param-brahman,* and then in other places simply referred to as *deva, iśvara,* and *brahman.*

These problems are common across all hierarchical concepts. For instance, color includes yellow, yellow includes color, yellow is color, but color is not yellow. Knowledge, beauty, renunciation, power, wealth, and fame are concepts. They exist in full and in parts. The whole is in the parts, the parts are in the whole, the part is the whole, but the whole is not the parts. All problems of understanding arise due to the use of object modeling along with binary logic. This is the legacy of Greek thinking upon the world, particularly embedded in all European languages, taught to everyone as part of modern education, and become part of our vocabulary and thinking whenever we begin speaking European languages.

We can now talk about the words God and demigod. The assumption in all of Prabhupāda's writing is that God means Bhagavān, the complete persona of the six qualities. Generally, he uses this word to mean Viṣṇu and Kṛṣṇa. He uses the word demigod for everyone else. The word God denotes the whole and the word demigod denotes the parts. This whole-part theory is described in many places in Vedic texts, including the Bhagavad

Gita. I will cite three verses here to illustrate the point about whole and part, the source and emanation.

Bhagavad-Gita 10.8:
ahaṁ sarvasya prabhavo
mattaḥ sarvaṁ pravartate
iti matvā bhajante māṁ
budhā bhāva-samanvitāḥ

I am the source of all spiritual and material worlds. Everything emanates from Me. The wise who perfectly know this engage in My devotional service and worship Me with all their hearts.

Bhagavad-Gita 15.7:
mamaivāṁśo jīva-loke
jīva-bhūtaḥ sanātanaḥ
manaḥ-ṣaṣṭhānīndriyāṇi
prakṛti-sthāni karṣati

The living entities in this conditioned world are My eternal fragmental parts. Due to conditioned life, they are struggling very hard with the six senses, which include the mind.

Bhagavad-Gita 9.4:
mayā tatam idaṁ sarvaṁ
jagad avyakta-mūrtinā
mat-sthāni sarva-bhūtāni
na cāhaṁ teṣv avasthitaḥ

By Me, in My unmanifested form, this entire universe is pervaded. All beings are in Me, but I am not in them.

The *samagrasya* (the original complete) of six qualities is *sarvasya prabhavo* (producer of everything). All that has been produced is *mamaivāṁśo sanātanaḥ* (eternally His part). After producing, *mayā tatam idaṁ sarvaṁ jagad avyakta-mūrtinā* (He pervades all the produced things in an unmanifest form). All that is produced is *mat-sthāni sarva-bhūtāni* (situated within Him just like an object in space). Thus, the idea of whole and part is also described as a space (whole) and its objects (individual locations). The Vedānta Sūtra says that Brahman is space. Kṛṣṇa says He is the space. The objects within this space are His parts. They have a location within Him, just like each object has a unique location in space.

We cannot understand all these statements with object thinking and binary logic. For example, if we remove something from an object, the object is reduced, what is outside the object cannot be inside the object, the source cannot be present in the emanation, and there is no such thing as unmanifest form (something either exists or doesn't exist). But we can understand all these statements with concept thinking and non-binary logic. Yellow exists inside color. Color produces yellow. After producing yellow, color is not diminished. Color is present in yellow, which is why we say that yellow is color. Thereby, color is both outside and inside yellow. And yet, the immanent form of color in yellow is unmanifest. Finally, yellow is within color at a unique location. The part is known through that location.

Returning to God and demigod, they are nothing but whole and part. Kṣīrodakaśāyī Viṣṇu is a part of Garbhodakśāyi Viṣṇu, who is a part of Kāraṇodakaśāyī Viṣṇu, and this process goes in several steps and culminates in Kṛṣṇa, who is *sarvasya prabhavo* (producer of everything). He is *mat-sthāni sarva-bhūtāni* (the resting place of everything). Shiva is produced from Kāraṇodakaśāyī Viṣṇu. Brahma is produced from Garbhodakśāyi Viṣṇu. Rudra, along with Deva, are produced from Brahma. Whatever is produced is a part. The producer is the whole. In English, the producer can be called God, and the produced can be called demigod. People feel outraged that Deva and Mahādeva are called demigods, but their outrage is baseless. All Deva and Mahādeva are parts of Kṛṣṇa. Since Kṛṣṇa is the complete God hence Deva and Mahādeva are demigods. We have to know the descriptions of Bhagavad Gita to understand how this terminology is employed and why it is employed correctly.

The meaning of words depends on the context and the speaker. The words energy, momentum, particle, and wave mean something in physics and something else in ordinary language. Similarly, the word demigod means something in Western context and something else in Prabhupāda's books. Those who don't understand or cannot appreciate the contextuality of linguistic usage should demand a full refund of their school fees.

The Abrahamic God is not Bhagavān because—(a) God is defined as omnibenevolent, omnipotent, and omniscient, while Bhagavān is defined as the complete origin of knowledge, beauty, wealth, power, fame, and renunciation, (b) God creates the world from nothing (which is why it is called *ex nihilo*) while Bhagavān manifests the world from Himself, and thus, the world is not created but manifested, and (c) the created world is separate from God while the manifested world is eternally a part of Bhagavān.

The fact is also that all Abrahamic religions are derived from pagan religions, which in turn worshipped many deities with one supreme deity. The Abrahamic religions retained the local supreme deity and abrogated the other deities. The Jewish Yawheh is the Greek Zeus and the Vedic Indra. The Christian Deus is the European Mithra and the Vedic Surya. The Islamic Allah is the Greek Dionysus and the Vedic Shiva. Monotheism is not defined by a single well-known deity with common attributes and shared viewpoints. If that were indeed the case, monotheistic religions would not be waging wars on each other for two thousand years. Monotheism is rather defined by its antipathy to Polytheism prevalent in the local pagan religions of the time. Different kinds of monotheisms were created by elevating the local pagan supreme deity (Indra, Surya, or Shiva) to the absolute supreme deity. The Vedic system doesn't accept their supremacy. They are all demigods as far as the Vedic system is concerned. Abrahamic monotheisms are redacted polytheisms.

And yet, because monotheism uses God to *mean* the Supreme Person, the situation is complicated. The word God *de jure* means the Supreme Person although *de facto* it was derived by elevating demigods to the status of the supreme deity. Since there is no other *de jure* word for the Supreme Person, therefore, to translate anything in European languages, we have to use the word God. That is not Bhagavān, as we have shown above. And yet, there is no other synonym for Bhagavān in European languages, so God works as the best possible substitute. Likewise, there is no other word than demigod to indicate the fact that some deities are parts of the whole, and yet, bigger parts than ordinary living entities. We cannot capture the complexity of Apsarā, Gandharva, Chāraṇa, Deva, Siddha, Asura, Devarṣi, Manu, Prajāpati, Mahādeva, and so on in the word demigod. So, we do what we have to do, as best as we can. Those who find faults in this cannot do better.

The fact is that European languages don't have the equivalents for most Sanskrit words. Bhagavān is not God. Ātma is not soul. Prakṛti is not nature. Ākāśa is not space. Graha is not planet. Śraddhā is not faith. Dharma is not religion. Pratyakṣa is not empiricism. Nyāya is not logic. We will be hard-pressed to find one precise synonym. Therefore, if we are pedantic about the translations, then we should also stop translating Sanskrit texts into European languages. The receiving languages don't have synonyms. All dictionaries are misleading. They are creating caricatures of almost every important word and obscuring our understanding of Veda. To avoid these problems, we could stop all translations.

This is probably why the Vedic tradition has almost always been insular. It did not learn about others and it did not teach them about itself. If we don't share ideas, how can we share knowledge? Those who have become accustomed to one set of words and ideas cannot appreciate a completely different set of words and ideas. They have to give up their thinking to embrace Vedic thinking. People of other cultures are called Mleccha, Yavana, Khasa, Pulinda, and Kirāta in Vedic texts. Their ideologies are not discussed, their claims are not refuted, and their questions are not answered. They are not integrated. They are quietly ignored. After that, the Vedic tradition goes round and round within itself.

The criticisms from Indian traditionalists are based on this insularity. They think that since we have always been insular, therefore, we should continue being insular. It means, for example, that we should not use words like God and demigod. Rather, we must use words like Bhagavān and deva. Just as we had to learn English to know the Western culture, similarly, the West must learn Sanskrit to know the Vedic culture.

However, the great Acharyas have chosen to go beyond this insularity. They translate Sanskrit words into European language words, to give people something rather than nothing, because have a very long-term view of transformation. Spiritual perfection takes many lifetimes. A person comes to a path and makes a little progress. He then dies and is reborn in a place where he gets to make more progress. As he progresses, he develops a deeper interest. If he had previously read an English translation, he will now develop an interest in memorizing the Sanskrit verses. Over time, he will go deep into the meaning of each word and form. He will understand that these words mean something different. Then he will revise his ideas. But if we forced the Sanskrit verses down the gullet of a newcomer, he would never come to the perfect idea. The great Acharyas try to bring people to perfection over lifetimes. They know that perfection takes lifetimes.

The critics of Acharyas don't have a long-term view of spiritual transformation. They also don't have compassion. Veda for them is a cultural, geographical, and civilizational identity. It is not the eternal truth that transcends races, species, geographies, nations, planets, and universes. They think that they are owners of Veda rather than its servants. They bind Veda to a land, such as India. But Veda doesn't belong to India. Veda was given by Lord Viṣṇu to Brahma, who divided it into seven parts and gave each part to one sage for dissemination all over the universe. No money was charged for this dissemination. There were no limitations on that dissemination except a person's genuine interest. Lord Viṣṇu did not say to Brahma: Make sure you don't give knowledge to those who don't know Sanskrit.

The truth is not confined to one land or language. The truth is given by Lord Viṣṇu for everyone, and He wants the truth to be known by everyone. Those who receive the truth don't become exclusive owners of the truth. At most, they are servants of the truth. They serve the truth by spreading it. We must be like Lord Viṣṇu, Brahma, or the seven sages to distribute the truth. This means there has to be knowledge, and there has to be compassion to give that knowledge to others. Hoarding knowledge on the pretext of the Sanskrit language is antipathy to Lord Viṣṇu, Brahma, and the seven sages. The narrow-minded hoard the truth, while the broad-minded distribute it. By this distribution, they are blessed by Lord Viṣṇu, Brahma, and the seven sages. Through such blessings, they attain perfection. Those who hoard the truth don't attain perfection because they don't receive the blessings.

To understand this process, we must understand dharma or duty. What is duty? It is the best a person can do under the given time, place, and situation. If the person is limited by his ability, or the constraints of time, place, and situation, then he cannot do the *ideal*. Binary thinking will tell us to either do the ideal or not do anything at all. Dharma doesn't do that. It tells us—do the best that you can under the given constraints. Doing the non-ideal thus becomes *contextually ideal*. For instance, the general rule is that we must not lie. But when there is no alternative, then the least amount of lying is accepted as dharma to preserve the truth longer. Likewise, the general rule is that we must avoid violence. But when there is no alternative, then the least amount of violence is accepted as dharma to preserve kindness longer. The general rule is to be ideal. But when there is no other alternative, then non-ideality is accepted as dharma. Dharma is the *contextually ideal.*

Prabhupāda did dharma. He brought people to the Veda, transforming the lives of people the world over. But even during his time, he was constantly criticized by the Indian traditionalists. In India, there is a proverb that summarizes their attitude—*lakir ke fakir*—which means blindly repeating what has been done in the past. They don't know that one with knowledge must distribute it to the eager. That dharma is doing the best possible under the given circumstances. That a person is transformed over many lifetimes. That the truth is not confined to a location, race, or language. They don't have the spirit of Lord Viṣṇu, Brahma, or the seven sages, nor their blessings. This is why they cannot teach the people in the way they can understand it. They cannot respond to the new questions, problems, and ideologies that emerge continuously. Veda for them is books rather than knowledge. Books cannot adapt. But one who assimilates the books adapts to the changing times. He imparts the truth in new ways suited to the time, place, situation, and the person receiving the truth. Thereby, Veda expands, but the truth remains unchanged.

The system of blind repetition of the past is not new. It was formerly practiced by the caste Brahmanas. They claimed ownership of Veda. Anybody not born in their family could not understand or practice Veda. Their exclusivism led to Buddhism in India. Shankaracharya then appeared to defeat Buddhists but did not solve the problem that had led to Buddhism. He cured the symptoms of the disease rather than the disease itself. He limited Veda to the Upaniśads and the Vedānta Sūtra and stipulated that the students of these texts had to take Sannyasa. The ownership of Veda transferred from Brahmanas to Sannyasis. If there were a few Brahmanas, there were even fewer Sannyasis. Earlier it was a problem of birth in a caste. After that, it became the problem of the inability of most people to take Sannyasa.

The Bhakti Movement in India reversed these trends. Knowledge was for everyone. If they could not get knowledge through Upaniśads and Vedānta Sūtra, they could get it through Purāṇa and Itihāsa. Only Brahmanas could perform Vedic rituals. But everyone could sing the names of Lord Viṣṇu. Brahmanas and Sannyasis lost control over Veda. It became widely accessible. Sanskrit was not the most important truth. Bhakti was the most important truth. This is why the saints of the Bhakti Movement composed songs and books in numerous regional languages rather than just Sanskrit. The songs were devotional and philosophical. These two were not divorced. Nobody tried to precisely map each song to some verse in some Vedic text. They gave people what was required. Those with Bhakti knew Veda perfectly. Everyone else was mugging up verses while forgetting that Lord Viṣṇu gave Veda to Brahma. If He was the source of Veda, then why should He not be the object of Veda? The Vedic system was completely transformed by the Bhakti Movement.

Prabhupāda did for the world what the Bhakti Movement did for India. The absence of precision is not due to his ignorance or malice. The problem is that the receiving language doesn't have the concepts and words. Therefore, he tried to approximate it. That is dharma. However, the caste Brahmanas and impersonalist Sannyasis in India cannot stand it. They try to regain control over Veda by talking about linguistic purity. They have a problem if Veda is given to common people, in a way that they can understand it, appreciate it, and transform their lives gradually and progressively. Their exclusivism contracts the reach of Veda rather than expanding it. That is just like caste Brahmanas and impersonalist Sannyasis contracted the reach of Veda before the Bhakti Movement expanded it.

The caste Brahmanas and impersonalist Sannyasis have been complaining for centuries. They were complaining even during the Bhakti Movement. They think that only intellectuals know the truth, contrary to Bhagavad-Gita 18.55, where Kṛṣṇa says: *One can understand Me as I am, only by devotion. Thereafter, fully knowing Me by such devotion, he enters that infinite enjoyment.* The intellectuals can keep licking the jar of honey from the outside. They don't have devotion, so they cannot enter the jar. They try to grasp the taste of honey in their words, without knowing what it tastes like. The devotees of Viṣṇu are not here to serve the agendas of the intellectuals. They serve Viṣṇu. If a Viṣṇu devotee is curious, all questions can be answered based on logic, philosophy, and quotes. This is a service to Viṣṇu. It is not the ownership of Veda. We are servants and not owners.

God Is Greatness

God is great, is an oft-heard statement. It relies on a separation between the idea of greatness and the thing we call great. The idea is always "above" the thing, in the sense that it is used to judge whether something is great. In the case of God, the statement "God is great" requires that greatness be above God, used to judge God, and deem Him to be an example of greatness. The criterion to decide whether something is God rests on an idea separate from God, above God, and used to judge God.

The situation is comparable to saying "He is President". In this case, there is an idea of a president separate from the president. The idea defines the criterion for something to be called president, used to judge whether someone is president, and therefore, logically before someone being president. If the idea of the presidency was undefined, there could be no president. The idea is itself impersonal. Thereby, when we claim that someone is president, we are using something impersonal to judge the person.

The same problem arises if we say that Kṛṣṇa is all-attractive. Now, there is an idea of all-attractiveness which must be logically before Kṛṣṇa, used to judge Kṛṣṇa, before He can be called all-attractive. Since the idea is impersonal, therefore, the impersonal is used to define, judge, or know the person.

Ideas are called *tattva* or essences in Vedic texts; they represent some ideal. The things that embody these ideals are called *bhava* or existents, which are used to judge, assess, or classify something based on that ideal. However, the *tattva* is also a *bhava*. For instance, there is an ideal fire in Svarga (the heavenly planets) and there are instances of fire in Bhu (the earthly planets). The ideal fire in Svarga is called Agni—the demigod fire—and the instances of fire in Bhu are also called Agni, even though the earthly instances of fire are not ideal.

The non-ideal is a *part* of the ideal. For example, Agni is divided into many parts, based on the five elements, the five knowledge senses, the five action senses, the five life airs, the four parts of the internal instrument, etc. All together, they constitute the body of the demigod Agni. In the demigod, they are in their ideal state (perfect, complete, and strong). In the earthly instances, they are in a non-ideal state (imperfect, incomplete, and weak). Since everything has some Agni, therefore, Agni is part of everything. Since all those instances of Agni are parts of the body of the demigod, therefore, everything is a part of Agni.

The separation between ideas and things (which later became the separation of essence and existence) began in Platonism. There was an ideal in the Platonic World and instances of that ideal in the Real World. However, the *ideal* was just an *idea*. The *tattva* or essence was in the Platonic World but the *bhava* or existent was in the Real World. This is known as the form-substance dualism. The essence is the form and the existent is the substance. Mostly, no existent perfectly embodies the essence because nothing is ideal, even though we call those things by the ideal name. Hence, the Real World was called an imperfect reflection of the Platonic World.

However, the relation between the perfect and the imperfect was never formalized because it requires (a) the complexities of dividing the ideal into parts, and (b) understanding their complete, perfect, and strong state. Without this complexity, we can never determine the extent to which something is ideal and in which of the numerous ways. Since the complete was never divided into parts, the ideal was depersonalized into an idea.

For instance, there was no subdivision of fire into parts based on the five elements, the five knowledge senses, the five action senses, the five life airs, the four parts of the internal instrument, etc. The demigod Agni was reduced to the idea of fire. Thereafter, we cannot talk about digestive fire, intellectual fire, creative fire, sexual fire, and perceptual fire. Fire is just photons. Each word either has one meaning or it is meaningless. Since the ideal meaning is not a person—i.e., a demigod—there cannot be many meanings of a word denoting the many body parts of the demigod.

The translation of the word Agni into the word fire, along with the reduction of fire to photons, destroyed the idea that photons are controlled by the demigod as they are part of his body. Instead, photons became independent particles. When we see photons, we are not seeing the body of a person. There cannot be unity or holism between these photons. The photons could not be ideal or non-ideal.

This results in an exponential reduction in vocabulary. If our vocabulary shrinks, then the mind shrinks. The world we create from this shrunken vocabulary and mind is shrunken. Infinite things fall outside this shrunken vocabulary and mind.

There is a simple solution to this problem—give up the form-substance dualism. Every word is a person. Earth, Water, Fire, Air, and Ether are persons. Each person has many body parts. Each of these body parts is a valid meaning of the word denoting the person. The reduction of each word to one meaning is infinitely false. All attempts to reduce words to just one meaning are infinitely incomplete.

With this conclusion, we can talk about "God is great". Underlying this sentence is a metaphysics in which "great" has one meaning. That meaning either exists or doesn't exist in something. We must either be great or not. We cannot be partially great. Thereby, we cannot grade people from great to greater to greatest. The presence and use of words like greater and greatest in ordinary language doesn't mean that they can be accommodated in a logical language. If an ordinary person is called great, then by the equivalence of two things that are equal to a third thing, he becomes equal to God. To avoid this problem, if God is great, then nothing else can be great.

We avoid these problems by talking about greatness. God is greatness. Kṛṣṇa is all-attractiveness. Every part of His body is a different kind of greatness. There are infinite such types of greatness, that correspond to the different body parts of Kṛṣṇa, and He is the complete form of greatness. Since our body lacks most of that greatness, our body is attracted to His body. Attraction is nothing more than the incomplete trying to unite with the complete to overcome its *sense* of incompleteness. Through such a union, the part neither becomes the whole nor remains incomplete.

Different subsets of the complete form of greatness exist in this world. There is greatness in rivers, mountains, seas, trees, flowers, fruits, animals, and humans. There are great rulers of the world called demigods and sages. Different kinds of greatness exist in men and women. Different kinds of greatness are found in different universes. Different combinations of different types of greatness are found in different things. Therefore, they are all parts of God—the complete form of greatness.

"God is great" rests on a separation between ideas and things, forms and substances. "God is greatness" dissolves that separation. There are no substances; there are only forms. There is a complete form of greatness and there are partial forms of greatness. The complete form is the origin of the partial forms. Some partial forms of greatness are limited ideals. They are personified as demigods. They are gods because they personify ideals. They are demi because they are parts relative to the whole.

The ordinary language use of words such as great requires infinite meanings of great to allow a great ocean, a great tree, a great land, a great animal, and a great human. These infinite meanings of great can be reconciled if greatness is a body with infinite parts. In different contexts, a different part of the body of greatness may be invoked. By calling two things great, they are not equalized because they pertain to different parts of the body. This in turn rests on the use of non-binary logic—the hand is the body but the body is not the hand, the part is the whole but the whole is not the part, yellow is color but color is not yellow, God is everything but everything is not God. The shift from "God is great" to "God is greatness" is not simple. It requires us to reject everything beginning with the elementary claims of binary logic.

Monotheism: The Objectification of God

Many people at present believe that Monotheism is the best idea of God, and some even use it in the context of the Vedic tradition. As a word, 'monotheism' was first used in 1660 and then developed during the Enlightenment. Before that, Abrahamic religions called themselves superior on the grounds of having received a revelation from God, and establishing the veracity of that revelation through miracles and victories in wars, rather than reason. Monotheism, as a doctrine, was an attempt to disprove pluralistic religions on rational grounds, by using Aristotelian ideas of universal truth to establish their exclusivism. The doctrine was then used to justify attacks on other religions on five continents, revealing its purpose.

While extensive formal application of Aristotelian ideas to religion is relatively recent, all Abrahamic religions have always been body-centric. The soul is a part of the body and never separate from it. As a result, a person is equated to a body in Abrahamic religions. Since man is said to be made in God's image, body-centric thinking is also extended to God. Now, if the body is modeled as an object, God too is modeled in the same way. The Aristotelian worldview of objects could be extensively applied to religion precisely because a person is always equated to a body in Abrahamic religions.

The way of thinking in the Vedic tradition is completely different—the world is a dream of God, so both mind and body are ideas. We can compare this to our dreams—we see a body in our dreams, but it is just an idea. This shifts the entire worldview from being body-centric to mind-centric, or from being object-centric to meaning-centric. An object is always in one place but a meaning can be simultaneously in infinite places. An object doesn't expand or contract, but a meaning can be expanded and contracted. An object is either inside or outside another object but a meaning is simultaneously inside and outside other meanings. When these ideas are applied to God, He is both in one place and in infinite places, He is one thing and yet He expands and contracts, He is at once inside and outside everything.

In this article, I will discuss how the use of Aristotelian objectivity and universality upon body-centric Abrahamic thinking transforms God into an object. I will also discuss the flaws of body-centric thinking and how they render Monotheism a logically incoherent and self-contradictory doctrine stilted upon double standards. At each juncture, I will contrast these problems to the mind-centric thinking in Vedic texts. In Monotheism, God is one. In the Vedic tradition, God is one, two, three, all the way to infinity. The Vedic tradition is not Monotheism and we should stop reducing God to fit our limited imagination. If we are interested in God, it is far better to upgrade our imagination, than to reduce God to fit into it.

Vedic Reality and Worldview

The Vedic Conception of the Body

In the Vedic tradition, a person in the material world is a soul, successively covered by layers of matter to produce several kinds of bodies; in the Yoga traditions there are five kinds of bodies called Annamaya (food), Prāṇamaya (life air), Manomaya (mind), Vijñānamaya (intelligence), and Ānanadamaya (pleasure). The subtle levels of matter expand into gross levels of matter until the soul is fully trapped in the world. This trap is not eternal; it keeps changing. In addition to these changing bodies, there is an eternal spiritual body, comprising the same levels as the temporary material body, with the difference between them rooted in the Ānanadamaya—the soul's idea of bliss. The eternal idea of bliss is loving service to the Supreme Lord. The temporary idea of bliss is becoming the Supreme Lord and enjoying like Him.

These five kinds of bodies are *ideas* of the soul—beginning with the idea of bliss, which expands into the judgments of truth, right, and good collectively called the intelligence, which expands into thoughts and sensations collectively called the mind, which expands into a life force, which expands into a system of organs created from food, which most people call a body at present. The expansion of deep ideas into shallow ideas (also called subtle and gross) is like a tree growing out of a root. The soul's idea of pleasure is the root, and its successive expansions are the tree. This expansion occurs during a dream where a temporary world that includes the body of a dreamer, is created without any effort by the dreamer. The same principle of construction of a body and a world applies to the waking stage.

The Vedic Conception of the World

The world in Vedic texts is the dream of God. The mind of God is the space, and things in the world are ideas in that mind. While dreaming, each person sees himself in the dream. Hence, the dream of God includes God, and everything exists in relation to the dreamer. Just as we see a world during our dream as objects, although it is our idea, similarly, the world we see while awake is an idea in God's dream which other people might call objects. Our dreams are shorter-lived compared to God's. The persistence about the world—e.g., that my home doesn't disappear and appear on a day-to-day basis—is due to God's longer-lived dreams. Persistency is not due to objects but due to these longer-lived ideas.

The Vedic description integrates all of reality into a single whole. The thought is in the thinker and the thinker is in the thought. Thinker and thought are distinct but cannot be separated. Thoughts themselves are distinct but not separate because they are each tied to the thinker. If the thinker is coherent, there is harmony in the thoughts. Even if there is disharmony, it is intentionally created by the thinker; there is always order behind the chaos. Changes to one thought are not just changes to that thought; they entail changes to many if not all thoughts. That is because the thinker is coherent and doesn't treat each thought independently. The alignment between thoughts ensures that each individual's interest is the collective interest and the collective interest is the individual interest. Thus, idea-thinking creates the worldview of eternal harmony and peace wherever it enters.

The Vedic Conception of Life

Life in the Vedic conception is a changing relation between the soul and its bodies. The soul is the person and the bodies are its attributes. The person is "I" and the body attributes "X" are joined together to form statements of the sort "I am X". This joining is temporary and is called bondage. The purpose of spiritual practice is to cut this bondage, initially to be situated in the self or "I" and then realize that the "I" has its own eternal attributes, or "I am Y". As the temporary attributes change, the soul moves from one body to another. All change is the effect of the soul moving from one body to another rather than the body moving. The soul moves from one idea of bliss to another, from one judgment to another, from one thought to another, from one sensation to another, from one life air to another, and from one body to another. Over time, it returns to the same bliss, judgment, thought, sensation, life air, and body. The soul's cyclical movement through temporary bodies is material science and its movement out of this cycle toward and into the eternal body is spiritual science. They are based on the principle of soul movement but are different as temporary and eternal. The concept of body change is integrated with the idea of change in bliss, judgment, thought, sensation, and life air.

There is no mind-body dualism in the Vedic conception of reality. Even life air, sensation, thought, judgment, and bliss are called "bodies". The world can remind us of God at every moment, as His creations carry partial imprints of His personality. The minimum level of God-consciousness is realizing that we are in God's dream. A little more advanced God-consciousness is being able to see the partial imprints of God's personality in His creations. Even more advanced God-consciousness is being able to see the complete personality of God face-to-face. The Vedic worldview constitutes a science, although quite different from Materialism. It is a science rooted in mind-and-idea thinking, so I call it *semanticism*. It is harder to imagine for those who assume a science-religion separation, with science dealing with objects and religion dealing with the soul and God. These three are inseparable in the Vedic worldview, as God is the mind, matter is thoughts, and the soul attaches itself to these thoughts.

Monotheistic Reality and Worldview

The Monotheistic Concept of Reality

Monotheism conceives the world as objects in space. Objects are things-in-themselves that don't need anything else to exist. In logic, philosophy, and classical physics, objects are seen as mutually independent entities. That means changes done to one object aren't done to other objects. Since objects are independent of each other and the space that contains them, such a world doesn't need God—if the world were eternal. A problem arises if the world is created and destroyed, and one might need to invoke the existence of God for creation and destruction, but God is otherwise unnecessary. Such a conception of the world involves the depersonalization of reality, which can be called objectification. It came out of Monotheisms which then created modern science. In this worldview, God plays a role only at the beginning and the end of the world.

When the world is conceptualized as objects, its creator God also becomes an object, which means separate from the world. Objectivity appears in society as individualism and competition for resources. Each person considers themselves separate from others, describes the world as separate objects, and believes that the world is separate from God. The objective world entails the separateness of things, and the separateness of God from the world, which in turn results in the objectification of God, which in turn reinforces an objectified conception of the world. The separateness of things in the world becomes science and the separation of God from the world becomes religion. They support each other.

The Monotheistic Concept of Order

All these separated things are then tied together in Monotheistic religions through contracts—religion is a contract between man and God, society is a contract between men, and nature is a contract between inert objects. These contracts are also called "laws". A religious law is a contract between man and God. A social law is a contract between men. A scientific law is a contract between inert objects. In each such contractual law, each side tries to minimize the giving and maximize the taking. Contractual laws often break down due to disagreements on giving and taking. At that juncture, a new set of laws are negotiated. Due to this renegotiation, Monotheisms have many sects which consider each other false.

Monotheism fundamentally doesn't believe in eternal truth because its conception of order is negotiable laws. It also doesn't believe in the principle of justice because at the heart of Monotheism is the idea that might is right. Those who can wield power can redefine the laws and thus change the definition of truth and justice. Ultimately, God has the greatest might so He is free to define all the laws. God's laws cannot be explained as truth or justice. They have to be accepted silently, as God is omnipotent. When the idea of power creating and enforcing laws is extended from God to humanity, Monotheistic religions create institutions of power that define laws for a society. These laws are also not proven to be true or just. They too are based on might is right. Some religions consolidate these institutions more while others distribute them more.

The Monotheistic Concept of Life

Due to the lack of concepts of truth and justice, and reliance on institutions of power, a Monotheistic society is always living in strife. The strife cannot be resolved by reason because truth and justice are replaced by the power to create laws. There cannot be harmony in a world in which everyone wants to minimize the giving and maximize the taking. Therefore, Monotheism becomes the ideology that gives birth to perpetual conflict and chaos. Monotheism doesn't see this conflict as a problem because the world is described in terms of a battle between good and evil, God and Satan. Each side describes itself as Godly and the other side as Satanic. In the good vs. evil battle, one side is expected to destroy the others.

Interspersed with war is the idea of pleasure. The world in Monotheism exists for man's enjoyment. God is said to have created a world and abandoned it and man is expected to take possession of the world and make it his personal property. Since objects are things-in-themselves separated from God, the world is not sacred. Trying to see God in the world is called false idolatry. Again, those who have the power can take whatever they want in their self-interest. Since might is right, the powerful take things in their self-interest, and justify that as God's will for them.

Life in the Monotheistic ideology is lived in the interplay between pleasure and war. By disregarding truth and justice, while trying to enjoy the world—by claiming that God created the world and abandoned it for man to own—man is caught in immense suffering. Monotheism is Materialism in disguise; war and pleasure are given a religious color to justify them intellectually. Materialism is the object conception of the world, in which each thing is separated from other things. Monotheism is a conception of God separate from a world of objects. The separation of objects from each other, the separation of God from the soul, the separation of God from the world, are varied symptoms of object thinking.

The Origins and Flaws of Object Thinking

The Greek Creation of Objectivity

Greek philosophers began marginalizing the soul and ignoring deeper realities to reduce everything to the food body. They postulated that everything is built from only four elements (Earth, Water, Fire, and Air), which were ultimately transformations of just one element—the Aperion. This substance was said to take many forms to create the food body. Thereafter, there were two main things in Greek thinking, i.e., substance and form. Initially, the forms were ideas that spanned the mind, intellect, and pleasure. In Plato's philosophy, there were pure ideas in another world of forms while impure versions of the same ideas existed in the present world. However, the Greeks had no understanding of ideas as their thinking was overwhelmed with substance ideologies. Hence, they could never define what these pure forms were. Aristotle subsequently separated forms into two categories—Theoretical and Practical.

The Theoretical forms pertained to the body, and were equated to shapes (such as triangle, square, circle). They were also embedded in the substance. The Practical forms pertained to the mind and were equated to culture (such as beauty, justice, virtue). They were not part of the substance but present in the psyche. The Platonic other world—heaven—comprised a fifth substance called the Quintessence, different from the four elements. Through his highly speculative claims, Aristotle synthesized various diverse streams in Greek philosophy—(a) the Monist tendency to think of one substance instead of four substances, (b) the Platonic tendency to think of a heaven beyond the earth, (c) the practical demand to study and describe the material world without invoking the supernatural, and (d) the need to continue the prevailing society, economy, and polity without having to define beauty, justice, and virtue.

Greeks were so impressed by Aristotle's synthesis that they decided that the whole world had to have this marvel of imagination. Alexander's conquests were seen as the vehicle for spreading all such Greek ideologies to the world. Eventually, when Alexander died, the Greek civilization began fragmenting. Nevertheless, Aristotle's ideas had a lasting impact on the world as they were picked up, expanded, and coopted in various ways even after the end of the Greek civilization. The Aristotelian merger of form and substance became *object.* Each object was one type of thing because it had just one shape. There was no meaning to a class, concept, idea, meaning, or type, other than the shape of a thing. There was only one objective truth about each thing because that objective truth equaled its indisputable shape.

Greek Thinking Pervades Science

Aristotle separated the body and the mind as Theoretical and Practical forms. Heaven and earth were separated as Quintessence and Aperion. The bodies within the earth were also separate as each shape existed independently of the other shapes. Through these separations, Aristotle gave birth to a worldview of the separateness of things, which is called objective truth. He essentially created three worlds—matter, mind, and heaven. Their interaction was not discussed. How Quintessence affected the Aperion, or how the Practical forms interacted with the Theoretical forms, were left as open questions. These questions have never been answered. Many subsequent thinkers, tired of these questions, have tried to reduce these three worlds into one, but have never succeeded. They are stuck in the worldview created by Aristotle—neither able to reject it, nor able to solve its problems, nor able to find an alternative.

Both Plato and Aristotle sowed the seeds of highly speculative types of thinking, which subsequently pervaded Western philosophy, religion, and science. For instance, mathematical Platonists claimed that geometric truths were not just embedded in matter but existed in a Platonic world; they replaced the Greek heaven—that formerly comprised Greek deities—with mathematical formulas. This tendency has survived till date as the three-world conception of reality as matter, mind, and mathematics. There is pure mathematics in heaven, an incarnation of that mathematics in human mind, which is embedded in the body. This tendency to think of the heaven and the mind in terms of the body—equated to numbers and shapes—solidified in Western worldviews the preeminence of object-oriented thinking.

When Gödel proved that mathematics is incomplete, he did not give up Platonism—i.e., that there is a heaven of mathematical formulas and theorems. The limitation of incompleteness pertained only to the human mind—*we* were incapable of knowing the mathematical heaven by our minds, but the heaven of mathematics still existed. Gödel's physics compatriots did not give up their belief that mathematics was embedded in matter. The limitation for them was that we could not prove the formulas and equations that govern the world from first principles—a limitation of the human mind—not that the world wasn't itself mathematical. If we kept inventing formulas and equations, and finding appropriate formulas and equations that described the material world correctly, science could continue forever although we could not prove why specific formulas and equations described the world correctly from first principles.

Mathematicians and physicists have never accepted the fact established by Gödel's incompleteness that if we try to describe reality mathematically then we will run into *contradictions*. This is because they firmly believe in Aristotle's system of objective truth—truth is shape, everything has only one shape, all shapes can be *described* mathematically, and once we describe everything as shape, we can logically connect the previous shape to the next shape, and that connection will be called the law of nature.

The Basic Flaw of Greek Thinking

The fundamental flaw with the Aristotelian conception of objective truth is that reality is not fixed shapes. Instead, reality is *potentials*. Everything is a collection of many potentials, some of which may *manifest* at one time, but that manifestation is temporary. After a while, a different set of potentials may manifest, making reality essentially a shape-shifting entity. We cannot say that reality is a fixed shape because it is potentiality of shapes—(a) the current shape is neither permanently true nor false, (b) the appearance of two shapes one after another is not logically contradictory, and (c) that something is one type of shape currently doesn't exclude the possibility of it being another shape in the future or the past.

If reality is a shape-shifting entity, then objective truth has essentially no foundation. The principles of Aristotelian logic—identity, non-contradiction, and excluded middle—are themselves false. That doesn't mean the absence of truth, because there is indeed an entity, that can take different shapes. We just have to start thinking in terms of entities that change shapes, rather than in terms of objects.

If this appears oppressive, then we can think of a mind. A mind is a shape-shifting entity. It produces ideas one after another and takes on the shape of the idea it produces. The ideas are potentials that the mind can produce. But all ideas the mind can produce are not simultaneously manifest. They manifest one after another, the mind takes on the shape of the idea, and hence it "becomes" that idea. But the very next moment, it may produce a different idea, and "become" that new idea. The mind's current shape is neither true nor false. Two conflicting ideas a mind produces don't entail a logical contradiction. The mind is not forbidden from thinking—and thus "becoming"—contradictory ideas and shapes. The mind is not one idea always, it is many ideas alternatively, and it can't be reduced to just one idea.

The entire foundation of Western thinking—Aristotelian logic, conception of objective truth, and reality as objects—is false if reality is potentials, which can be correctly modeled only if we think in terms of mind and thought. Mathematics works for objects because it relies on binary logic to say that something is either X or not, it cannot be both X and not-X, and it cannot be neither X nor not-X. All these claims are false for potentials. Therefore, mathematics is not a model of the material world, let alone a heaven.

Even numbers are concepts, which is why a number (such as 5) is just one thing that exists in many places at once (five horses, five cows, five shoes). That contradicts binary logic according to which each logical entity must be either inside or outside another entity; it cannot be both inside and outside, it cannot be neither inside nor outside. The number 5—as a concept—is both inside and outside sets of five things and neither inside nor outside. Logic only allows something to be inside or outside, which is incompleteness. Hence, if we use Aristotelian logic for concepts, we can only prove a small subset of truths—either something is inside or outside—because the vast majority of truths depend on one thing being both inside and outside and neither inside nor outside. The main problem is that Aristotelian logic applies to objects and not concepts, which doesn't work even for something as simple as a number.

Objectification and Body-Centrism

The Greek Objectification of a Person

Aristotle's objectification means that if a person grows older, he becomes a different person because the shape of his body has changed. After all, objective truth is shape. If a circle becomes a square, and then becomes a triangle, and then becomes an octagon, we can't say that it is the same thing. Likewise, for us to say that the body with a different shape is the same person we have to say that the soul is a shape-shifting entity. But reality is not a shape-shifting entity in Aristotle's worldview. Hence, as the shape of the body changes, a person must change. Through his objective truth, Aristotle destroyed the soul.

At most, a soul is a Practical form in Aristotle's worldview, which is a euphemism for private and personal beliefs like one's belief in some particular notion of beauty, justice, or virtue. It can't be called a truth. If Aristotle had described reality as potentials, there would be no dualism of mind and body, private and public, practical and theoretical, belief and truth, subjective and objective. Reality would be potentials and a soul would be a shape-shifting entity moving from potential to potential. Aristotle's objective truth became the source of dualisms in Western thinking because the mind could not be objectified. The mind remained a shape-shifting entity, different from objective truth, so every successive generation of thinkers shunned the discussion of the mind as their comfort zone rested solely in the body.

Abrahamic Religions Copied the Greeks

Abrahamic religions coopted Aristotle's philosophy in nearly all respects. The soul in these religions was described as *breath* (similar to the Prāṇamaya body)—God made the body and breathed life into it. Genesis 2:7 says: *Then the Lord God formed a man from the dust of the ground and breathed into his nostrils the breath of life, and the man became a living being.* In this description, the substance is dust and the breath is the form. If the breath goes away, the dust disintegrates into particles as the loss of form. If the breath comes back, the dust regains forms. The breath does not exist outside the body.

Abrahamic religions postulated that the baby in the mother's womb does not breathe, and yet it is alive. Similarly, death is when the body stops breathing although it is alive like a baby. Of course, the baby's body does not decay although a dead body decays. But that has been a minor aberration. Upon the end of the world, and the arrival of Judgment Day, all the decayed bodies supposedly come alive again—i.e., start breathing. The dust regains form of the body because the form is breath. The soul—breath—is the *form* embedded within the *substance.* Aristotle's philosophy was thus coopted for humans.

Plato's philosophy was coopted for heaven and God. There is another world of pure forms, of which the present world is an imperfect reflection. Genesis 1:27 says: *So God created man in his own image, in the image of God he created him; male and female he created them.* God is the form of purity in heaven and He made man after Himself. But then man fell from heaven due to sin, and after salvation from sin, man will return back to heaven. At the moment, man is an imperfect reflection of God, just like the Platonic world is a world of pure forms and the present world is an imperfect reflection of the pure world. God did not make animals in His image, so even if they are breathing, they are not God's reflections. In fact, God gave man dominion over the animals, so they are more imperfect compared to humans.

This idea of God making man in his image, where image really means shape due to Aristotle's thinking, has been at the root of racist ideas in Abrahamic religions. Race is not just skin color; it is body shape, body size, facial features, eye color, and skin color. They depict God (in religions that are permitted to depict God) after their own bodily shape, facial features, body size, eye color, and skin color. For instance, Europeans depict Jesus as a tall man with blonde hair and blue eyes, although he was a Jew born in the Middle East. God making man in His own image has been strictly interpreted in terms of the body, not in terms of virtues, values, beliefs, etc., which shows the body-centric thinking.

Body-Centric Abrahamic Thinking

Abrahamic religions don't consider the present body material because man goes to heaven in the same body and lives eternally thereafter. Each person is a body, which is the body in heaven after salvation, so it is also a spiritual body. Feeding, clothing, and pampering the present body is not a material activity; it is also a spiritual activity. Hence, there is no fundamental difference between material and spiritual in Abrahamic religions.

This is why when people from Abrahamic religions accept traditional philosophies and practices, they start calling themselves "spiritual" rather than "religious". They are saying that they believe in something beyond the body, which their religion has never recognized. Things such as Chakras, breathing exercises that stimulate the Chakras, and astrology which affects the Chakras—are material in the Vedic tradition. But they are called spiritual by the erstwhile followers of Abrahamic religions because for them there has never been anything other than the body made out of food. A person equals a body, as long as he is breathing.

Both secular and religious ideologies in the West are materialistic. It began with Greek philosophy as they separated truth and belief as body and mind, had no explanation of how the mind went from body to body, or how it went from earth to heaven. After that, Abrahamic religions merged mind and body into body, and added miracles to materialism—such as expecting a body to be automatically revived after decay—which is not possible or expected in materialism. In scientific thinking, there is a duality of matter and mathematics. In religious thinking, there is a duality of matter and miracle. Matter is common to both, but miracle can't be reconciled with mathematics. The fact that mathematics fails to explain matter often creates the illusion that miracle must happen. But factually both are false.

All traditional religions were an antidote to materialism as they talked of realities beyond the body that could exit the body, enter another body, and transfer from one body to another. In the Vedic tradition, the moving soul is the concept of jīva that leaves one body and goes to another body, such that the old body becomes dead and the new body becomes living. All change in the Vedic tradition is modeled as an effect of a moving soul—i.e., jīva. But the soul in Abrahamic religions never leaves the body. Change is not the effect of the soul moving but of the body moving, with the soul—i.e., breath—just tagging along. The psyche in Greek pagan religions meant something that went from one body to another. Abrahamic religions took that word and changed its meaning to something that never leaves the body; their soul is embedded in the body as breath. Therefore, Abrahamic religions have never been an antidote to materialism.

Objectification in Religious Contexts

Monotheistic God is an Object

Monotheisms have a serious problem with the different forms of God, which means different shaped images. God can only have one shape. If God is worshipped in various shapes, then it must mean many gods. This is an extension of Aristotelian thinking where an object has one shape and if there are different shapes then there must be different objects. If reality were a potential—i.e., a shape-shifting entity—it could have many shapes. But God is not a shape-shifting entity. God must have only one shape like an object. Since God made man in His own image, that shape must be human. God cannot take the shape of a boar, tortoise, snake, fish, or lion. God cannot have more than two arms or more than one head because humans have only one head and two hands. Since God only made man in His image, a feminine image of God is impossible. Man's limitations are transposed to God. Monotheists call the varied shaped images of God Polytheism.

An object is only in one place at one time; it cannot be in many places at once. Hence, God must only be in heaven. He cannot come to earth without leaving heaven, and since leaving heaven would make it a godless place, God cannot come to earth. Instead, God sends His messengers. Likewise, God cannot be in everyone's heart because an object is always in only one place. If God were factually in many places at once, it would be many gods—contrary to Monotheism—designated by the word Pantheism. In fact, we cannot make images of God also because if that image were God, then it would mean two gods. God produces the world out of nothing because if He produced it from Himself, He would be reduced, following the principle of conservation of matter and energy.

The Depersonalization of God

Monotheists define God as the Supreme Being. There can't be more than one Supreme Being, and hence God is one. However, in this description, God is defined *relative* to other things, over which He has supremacy, which is not a description of God in itself. By saying that God is the Supreme Being, we don't know what he looks like, how he lives, what he eats, how he talks, how he thinks, what he feels, etc. The focus on God's supremacy defocuses from His persona. Other descriptions, such as those that call Him omnipotent, omniscient, and omnibenevolent, are also relative to other things: God knows, controls, and loves everyone. What about God Himself? Monotheistic religions don't answer that question.

A person is different things in different contexts; an object is the same thing in every context. Factually, objectivity is an imaginary creation of Aristotle that approximates to non-living things like tables or chairs, not trees, animals, or humans. Contextualization is the essence of personhood. The moment we try to universalize the truth, we also decontextualize and depersonalize the truth, and convert it into objective truth. If truth could be contextualized, then different cultures could conceptualize God differently. Some cultures may call God a father, others a friend, and others a master. If each culture was allowed to think of God differently, there would be no objective truth and no exclusivism. Since Abrahamic religions rely on exclusivism, they reject contextualization and personalization of God. Their claims about God, in the framework of objective truth, require that God be an object. Abrahamic exclusivism is married to Greek universalism which is married to Aristotle's idea of objective truth.

Every person is described in many ways through their various attributes such as father, husband, employee, citizen, artist, musician, writer, etc. However, all these claims are not simultaneously true for a person, nor is "I am a father" contradictory to "I am a citizen". Every person is the potential of many traits which are seen at different times, places, and situations by different persons. If God were allowed to be as much of a person as an ordinary human, then there would be no exclusivism or universalism as humans are many different things. Everyone doesn't know each human in the same way. So why do they need to know God in the same way? Exclusivism and universalism require that God must be an objective truth. To attain it, we must remove contextualization of the understanding of God and then universalize God to just one understanding. This kind of truth applies only to objects. Monotheisms try to attain universal truth and they transform God from a person to an object.

The Minimization of God's Power

Even if we just accept God's omnipotence, it entails that God could be a boar, tortoise, snake, fish, or lion. He could have more than two arms or more than one head. He could be both masculine and feminine. God could sometimes be a child, at other times a youth, at yet other times old. Omnipotence is enough to guarantee infinite forms of God and there could be no opposition to so-called Polytheism. Since that is unacceptable to Monotheism, by their own advocacy, God's omnipotence is greatly limited, reducing God to one thing, which is a non-omnipotent God.

Thomas Aquinas in fact went so far as to say that there were many things that God could not do. Among these were making copies of Himself, disobeying the laws of mathematics (such as the sum of the angles of a triangle were 180^0), and undoing the past. Monotheisms have tried to reduce God's omnipotence to preserve objectivity, universalism, and exclusivism. It is not simply a case of ignorance or innocence. They went to great lengths to preserve universalism and exclusivism, even if that meant God was losing omnipotence and personhood. Having employed these techniques relentlessly in pursuit of an ideology, they reduced God to a powerful machine. That machine is always one thing—i.e., it has just one shape. It created the world and left it to work according to mathematics. The machine cannot violate mathematics. In fact, it delivers punishments and rewards based on a rule-based system of covenants. Humans modify these covenants and reprogram them into the machine.

By the absence of personal information, the decontextualization and depersonalization of God, and the relentless advocacy of exclusivism and universalism (God has only one shape, God has only one gender, He only exists in heaven, He talks to humans through messengers, He is not present in everyone's heart, we cannot make images of God), Monotheism objectifies God. The absence of personal information could be ignored as an incomplete understanding if there was no advocacy of object thinking, or if God could be understood in different ways based on different contexts. However, the advocacy entails that a non-object conception of God—e.g., that God has many personas in different times, places, and situations, or in relation to different people (like ordinary humans are shape-shifting entities)—would totally destroy Abrahamic theology.

How "God" is Used in Monotheism

"God" is a Name, Not a Meaning

The word "God" in Monotheistic religions is a name, quite like John, Peter, or David. We could replace it with X, Alpha, or

Omega, which are equally meaningless names. Each name identifies one thing, but that name means nothing. In English grammar, this is expressed as the distinction between proper noun (name) and common noun (meaning). "God" is a proper noun and not a common noun because if it were a common noun, it could denote many things that belong to the class denoted by that noun. The claim of Monotheism can now be rephrased by saying that "God" is a name and not a meaning.

Let's contrast this to the situation in which God means a common noun like "good", not confined to God. Factually, we can say that the food is good, the medicine is good, the boy is good, and the country is good. While they may not be all-good, i.e., embody all kinds of goodness or be good in all situations, due to the presence of some goodness, we could say that goodness was present in them partially. They would now become parts of God—God being all-good and the food being some of that good. Now, we can make non-binary statements such as "food is good, God is good, but food is not God, and God is not food" because while God is all-good, food is some good, so there is a difference between the two.

Factually, if the word God meant all-good, then God would be nearly impossible to understand *fully* given that there are infinite types of goodness. As a name, God would mean just one thing—all-good—but as a meaning, God would be infinite types of goodness, which are seen in different contexts partially so seeing them would in one sense mean seeing God in everything and yet not seeing Him fully. In so far as we cannot see everything, we cannot understand all-good completely. And yet, as we see more types of goodness, we would understand God better. Seeing good in everything would now become our way of understanding God better. All good things would be part of God and parts of God would be in all good things. Unless we were referring to all-good, there would be goodness—Godliness—everywhere.

Monotheism confines God to heaven. Even if a spirit in the world guides people, it doesn't pervade everything like goodness. If sacredness pervaded everything, man would not be the owner and enjoyer of the world. The conception of an all-pervading spirit is actually inconsistent with man's dominion of the world. Therefore, in Monotheism, God is a proper noun, not a common noun.

The word "God" *refers* to one thing, but *means* nothing. If the word meant anything at all, it would be present in infinite places at once (since every common noun is present in infinite places at once) but in each place God would seem different as a different part or aspect of that common noun would be seen in different places. Due to these infinite partial visions of God—e.g., different kinds of goodness in different kinds of food—we could not say that God was only in heaven. We would rather say that the common noun He personified was concentrated in heaven but diffused in the world. This is strictly unacceptable to Monotheism. To concentrate God, rather than diffuse Him, the word "God" must be a name and not a meaning.

Meaning-Naming Separation

The disconnection of meaning and naming has a long history in Abrahamic religions—after God gave Adam dominion over the world, He asked Adam to name the creatures that God had made. Genesis 2:19-20 says: *The Lord God formed all the wild animals and all the birds out of the ground. Then he brought them to the man to see what he would call them. Whatever the man called each creature became its name. So, the man named all the domestic animals, all the birds, and all the wild animals.*

This separation between naming and meaning has always been an essential feature of Western thinking. Shakespeare noted it when he said, "a rose by another name would smell as sweet". All philosophers of language in modern time have upheld this distinction, calling words human labels to refer to things or classes of things. That class, in turn, has never been a mental entity, a meaning, or a concept. As Aristotle would say, a triangle, circle, and square are defined by mathematical formulas, so all Theoretical forms (truths) must be defined in the same way and confirmed through objects. Anything not definable in this way, is a Practical form (belief), and while it might exist in the mind, it can never be proven true. For Aristotle, "good" is a private belief, not a provable truth. All truthful words only refer to mathematical formulas or objects, not mental entities.

20th century Analytic Philosophy dissolved this separation

between Theoretical and Practical forms by replacing concepts with *sets* or a collection of things. Things were *in* the set, but the set was *not* in the things. Thereby, there was a set of shades called "color" but color as a concept was never in the shades. The statement "yellow is a color" simply meant that yellow is a member of the set given the arbitrary name "color". The question of how we put shades in that set, instead of dogs, cows, smells, or tastes (which required seeing a concept in each thing), was never resolved.

To say that "God is one" can thus be interpreted in two ways—(a) there is a set called God with only one member, and (b) there is an object called God. We don't know how we put that one member in the set called God (just like we don't know how we put shades in a set called colors) because to do so would require us to define God based on a meaning (e.g., goodness) before we find it in the member. However, if we try to define God based on meaning, then any meaning we use can be found in infinite other things, not just God. Hence, we can never construct a set called God with just one member in it. God can now only be an object, with "God" being that object's name. To say that "God is one" is like saying "Earth is one", a meaningless claim if "Earth" refers to one thing as a proper noun rather than a common noun with one member in it.

Monotheism simply asserts monopoly on the word "God"—I use it to refer to one thing, so nobody else can use it to refer to anything else, quite like we use "Earth" to refer to one thing, so nobody else should use it to refer to anything else. This monopoly can be broken only by saying that "God" is a meaning, such as "good", not a name. But that would also entail the multiplicity of good, not Monotheism. There could always be a Supreme Good, but that would not eliminate the presence of other types of good. Hence, to assert Monotheism, one has to insist that God is a meaningless name, like Earth. It refers to an object, not a class. Pretending that God is a class, to claim that "God is one" is self-contradictory.

God is Name and Meaning

The solution to this problem requires us to describe reality in terms of concepts or meanings. A concept is not a collection of objects—denoted mathematically as a set. Concepts are the fundamental reality.

An ordinary concept like "color" is both one and infinite—it is one because "color" is a single concept, it is infinite because there are infinite shades subsumed within color. If we actually tried to explain what "color" means, we would have to enumerate these infinite shades. This solution is presented in the Vedic texts when the Supreme Person is described as "knowledge", the original concept. It is one concept, and yet, if we tried to enumerate what we mean by knowledge, or what it includes, it would be infinite.

In the Vedic tradition, knowledge is the body of God. It is one, and infinite. There are partial forms of God, who embody "knowledge" partially. They create smaller domains of reality like an expert in one area produces books in that area. The "original" form of knowledge produces authors who produce books. Thus, God is one, two, three, all the way to infinity. All the authors have existed for eternity, but their books might be created or destroyed. Hence, at no time could we say "God is one". That claim pertains to the original reality—i.e., knowledge—which has always been expanded infinitely.

Note how the Vedic tradition shuns object-thinking at the outset—God is described as knowledge, not as an object. Of course, knowledge is a form. It is diffused everywhere and concentrated in one place; the diffused reality is expanded from the concentrated reality. Hence, there are infinite forms of God—progressively better forms of knowledge—with one perfect form of knowledge. Thereby, God is one, two, three, all the way to infinity. In fact, the one is infinity because if we tried to enumerate what we meant by knowledge, we would have to enumerate infinite types of knowledge to fully know it.

The Vedic texts don't use any meaningless names, even while referring to God. For instance, the name Kṛṣṇa means all-attractive. It doesn't mean nothing else is attractive. Even a river, mountain, land, house, and car are attractive. However, they are not all-attractive. There is some attraction in them, while Kṛṣṇa is all-attractive. Thereby, Kṛṣṇa is not a meaningless name. The result of using a meaningful name is that Kṛṣṇa's attractiveness is distributed in everything in the universe partially. There is also a hierarchy of attractiveness with some things being more attractive than others. Likewise, the name Vāsudeva, which means "lord of light" is not contradictory to the name Kṛṣṇa because the lord of light is also attractive. He may not be all-attractive—because there is some attraction even in darkness—so the situation is not binary, i.e., only one God and everything else not-God. There is some godliness in everything and we can use the term "God" for many personalities if they are near the top of the attraction hierarchy.

A hierarchy of deities appears the moment we use meaningful names, such as Kṛṣṇa. That hierarchy disappears when we use meaningless names—such as God. If this name is given any meaning, such as "good", immediately the hierarchy of goodness appears, undermining Monotheism. Hence, the claims of Monotheism can only be sustained if meaningless names are used to *refer* rather than *describe*. The focus in the Vedic texts is description. When that description is accurate, it also becomes a name. However, it is a meaningful name which simultaneously describes and refers, not just refers.

Objectification Creates a Formless God

The Religious Problem of Infinity

When Christians tried to marry their religion with Greek philosophy, they ran into a serious problem that all forms had to be finite and if God was a form in the Platonic heaven, then He too would be finite. Since Greeks were reducing truth to shape and size, God having the same shape and size as man (since God made man after Himself) would mean that God was on par with man. We could address this issue by saying that God was taller and heavier than man, but no matter how much height and weight we assign God, it is always conceivable that there could *be* someone even taller and heavier than God.

When children fight with other children, they talk about how their daddy is the greatest. They might refer to great deeds their daddies might have done. Every child tells more and more exaggerated stories of their daddies. Hence, if Monotheism said that God had a certain height and weight, then someone else could say that their God was even taller and heavier. This problem can only be solved by making God infinite. Was God the greatest as a matter of fact (i.e., taller and heavier than any other God) or as a matter of principle (i.e., having infinite height and weight)?

There is factually no solution to this problem because in the limiting case of infinite height and weight, God would be inconceivable since infinite is inconceivable. Likewise, if God were infinite, then how could God have made man in His image—i.e., finite? Factually, most Greek philosophers abhorred infinity as it led to paradoxes such as Zeno's Paradoxes. But if God was finite, then any competitor religion could simply do +1 to the Monotheistic God's height and weight and claim that their God was greater.

The Iconoclasm of Monotheisms

The Christian solution to this problem was to stop talking about God's form. All pagan deities had hands, legs, face, eyes, nose, ears, etc. But having these features made God finite. Therefore, Christians simply stopped talking about God's bodily features to end any kind of competitive claim from other religions. In her book, God—An Anatomy, Francesca Stavrakopoulou describes in great detail how God originally had a body. However, the influence of Greek philosophy, specifically the finitude of all forms, made God formless. Images of God made God finite and hence destruction of images became an essential part of religions. Thereafter, Christianity replaced numerous Greco-Roman images with a formless deity.

Romans, who created Christianity, were keen on conquering Europe, not on theological problems. Their "solution" to the problem of infinity was to stop making images. All Greco-Roman deities had images. Roman Christianity stopped making images. They talked about Jesus as the "incarnation" of God—i.e., an infinite spirit entering a finite flesh, allowing them to make images of Jesus, while not making an image of God. To allow Christian authors who had never met Jesus to write about God, they created another infinite spirit they call the "Holy Ghost", which is also incorporeal because it exists everywhere. And yet, that infinite spirit doesn't make everything sacred. It is kind of hovering above the world, in a way that is not explained or understood properly.

In simple words, if "God is one" then He must be formless, incorporeal, and infinite spirit. However, if God has a form, then He can't be infinite and hence not God. This problem sets up the stage for the Christian Trinity of Father, Son, and Holy Ghost in which the Father is the infinite formless incorporeal spirit present only in heaven, the Son is finite, formed, and embodied spirit who temporarily appeared in this world, and the Holy Ghost is the infinite formless incorporeal spirit present everywhere in this world and yet it doesn't make the world sacred.

Aristotle had imagined two kinds of substances—Quintessence in heaven and Aperion in the world—while applying form to both. Greeks could say that deities in heaven were different from bodies on earth because they were built out of different substances (Quintessence vs. Aperion). But that also meant that the heaven and earth were completely different and never the twain shall meet. Christianity required the spirit of heaven—i.e., Quintessence—to descend into the Aperion in the form of Jesus, and then be present in the Aperion as a formless Holy Ghost breaking two essential dualisms—(a) between heaven and earth, (b) between form and substance. The Christian Trinity says that God is both formless and form, Quintessence and Aperion, without having the capacity to resolve the Aristotelian dualisms.

Islam and Judaism face this problem less because they don't need the Holy Spirit; their books are said to be direct revelations from Mohammed and Moses, not written post-facto by Greco-Roman authors (although they have been modified considerably over time). However, they too cannot reconcile the finitude of a form with the infinitude of God. Hence, they too never talk about the form of God.

Many people think that Monotheistic iconoclasm is an accident, not essential to Monotheism, because they are unaware of the problem of establishing how God is the greatest based on the Greek ideas of objective truth as shape. We have to either accept iconoclasm or discard the Greek system of objectivity, universalism, and exclusivism, which would destroy Monotheism itself. Iconoclasm is a fundamental feature of Monotheism, that can never be disregarded without rejecting Monotheism itself.

The Exclusivism of Formlessness

If we can't say anything definite about God, then whoever says something definite implies a limitation on God. Abrahamic exclusivism now takes on a new form, where saying anything definite (e.g., that God has any particular shape) is tantamount to saying that it is a false god. Now Monotheism doesn't even have to prove why that deity is false. Simply the fact that the deity has a shape implies a limitation on the indefinite and hence false. Thus, every deity in every religion that talks about God's pastimes, or that He bears a specific set of implements, becomes a false God.

The problem with Monotheism can be described easily by reframing God as knowledge. Can we really say that "knowledge is only one", when there are hundreds of subjects—logic, mathematics, physics, chemistry, biology, economics, sociology, cosmology, psychology—that are all knowledge? When each subject respects other subjects, there is no conflict between them, and the claims of other subjects are affirmed in each subject. This is how the Vedic texts describe varied forms of God—each form respects all other forms, and so, there is no conflict between them. They are just like psychology and physics if these two confirm each other, rather than contradicting each other (as in present academia).

Exclusivism is dangerous if our idea of truth is inspired by one specific type of truth (e.g., mathematics) because then we can't reconcile it with other types of truth (e.g., psychology). Greeks chose to model the whole world based on their ideas about inanimate objects. Their model of reality wasn't a living body, a social body, or a mind, or even an encompassing conception of truth. They specifically chose inanimate objects. Abrahamic religions elevated it to the only truth. If a limited conception of reality is elevated to the only truth, it runs into contradictions with other truths that can't be denied. As time passes, there are so many exceptions to the exclusivist claims that one has to totally abandon the truth claims, which in the case of Abrahamic religions means giving up on God's shape after using a system of thinking in which shape is the only kind of truth.

Formlessness in Indian Philosophy

The Birth of Indian Impersonalism

The iconoclasm of Monotheistic religions appeared in India as Advaita impersonalism in which two statements "God is one" and "God is infinite" were reconciled by merging all of reality into an infinite, incorporeal formless spirit that pervades everything. Advaita further claimed that their segregation into finite forms is the result of illusion or Māyā, indicated by the temporary nature. Advaita rejected eternal forms. In that process, all forms of God were rejected, along with their images worshipped in temples. At most, the worship of finite images was a stepping stone to the infinite, meant for the "less intelligent".

Advaita impersonalism thus aligned with Abrahamic Monotheism in India in the sense that God was an infinite incorporeal formless spirit for them. Monotheistic iconoclasm was just like Advaita rejection of images of God. Of course, Advaita did not violently destroy images while Monotheisms did. But this difference in practice is not substantiated by Advaita philosophy. According to philosophy, all images of God are limiting the infinite into something finite, and hence, they must be false representations.

Vedic philosophy had declined by this time to an extent that they did not conceive reality as concepts or meanings, which are simultaneously one and infinite. No personalist Vedānta interpretation after Advaita offered a clear resolution to the problem posed by the twin requirements of "God is one" and "God is infinite". Despite the appeal of personalist Vedānta interpretations on devotional grounds, they have never been able to explain how a finite form is infinite, which is why Advaita still lives today. Factually, the finitude of a form in Advaita is also based on form being equal to shape, just like Greeks.

Neglecting Many Kinds of Infinities

The solution to the formlessness in Advaita (just like in Monotheism) is semantics—i.e., that reality is concepts. Each concept is one and infinite. These concepts are organized in a hierarchy, making all of reality an inverted tree of concepts. The root is one, the trunks, branches, and twigs are many, and the leaves are infinite. Even the smallest leaf on the tree is infinite because it is a concept and can expand unlimitedly. And yet, the twigs, branches, trunks, and the root are successively bigger infinities because whatever the leaf can expand into, the twigs, branches, trunks and the root can expand even more.

Therefore, there is no contradiction in saying that each person is Brahman, and Brahman is infinite, and yet, there is a Param-Brahman who is a far greater infinity than Brahman. That is just like saying that "color" is infinite and yet "knowledge" is a bigger infinity. Each person can factually know infinite things, and so, each person is infinite. And yet, they cannot know as much as Param-Brahman. The duality between finite and infinite doesn't exist; it is many levels of successively larger infinities. The idea of finitude emerges from object-thinking. The idea of infinitude comes from concept-thinking.

Why Size Truly Doesn't Matter

Factually, the Vedic texts describe both large and small forms of God, with the large ones being inferior to the small ones! For instance, there is a conception of a Virāta Puruṣa in the Vedic texts—the cosmic form of God—in which God is as big as the universe. Anyone can keep adding to their height and weight and reach the size of the universe, and they would still not be greater than the Virāta Puruṣa. And yet, the same universe, looked at from the outside, is described as just a mustard seed with greater forms of God creating millions of such universes in a blink, although looking far smaller than Virāta Puruṣa. This is because form doesn't equal shape and size. God's form is a meaning, not a geometrical object.

The situation is akin to saying that we can condense a section into a section title, a bunch of sections into a chapter title, a bunch of chapters into a book title, etc. There is no limit to condensation until we reach the most basic concept—knowledge—which cannot be further condensed. Whatever any other concept can expand, knowledge can expand even more. Even as everything can expand infinitely, knowledge can expand more than everything else. For instance, botany is infinite, but biology is a bigger infinity than botany, and knowledge is an even bigger infinity than biology. The duality of finite and infinite, which results in the claims about formlessness, is entirely a result of using physical-object conceptions of reality.

Rational Proofs of God's Existence

The Impossibility of Rational Proof

Abrahamic religions try to construct proofs of God's existence without recognizing the basic problem of proof as conceived in Aristotelian system of reasoning—each rational proof begins with axioms, which must be assumed to be true, and which can't themselves be proved. A proof doesn't entail the truth unless the axioms are proven to be true. However, the axioms, by definition are unprovable. In fact, it is well-known that a rational proof regurgitates in a new way what is already assumed in the axioms. A rational proof is not a truth because axioms are unproved.

During Enlightenment, the scientific method postulated that we can create axioms by observing the world, then derive their logical predictions, and test those predictions against the facts of the world. In short, axioms were hypotheses based on world observation and their truth was confirmed or denied based on world observation. However, according to Monotheism, God is either absent from the world, or even if He is present (e.g., as a Holy Ghost), we cannot see Him, for seeing means having a form, which would allow us to draw an image, but drawing images of God is explicitly forbidden. Hence, we cannot make a hypothesis about God's existence based on world observation nor can we confirm or deny that hypothesis based on world observation. There is simply no basis for hypothesizing God because a scientific hypothesis requires a world observation.

Christian Apologists have recently come up with a solution to this problem through the Fine-Tuning Design Argument which states that the mathematical laws of nature must be finely tuned to produce life and since life exists therefore some superior intelligence must have tuned the laws. This is a hypothesis. For it to be proven, we must make predictions and then test them against observations. But nobody has been able to make a verifiable prediction either about other finely-tuned laws or about the kinds of life forms that must arise from such fine-tuning. In fact, all the mathematical laws are known to be either incomplete in explaining some observations or contradictory to some other observations. How can we talk about the fine-tuning of the laws by some intelligence when the laws themselves are not proven to be consistent and complete explanations of what we can already observe? The meta-inference of intelligence tuning the laws would make sense only after the laws were proven.

The proofs of the existence of God have thus relied on human ideas—e.g., the Ontological Argument for the Existence of God says: By definition, God is the most perfect being, and a being that exists is more perfect than one that does not, hence God must exist. The essential claim here is that perfection exists. The counter to this argument is the Problem of Theodicy or the existence of evil. If God is perfect, and He created the world, and happiness is greater perfection than suffering, then why did God make an imperfect world? There has been no response to this problem in any Monotheistic religion. Therefore, the claim that perfection exists is itself in question. Yes, we have ideas about perfection but if evil exists, then perfection doesn't. Therefore, to say that just because I can think of perfection, and perfection must exist, becomes a false claim.

In the Vedic texts, God is both good and evil and He shows His good face to the good and the evil face to the evil. When God shows His evil face to evil, He reforms it into good, so even the evil is good. However, that requires God to have at least two forms—one gentle and the other fierce—which would mean two gods. It is impossible to prove the existence of a Monotheistic God because of the existence of evil, which requires God to be both good and evil, which is inconceivable in Aristotelian logic. This is also the recurring pattern of incomplete vs. inconsistent—if God is both good and evil, then the situation is inconsistent, but if God is only good, then the situation is incomplete as we cannot explain evil.

When reality is conceived as meaning, then it is structured as an inverted tree, and the proof of the existence of God becomes trivial—since we can see the leaves, therefore, the root must exist. If there is a hierarchy of meanings, then for anything to exist, this hierarchy must terminate into a pinnacle, and at the top of the hierarchy is the Supreme Meaning. Hence, if this world exists, then God must exist. This is probably why Vedic texts never gave any proof of God. They describe reality as meaning, organized into multiple tiers of meaning, which originated in a Supreme Being. We only need to understand that reality is meaning to know that it is hierarchical and for a meaningful world to exist, God must exist.

Even as God is both good and evil, He shows His good face to the good and the evil face to the evil. By showing the good face, the good is confirmed and enhanced. By showing the evil face, the evil is denied and reduced. Thus, God's evil face is not contradictory to good, even though it is distinct from good. Good and evil are also potentials in God. He is neither always good nor always evil. Likewise, good and evil are potentials in each soul. No soul is either always good or always evil. That potential to be evil never dies, although when one knows that evil is reciprocated by evil, the potential is not activated. The evil appears only as a result of forgetting that evil will be reciprocated by evil—i.e., ignorance.

Thus, both good and evil are eternal potentials, and yet, the activation of the evil potential is not eternal because it is activated only by a person's forgetfulness and corrected by their remembrance. We need a philosophy rooted in potentials to solve the problem of evil. We need a worldview of meanings to create a hierarchy of meanings to say that good and evil are two branches emanating out of a root that exist as the spiritual and material realms, which are non-intersecting, but we can go from one realm to another because good and evil are eternal potentials that are activated by our choice to remember or forget. When there is a hierarchy of good and evil, then it must terminate in an ultimate source.

Factually, there is no good or evil in a world of objects because objects don't suffer or enjoy. There is no pain or pleasure in an object, therefore, there cannot be any good or evil. Of course, our bodies have pain and pleasure, which means they can't be objects. Hence, when objective thinking is used in religion, a double standard is created—(a) on one hand, there can be no pain and pleasure and hence no good or evil, and (b) on the other, there is pain and pleasure, and hence evil and good. This contradiction can be resolved only by rejecting objects and embracing meanings. Objects are studied as quantities and meanings are studied as qualities. Pleasure and pain can't be measured as numbers but they can be experienced as qualities. We cannot reconcile these two kinds of worldviews because in object-quantity world there is no pain and pleasure.

Obstinacy on Object Ideologies

Everything created in the West since antiquity in the name of philosophy, religion, and science is the byproduct of object thinking pioneered during Greek times. Object thinking brought in decontextualization and depersonalization. All persons were reduced to bodies, which were then modeled as objects. This entire trajectory of developments is false because reality is meanings, not objects. Religion is wrong because God is the original meaning, not an object. Science is wrong because the world is meanings, not objects. Philosophy is wrong because thinking in terms of objects is wrong. Logic is wrong because it is evolved from object-thinking, which is wrong. Since everything is wrong, and can be proven to be so, therefore, object ideologies are enforced through violence on people, animals, and nature. Violence and falsehoods are two sides of the same coin. Since we cannot rationally and empirically prove the lies, therefore, they are forced on everyone through coercion and violence.

The West developed institutions of power to brainwash people into thinking that falsehoods are the truth. All these institutions claimed to have received the imputed power of God as the omnipotent lawmaker. As evidence against this brainwashing accumulates, and people see through the false claims, the institution uses greater and greater violence. Most people can't believe that everything they have created is false. They think that if others would stop contradicting them, then their worldview would be proven true due to the absence of contrary opinions. They don't realize that a false system is self-contradictory. It doesn't need external disconfirmation; it collapses under the weight of its own contradictions.

And yet, until it fully collapses, a lie repeated often enough appears to be true because most people don't undertake a rigorous analysis. They remain ignorant of the problem, and can't see beyond the propaganda because they don't invest effort into seeking. The brainwashing succeeds because people are unwilling. Hence, there are only two solutions—(a) wait for everything to collapse under the weight of its own contradictions or (b) proactively study, find the truth, and disengage yourself from the falsehoods. The latter can be done by reason and observation; hence, violence is unnecessary. Institutions of power are not required to force the truth if everyone is serious about the truth and eager to find it.

The Intellectual Hypocrisy of Iconoclasm

Public Interest Litigation in India

Recently, a public interest petition was filed in the Supreme Court of India, requesting the Supreme Court to direct the Government of India to restore an ancient deity of Lord Viṣṇu in the Javari Temple, Khajuraho, beheaded during the invasions of India. Rejecting the petition, the Chief Justice of India, BR Gavai, noted: "This is purely publicity interest litigation. Go and ask the deity himself to do something. If you are saying you are a strong devotee of Lord Viṣṇu, then you pray and do some meditation."

The court also mentioned that the matter fell into the jurisdiction of the Archeological Survey of India (ASI) and was therefore outside its jurisdiction. The petitioner could either approach Lord Viṣṇu or ASI. These comments led to some furore among the Indian public, to which Justice Gavai responded: "the comments I made have been portrayed in social media in a certain manner...I respect all religions". However, he also refused to withdraw the comments he made from the official court records.

Judges in India have never asked the followers of other religions to pray to their deity for help in legal matters. In fact, if religious people always prayed to a deity, rather than asking courts for help, courts would exist only for atheists. Such comments could be valid only if the court reduced its judicial powers to the atheists, after which 97% of Indians who are religious would be outside the court's purview.

The Practice of Hypocritical Iconoclasm

Such comments hark back to the times when invaders into India would ask the invaded people to pray to their gods and goddesses for protection, and many of them said that if stone, metal, and wood images could not prevent their own destruction, how would they protect the people praying to them?

By the same yardstick, even those who prayed to a formless deity haven't been protected from invasion or slaughter. Do we have to recount the stories of monotheistic religions attacking each other to prove that their deities did not protect them from attacks despite prayer, and the legal system had to intervene to help them? So, why should those praying to an image seek help from their deity while those praying to a formless deity do not, when the problems in both cases are exactly the same? For instance, would the court ask Christians and Muslims to pray to their deity if Hindus attacked their religious places?

This double standard makes judicial pronouncements on prayer hypocritical. They say, without saying it, that those who worship stone, metal, or wood deities worship false gods, while those who pray to a formless deity, or oppose images of a deity, worship true gods—(a) the deity was helpless when it was beheaded, so it can't be divine, (b) requesting the restoration of a false god is a waste of time, (c) if you still insist on restoration, pray to the deity, discover the futility of prayer, and get convinced that it is a false god, and (d) these deities belong to the past, not the present, where a deity can either be formless or absent, and (e) if you want a cultural memory of false gods, you can ask the ASI, because it deals with excavation and restoration of the past for cultural tourism. The selective targeting of the religion that makes images of their deities, while never making the same demands for those religions that pray to formless deities, reveals the bias toward iconoclastic religions and against the deities of the Vedic tradition.

The Fundamental Issues of Iconoclasm

So, in this article, I will discuss the problems with iconoclasm, namely, that iconoclastic religions demand respect for their symbols and texts, which are religious icons, while they attack others' religious symbols and texts, although they cannot prove that their icons are sacred or that others' icons are profane.

The hypocrisy of iconoclasm is that it applies to images of deities, while not to symbols and texts, when they, too, are given sacred meaning. The selective use of iconoclasm for deity images, while not using them for sacred symbols and texts, is a mark of the arbitrariness of the sacred, devoid of any philosophy of sacredness, which puts all claims of sacredness into the bucket of irrational, blind faith beliefs.

I will then talk about how everything in nature was earlier considered living, including a stone, wood, or metal, and the idea of dead matter is a monotheistic creation. This ideology has now stagnated modern science, and to get out of that stagnation, we have to return to pre-monotheistic ideas of an alive nature and understand how matter is living, meaningful, and purposeful, not an inert substance. The Vedic tradition explains how everything is living, but different living forms symbolize sacred, mundane, and profane meanings. If life and meaning are scientific topics, then sacredness cannot be conjured based on blind faith.

Universal Ideas of Sacred Symbolism

All ancient cultures denoted natural principles through symbols. The Mesopotamian Pentagram (five pointed star) represented the five elements of nature; the Sumerian Pentacle (a pentagram in a circle) denoted the oneness of the five elements, and represented Ishtar, mother nature; the Egyptian Ankh (depicted as a cross with a loop at the top, using as a Christian symbol by Coptic Christians in Africa) symbolized life, vitality, and eternity; the Celtic Triskelion (a three-branched spiral) and Triquetra (a triple-interlaced knot) represented eternal temporal cycles; the Ouroboros (a serpent consuming itself) represented how nothing truly disappears but only transforms from one thing to another cyclically.

In the Vedic tradition, sound itself has meaning, which is the basis of all mantra chanting—it doesn't matter if we know the meaning of the sound, the sound automatically has mental and bodily effects. Similarly, in the Vedic texts, touch, sight, taste, and smell successively expand from words, explaining why the word could not be something else. This sound is divine and the true description of things. It becomes mundane or profane only when we describe the world differently than its divine description.

Plato believed that the world is a combination of substance and form; the substance is earthly, while the forms are heavenly, and when the two combine, we get ordinary things. However, Plato also believed that when heavenly forms descend into earthly substance, they become imperfect. For instance, there is a perfect (form of) circle in heaven, but there are no perfect circles on earth. Strictly speaking, the entire world was sacred in Platonism because all forms descended from heaven, so they made everything sacred. We could say that some things were less perfect than others (e.g., a less perfect circle vs. a more perfect circle), but we could not confine sacredness to just one religion, culture, ideology, or society.

The descent of perfect heavenly forms became the basis of mathematical Platonism, as mathematicians equated heaven to a world in which all formulas, equations, symmetrical shapes, and numbers resided. Even if reality did not perfectly work according to mathematical equations, it was because the earth was only an imperfect reflection of heaven. The scientists who described nature through mathematics called it the discovery of the mind of God. God's mind wasn't just known through religious scripture; it was also known through nature, so in a sense, the world was itself a scripture, revealing the mind of God.

Failed Philosophies of Sacredness

The above universal, rational, and provable ideas of sacredness don't work for monotheisms. If these religions truly followed Platonism, they would have to accept that every religion's symbols and texts were more or less sacred, contrary to their exclusivist claims. The problem in Platonism is that if all forms are heavenly, evil must also be a form in heaven, and so the distinction between good and evil can never be made. Abrahamic religions require that good comes from heaven (the place of God) and evil comes from hell (the place of Satan), so forms are not just descending from heaven but also ascending from hell. How do we know which form comes from heaven or hell? This became a matter of blind faith.

Platonism died after Gödel proved the incompleteness of all mathematical descriptions; even numbers have many interpretations, such as one and first, and theorems proved for one interpretation are not true for other interpretations; in fact, using multiple interpretations leads to contradictions, but if we restrict ourselves to just one interpretation, then we cannot capture all the possible truths. And thus, science ceased to be divine truth, the attempt to know the mind of God, and uncover the sacred in the mundane. Instead, science adopted Pragmatism—developing different theories for different phenomena, which contradicted other theories, so they could never become one theory. Then, science found out that it could not build a complete and consistent theory for any phenomena, such as the observations pertaining to the subatomic particles (in quantum theory) or those pertaining to the cosmos (in the theory of general relativity).

And so, there is no way to distinguish sacred, mundane, and profane, or good from evil, because the attempts to do so failed in philosophy, religion, and science: (a) science cannot be divine because its application to the world results in contradictions, (b) there is no way to tell which form descends from heaven or ascends from hell, and (c) different people just call their beliefs, ideas, and theories divine because they need these for pragmatic organization of their societies, countries, and institutions.

The Abrahamic Failure to Prove Sacredness

For centuries now, Abrahamic religions have tried to develop a philosophy of religion, or specifically, how to prove that their sacred symbols (Star, Cross, and Crescent) and books (Torah, Bible, and Koran) are sacred, while those of the other religions are not. Not one of them succeeded, which is why sacredness was detached from rational or empirical proof, and the state (judges, courts, and governments) had to be secular, i.e., non-discriminatory to all faiths or beliefs. In fact, matters of faith and belief can never be decided by the state, owing to the definition of secularism as the separation of religion and state.

There is no way any Abrahamic religion can justify respect for a religious symbol or a book because (a) the symbol is a piece of wood, metal, stone, plastic, paper, or ink, so on par with other things made out of the same materials, (b) that symbol cannot be living because life means something that breathes, which these symbols do not, (c) respecting, revering, or worshipping some non-living thing is actually worshipping false gods by their own yardstick, and (d) some people may want to believe that their false gods are true gods because they want to see the divine in some tangible form within their lives.

The unprovability of religious beliefs is not a problem per se if one keeps those beliefs private and lets others believe in whatever else they want to. But Abrahamic religions want to globalize their ideology as divine revelation and use it to control, conquer, and exploit the world. Their theology says that they are exclusively blessed by God with a revelation, and they will eventually rule the world. Unable to prove that their revelation is true in any other way, these religions try to prove their truth through violence.

The Response of Godless Religions

Given these problems with trying to demarcate sacred, mundane, and profane, godless religions (Buddhism, Advaita, and Jainism) reject ideas of a God, describe life in this world as a result of desires for pleasure, which lead to endless suffering, and hence, liberation from the world as the renunciation of these desires. They differ in their doctrines, as Buddhism accepts no soul, Advaita one soul, and Jainism many souls. But without desire, nothing is actually meaningful or purposeful in this world. Buddhists call the world codependent opposites created by desire, Advaitins call the world an illusion created by desire, and Jains call the world a reality into which the soul falls due to desire. Since renunciation of desire is the eternal state, the worship of a deity is at most that of a mediator to the ultimate state, and that worship is discarded after attaining the eternal state, because it does not have any eternal significance.

In godless religions, the eternal state of an individual is the same as that of the deity they worship. There isn't an eternal difference between the worshipper and the worshipped. In fact, worshippers worship to attain the state of the worshipped. The deities are gurus and not God, and one attains the guru's state, after which one can be a guru, so equally entitled to worship. Since all individuals can ultimately become guru, worshipping a deity is ultimately worshipping a human, although enlightened and not ignorant.

Buddhism and Jainism don't accept the creation or the end of the universe; the world is timeless for them. History still evolves in cyclical ages of rise and fall, but there is no beginning or end to these ages. These claims are essential to allow Buddhism and Jainism to remove deities that create, maintain, or destroy the world. While Advaita accepts that the universe is created, maintained, and destroyed, this acceptance contradicts its rejection of deities that create, maintain, and destroy the universe. Clearly, if some deities exist before and after the universe, then their existence during the universe cannot be equated to the existence of other living entities that don't exist before and after the universe. And so, godless religions either directly or indirectly reject a creator deity, which is their rejection of God.

Godless religions can never explain how living entities who have transcended the material body are, in fact, immanent in some image, because that presence indicates that they haven't yet transcended. In their original forms, godless religions did not make deities and did not even have a cosmology with varied types of deities. All these were added later to compete with the Vedic tradition, allowing people who were leaving the Vedic tradition to worship deities just as before. However, even as these deities in the cosmos were added, how they are simultaneously transcendent and immanent wasn't explained.

These difficulties in godless religions eventually led to the creation of sects that accept or reject deity worship. For instance, Mahāyāna Buddhism accepts deity worship while Hināyana Buddhism rejects it. The Saguna Brahman sect of Advaita accepts deity worship while the Nirguna Brahman sect rejects it. Sthanakvasi, a subsect within Śvetāmbara Jains, and Taranpanthi, a subsect within Digambara Jains, do not worship images, while other sects do. The real issue is not whether a sect accepts deity worship. It is that the acceptance cannot reconcile how a transcendent person is immanent within an image.

Brahman, Paramātma, Bhagavān

Does that make the divinity of all deities a blind faith, in which case, everyone should be allowed to hold their personal blind faith? Or, is there a rational explanation for why deities can be sacred and alive?

The answer to this question goes through what Mīmāṃsā calls Arthavāda, and I call semantic reality. Let's try to solve the problem of immanent and transcendent through the example of concepts of yellow and color. The concept color is at once finite and infinite—we can grasp the concept color in a moment, so it is finite, but the concept includes infinite shades, which we can't grasp even in infinite time. Hence, yellow is a part of color, and color is a part of yellow, and yet, color precedes all the shades as the whole, while the shades that follow from color, are a part of color. We can never understand this in physical thinking because it requires something to be either inside or outside another thing, so one thing can either be transcendent or immanent, but never both. The simultaneous truth of both needs semantic thinking because color is at once outside all shades and inside all shades. We express this fact by saying that yellow is a color, but color is not yellow. Color is both transcendent to and immanent in yellow.

Semantic reality is described as the triad of Brahman, Paramātma, and Bhagavān in the Vedic texts. Bhagavān is like the transcendent form of color, from which innumerable shades—yellow, red, green, blue—expand like Brahman, within each of which Paramātma enters like the immanent form of color. Due to Paramātma's presence in all things, everything is at once divine, but not identical to Bhagavān. However, some things *represent* Bhagavān much better than others, quite like white is the complete color, and therefore, different shades of white come closer to representing color much better.

There is no culture in which the divine has not been described as light and the demonic has not been called darkness. In one sense, these are just colors, and yet, they represent divine and demonic. In the Vedic tradition, Bhagavān is the source of both divine and demonic, so He is portrayed in the color of light shining through a dark cloud, called Megha Varṇam, and hence Viṣṇu is depicted as blue.

The point is that while Bhagavān is immanent in all things as Paramātma, He is *described* better by some things and not others. The things that capture more and more qualities of Bhagavān become better and better representations of Bhagavān. A deity of Bhagavān is such a representation, even if it is made out of stone, wood, or metal. By looking at that deity, we are seeing Bhagavān far more than by looking at other things, such as tables, chairs, or beds. That doesn't mean the Paramātma is absent from tables, chairs, or beds. It also doesn't mean that Bhagavān is confined to the deity we see. The deity is simply a representation of Bhagavān, like a book can be a description of some reality. If we burn the book, we don't destroy the reality. But if we read the book carefully, we can know reality, as if we were seeing reality, not the book. The book is a substitute for reality for those who can't perceive reality.

The Process of Remote Sensing and Control

The Vedic tradition goes beyond the description of divinity into images and makes them alive, through a process called Prāṇa Pratiṣṭhā. Prāṇa is translated as life-force, to contrast it to the mechanical forces of modern science (such as gravity or electromagnetism). Prior to the advent of monotheism, the earth was considered alive even in Greek and Roman societies, and was treated as a mother. But the mother couldn't be seen just by digging the earth. The earth was alive in the sense that all that happened on the earth was controlled by a heavenly deity called by varied names, such as Gaia by the Greeks and Terra by the Romans. And so, people worshipped Gaia and Terra in images; the earth and her image were both Gaia and Terra.

How could Gaia and Terra at once be the vast earth and an image in the earth? The answer is that Gaia and Terra were not identical to either the earth or the image. Both lived in heaven, not on earth, nor in the image. But they controlled the earth from heaven, like the mechanical forces of modern science, with action-at-a-distance. Similarly, their images described them better than anything else on earth, and they were in control of those images, just like in control of the earth. One could touch the image, and it was as good as touching the heavenly deity, or offer her something, as if she were face to face.

This process of remote control is just like controlling a TV with a TV remote. The TV remote does not touch the TV, and yet it controls the TV. The process of remote presence is just like seeing a remote person during a video conference. The person is not actually face-to-face but appears to be face-to-face, and all things said to the image on the videoconference screen are said to the remote person. A deity of a heavenly personality is just like a videoconference screen—the person is seen, the person controls what we see on the screen, and all things said to the videoconference screen are, in fact, communicated to the person. However, breaking the videoconference screen doesn't hurt the remote person.

These processes of remote presence and control are called Prāṇa in the Vedic texts. Prāṇa is translated as life-force because it can be controlled by will. The soul interacts with the mind and the body through Prāṇa. But Prāṇa is not confined to a body, and can spread beyond it, creating telepathic and telekinetic powers. This concept was used in movies such as Star Wars, with yogi-like Jedi knights dealing with The Force, spread all over the universe, just like telepathic and telekinetic powers in some humans.

Modern science tried to depersonalize Prāṇa as deterministic mechanical forces, such as gravity and electromagnetism. But that attempt failed after the discovery of quantum phenomena, because force was quantized as packets, whose emission and absorption were no longer deterministic. We can still use Prāṇa for remote sensing and action, but the actions are not deterministic, quite like (a) we can control our minds and bodies by will, but that control is not predictably deterministic, (b) we can control a TV using a TV remote, although that control is not predictably deterministic, and sometimes we have to press the TV remote buttons multiple times to get the desired effects, and (c) the images and voices during a videoconference sometimes flicker and jitter, which is not predictably deterministic. Science is also unable to describe the deterministic gravitational force and the quantized electromagnetic force in the same theory because of the fundamental contradictions between the two force paradigms.

All these problems require the renunciation of the idea of

mechanical force and its replacement with life-force—our own and those of heavenly personalities controlling the world through telekinesis and telepathy. The world under the control of will is neither random nor deterministic. It works according to a mind imbued with meaning and purpose, which change based on time, place, situation, and person. The problem is not nature's randomness but science's attempts to model the mind as a machine.

Deities Are Not the Same as Idols

That brings us to the difference between an *idol* and a *deity*. An idol is an impersonal representation of a deity, just like a picture or photograph. A deity is instead Prāṇa expanded from a divine personality into that idol, picture, or photograph. Thus, in the case of Vedic deities, a sculptor carves an image of the divine personality, which is an idol, image, or picture. This idol is then installed in a temple through a process called Prāṇa Pratiṣṭhā, during which the deity is invited to be present in his or her image, and the Prāṇa of the transcendent personality becomes immanent in that image, to make it a living deity.

We can explain Prāṇa Pratiṣṭhā through the example of a dream. During a dream, our mind creates an image of the self, which is neither identical to the self nor completely different from it. The image is projected out of the mind by Prāṇa, and that Prāṇa enters the image, after which the dreamer thinks that he is that image. If something happens to that image, the dreamer considers it to be happening to himself. The image is of the dreamer, by the dreamer, and for the dreamer. If the dream is pleasant, the dreamer enjoys it, but if the dream is unpleasant, the dreamer wakes up, the Prāṇa is withdrawn from the dreamt image back into the mind, such that the mind doesn't see that image anymore. Even if the dreamt image was attacked and killed during the dream, the dreamer is not factually attacked or killed. Of course, the dreamer doesn't enjoy that experience; only the pleasant experiences are enjoyed.

Prāṇa Pratiṣṭhā is just like a person identifying with a dreamt image for pleasurable experiences, but not with painful experiences. This is why if a deity is broken after Prāṇa Pratiṣṭhā, it becomes an idol, and no longer remains a deity—the transcendent personality withdraws the Prāṇa, after which a new image has to be carved, and reinstalled using the same Prāṇa Pratiṣṭhā process as before. This requires the cosmos to be the dream of a cosmic dreamer—called Nārāyaṇa in the Vedic texts—with other life forms, created as secondary dreamers by the primary cosmic dreamer, being capable of creating their own dreams. The deities of the cosmic dreamer they install in temples, are also dreamt personas of the cosmic dreamer.

The Hypocrisy of Monotheistic Theology

Monotheisms advance an objective conception of reality, in which only humans are living, while all other things (including animals, plants, reptiles, birds, and fishes) are non-living. God fashions all species of life on earth out of dust, and originally, they just live on earth, without humans. Meanwhile, God fashions Adam and Eve in heaven out of dust, and then breathes His life into them. Subsequently, when Adam and Eve are sent to earth due to their original sin of eating the forbidden fruit, humans remain heavenly creatures, while all other species remain earthly creatures. Dogs and cats, for example, cannot go to heaven under monotheistic theology, even as some people claim that they are going to heaven.

When humans return to heaven, they do so in the same human body as they had on earth. Therefore, there is no difference between soul and body in monotheisms, other than something intangible that makes humans divine creations, while animals, plants, reptiles, birds, and fishes are earthly creations. Since the soul and body are forever bound in monotheisms, the soul is always immanent in the body, and never transcendent to it. Salvation requires body rejuvenation, ascension of the body to heaven, because the soul cannot leave the body and get a new body, as that would be reincarnation.

Just as humans have a forever-bound body and soul, even God's body and soul are forever bound. God cannot leave His body and become immanent in another body on earth, to produce a sacred symbol. As a result, God is always transcendent. Even if He enters one symbol or text, He cannot be at once present in another symbol or text—including one of the same religion—which means there can only be one sacred symbol or text at one time. Finally, if God could be immanent in this way, there would be no need for messiahs as God could appear in this world exactly like He becomes immanent in a book or symbol.

Therefore, monotheistic religions cannot in principle have a sacred symbol or text, because sacredness has to be transferred from God to the symbol, which would require the reduction of God's sacredness, and ultimately the separation of God's soul and body, which would destroy the entire theological system. When monotheistic religions talk about sacred symbols, they are talking about something incompatible with their theology. They allow people to believe that books and symbols are sacred, without explaining how God became immanent in millions of symbols and books, while being the one transcendent deity. In fact, if God could be present in millions of sacred symbols, they would all be images of God, as good as God, and therefore, millions of copies of God, contrary to the monotheistic idea of just one God.

The History of Iconoclasm Within India

Deity worship requires—(a) the Mīmāṃsā doctrine of Arthavāda, (b) the Sāñkhya description of Prāṇa moving beyond the body, (c) the Nyāya description of how a world is produced as the dream of a cosmic dreamer, and (d) the Vedānta description of the whole reality as Brahman, Paramātma, and Bhagavān. Without these, we cannot explain how an image represents God and how that image is living.

All these fundamental principles were lost in the last 1,200 years after the advent of Śankarācārya, who rejected Mīmāṃsā, Sāñkhya, and Nyāya as mundane ideologies, reduced Vedānta to Brahman, equated the living entity to Brahman, and rejected the reality of anything beyond Brahman, i.e., Paramātma and Bhagavān. Advaita is the Indian version of iconoclasm, with the Saguna Brahman sect allowing deity worship while the Nirguna Brahman sect rejecting that worship, and the dominant thesis is that those who worship images are the less intelligent sentimentalists, while those who reject that worship are the more intelligent philosophers, and philosophy leads to liberation while sentimentalism binds us.

In this degraded condition, the only recourse for deity worshippers is secularism—we are all following blind faith religions, no blind faith can be proven to be better or worse, and the judiciary must equally respect all blind faiths. I don't have any problem with secularism because it enables the minimal level of freedom in a degraded condition. My realization is that it is impossible for believers in one religion to be unbiased toward believers of other religions. If you believe that the world is about to end, or that one religion will soon rule the world, how can you see those who don't have such beliefs with equal vision? Those who can accept that the world has been going on for billions of years in the past, and so it will go on for billions of years in the future, can ignore the claims of an apocalyptic future conjured in monotheistic religions (based on a six-thousand-year world history) as childish nonsense. However, the reverse is not possible.

Therefore, when we lose the Vedic understanding of a living deity and adopt secularism to continue our practices as our blind faith, we create several false equivalences. We equate beliefs that can be rationally explained with those that can never be rationally explained. We equate the sacred symbols of religions that cannot have sacred symbols according to their own theology, with the sacred symbols of religions that can have such symbols according to their own theology. We equate ideologies that are based on an empirically falsifiable few-thousand-year history of the world with those that are based on an empirically provable several-billion-year history of the world. We equate a worldview that can solve the currently unsolved problems of modern science with those that cannot even comprehend those problems.

The Law Doesn't Recognize Sacredness

The present Indian legal system is copied from the Western monotheistic legal system, which came out of the depersonalization of reality during the European so-called Enlightenment in which the world is governed not by persons (God, gods, kings, or priests), but by impersonal laws (written in sacred scriptures, which their believers themselves don't strictly follow, or man-made constitutions, which their creators keep amending). The legal system applies only to humans, not to animals, birds, fishes, trees, or reptiles, let alone rivers, mountains, oceans, or lands, because all these are considered non-living.

The legal system defines a person as someone with rights—such as of free speech, voting in elections, signing contracts of marriage, employment, and citizenship, ability to buy, hold, and sell properties, appoint solicitors on his behalf, stand in his defense in a court of law, and fully subject himself to the law of the land enacted by a government, including sentencing by a judiciary, imprisonment in a jail, and execution by hanging. Since none of these definitions of a person apply to a deity, while nothing else is living, a deity is not even a person under the legal system. Meanwhile, corporations are legal persons, and their directors are legal representatives capable of meeting all the person requirements.

This means that every religious place, including a temple, must formally register itself as a corporation, after which it must be administered as a corporation, and could be tried as a corporation in a court. The temple deity is not the maker of the laws, and the judges don't have to follow the deity's laws. Rather, judges make the deity appear before the judges—through representatives—to pass judgments on the deity, based on laws made by a parliament, which includes people opposed to the deity's existence.

Under the monotheistic conception of law, the places of worship are inanimate buildings made out of brick, stone, wood, lime, steel, and cement. The deity in the temple is a part of the building structure, no different from a pillar, staircase, dome, or arch. The deity is, in fact, not the owner of the temple in which he or she resides. Rather, the deity is owned by the proprietor of the temple structure, who can buy and sell, modify or demolish, the temple and the deity, quite like any other building, with no objection from any third party. Since monotheistic religions don't have deities, their places of worship are not actually sacred because God is always transcendent and never immanent. All places of worship are just buildings, no different than palaces, forts, apartments, houses, theatres, and malls owned and managed by people. They can at most have some historical significance, but under the law, they have no sacredness.

Dharma Can Never Thrive Under Laws

While people may cry hoarse regarding the impersonal and objectified treatment of deities by the legal profession, the fact remains that the problem is the law itself, not just the courts. Under that law, a temple is not anything more than a building—like a Church, Synagogue, or Mosque—because law itself comes from monotheistic depersonalization of reality and purging of God from this world. Legally speaking, anyone can buy and burn a religious text, and the law can do nothing about it, because that text is private property, and everyone is entitled to the destruction of their private property. So, one man can worship a text and another man can burn it, because those are simply different ways of handling private property, allowed by law. Unless we apply a religion-specific law, secular law can do nothing about it.

This is why no society factually practices secularism. In every so-called secular country, judges of the dominant religion protect their religion and interpret the law in ways favorable to the dominant religion. However, in India, Hindu judges try to be secular or follow legal precedents set by followers of other religions, as if the burden of secularism rests only on the Hindus, while followers of other religions protect their religions and interpret the laws in ways favorable to their religion. Insofar as this judiciary is committed to upholding the law, it is committed to upholding monotheism because law is itself a monotheistic construction designed to work for monotheistic societies, not dharmic societies.

All followers of dharma must realize that the rules of the game were rigged against dharma and in favor of monotheistic religions, the day India adopted the Western system of law. India's legal system is itself the biggest threat to the survival of dharma in India. India's secularism is also the greatest threat to the survival of dharma in India because it equates provably false claims to provably true claims, and then judges the provably true claims according to the norms and standards set by provably false claims. When the truth is judged by standards of falsehoods, the truth is destroyed, and falsehoods are elevated. The adoption of the Western monotheistic law, and its continuous use by the government and judiciary as the way to govern India, is the continuation of three centuries of colonization under British rule. The Vedic religious places can never be restored to their truthfully deserved status under colonized rule.

Iconoclasm is an Untenable Position

All systems of blind faith, and that includes all monotheisms, rest on self-contradictory dogmas—such as never making an image of God, while making millions of sacred symbols, not realizing that their sacred symbol is itself an image of God. Similarly, when they talk about never worshipping idols, but worship religious texts, they are worshipping millions of idols, while claiming to never worship an idol. Likewise, they don't realize that even writing God's name is producing an idol, icon, or image. After all, the name written on text as much represents God as the image of God within a temple. How does it matter if the icon, idol, or image is made out of ink and paint and called letters, rather than made out of wood, metal, or stone and called an idol? Nobody can provide a method to demarcate one from the other. It's not that they haven't yet tried to provide such methods; they have tried for centuries and failed to do so.

Even godless religions need icons, images, and idols of books. They don't want to trample their books under their feet, but they are ready to trample on the floor and their slippers. That means they consider the books sacred, but the floor and the slippers not sacred. So, what makes the book sacred and the floor or slipper not sacred, when both are made out of the same materials, or could be made out of the same materials? Since nobody made the world, these materials could not be a fuller representation of the maker, so nothing in this world could be more sacred than others. Or, if humans made these things, then all man-made things would be equally sacred, and nothing could be called more or less sacred.

Nobody would have attained enlightenment without the first enlightened person, and the only way he could be enlightened is if he was always in an enlightened state, and he came to tell others how to attain it, without any fear of falling back into the state of ignorance while teaching enlightenment. If the first person to attain enlightenment began in ignorance and attained the enlightened state of nothingness, oneness, or self-absorption, they would never return to tell others about it. Every enlightened person would repeat the same process—attain a state from where you never return, and tell nobody about it. After that, there will be no books telling people how to reach that state, and without such books, even an idea of who reached that state, so there will be no books to read and nobody to worship as a guru.

This is why the Vedic tradition says that God is the original guru. If there is no God, there is no original guru, nobody can attain enlightenment, nobody will author a book on enlightenment, and after that, there will be no book to read and no guru to worship. Hence, the Vedic tradition reveres even Buddha, Ṛṣabhadeva, and Śaṅkarācārya (the founders of Buddhism, Jainism, and Advaita) as forms of God, not simply gurus. They are eternally enlightened, not enlightened by some meditation, philosophy, or lifestyle. Once we understand that God is the original guru, then He creates the world, He appears in the world to teach (without leaving His world, exactly like a person appears in a remote place through a video conference), His words become the sacred books to read, and all those who explain those words become the subsequent sacred gurus. God always protects those devoted to Him, and they return again and again to teach what God has already taught previously, without fear of falling back into ignorance. All things that describe God accurately are sacred, and some such things can also become deities if God agrees to identify with them. Through such identification, He takes infinite forms, and these forms cannot be equated to idols or false gods.

Viṣṇu is the True Icon for Everyone

Factually, no religion can ever truly practice iconoclasm, because iconoclasm entails the absence of all sacred symbols, books, and teachers, after which religion would itself be absent. Iconoclasm is either envy of God (after He gave a process of enlightenment, people said that they got it on their own), or it is deceit (those who made up their own process of enlightenment had never seen God, so they rejected all images of God, not realizing that their books were the self-proclaimed images of sacredness).

Iconoclasm always ends in hypocrisy—my icons are true and your icons are false—without a shred of evidence for either. They try but fail to find explanations of sacredness in symbols and texts, because if there is a sacred symbol or text, it is an icon or image of God. Unable to recognize the problems with their ideology, they encourage people to pursue their provably false beliefs and call it secularism. They also use laws to persecute others through passive-aggressive, if not outright violent, methods. If they were honest and truthful, this article would itself debunk all their false proclamations over the centuries.

All great societies are governed by great heroes, not by laws. God is the greatest hero who personally governs the world, and a society that understands His governance also becomes the most heroic. God delegates His control to Devas and Devis, all of whom have powers of remote control. By the same powers, they can be present in deities. All these things can be explained rationally and scientifically.

And yet, people envious of God's control, or desirous of escaping this control, postulate that He doesn't exist. Some of them claim to have received the authority to rule the world on God's behalf, while they replace God's system of fair justice with an unfair system of laws designed to empower themselves and disempower others. Others conjure fictions of equality and end up equating provably true claims to provably false claims. Their claim to fame is a divine revelation without seeing the divine, an enlightenment without seeing the one who enlightened them, or empowerment without knowing who temporarily delegated their power to empower them. As a society replaces real heroes with fake ones, it progressively accepts worse and worse icons. Eventually, everyone becomes a villain as all their heroes are destroyed.

Viṣṇu devotees don't go to a temple to *pray* (i.e., beg for something) but to *praise* (i.e., offer something). So many people go to God to beg for something, but Viṣṇu devotees go to Him to offer something. A hero is one who gives without taking, and a thief is one who takes without giving. Prayer makes us a thief, and praise makes us a hero. The Lord is not a beggar to ask for worship, and His devotees are not beggars to ask for gifts. Both give each other selflessly and unreservedly, and through this process of praise, rather than prayer, both the Lord and His devotee are known as heroes. The cycle of receiving (without asking) and giving (without being asked) is the eternal spiritual play between the Lord and His devotee.

Viṣṇu is the greatest hero of any society, and when He is worshipped in a deity form, it is simply hero worship. By such worship, the entire society is elevated to a heroic status. Iconoclasts are envious minions who can't stand Viṣṇu worship because His excellence shames their mediocrity. They try to remake the hero in their own image, not remaking themselves in the hero's image. They replace Viṣṇu with alternative heroes, all of whom suffer from their kind of mediocrity, which actually comforts them. They call Viṣṇu's heroic deeds mythology because they can't stand a hero whose deeds far exceed theirs in greatness. They erase images of great heroes to not feel ashamed of their own mediocrity. They accept a hero who is just a guru, or one filled with jealousy and wrath, because it approximates their condition, never far superior to theirs. And yet, the worship of mediocre heroes normalizes mediocrity and pushes a person toward greater mediocrity, which increases his shame, never reducing it. Iconoclasm is a failed attempt of the mediocre to erase excellence, to feel less shame, which increases shame. Therefore, we should not be perturbed by iconoclasm but understand the pitiful mindset that creates, perpetuates, and practices it.

www.ingramcontent.com/pod-product-compliance
Ingram Content Group UK Ltd.
Pitfield, Milton Keynes, MK11 3LW, UK
UKHW041312190726
13845UKWH00025B/223